Netscape®
Mozilla™
Source Code
Guide

D1519139

Netscape® Mozilla™ Source Code Guide

William R. Stanek

Netscape®
Press

Mountain View, California

Netscape® Mozilla™ Source Code Guide

Published by
Netscape Press
501 East Middlefield Road
Mountain View, CA 94043

Library of Congress Card Number: 99-066774

ISBN: 0-7645-4588-4

Printed in the United States of America

10 9 8 7 6 5 4 3 2 1

1O/RV/RQ/ZZ/FC

Distributed in the United States by IDG Books Worldwide, Inc.

Distributed by CDG Books Canada Inc. for Canada; by Transworld
Publishers Limited in the United Kingdom; by IDG Norge Books for
Norway; by IDG Sweden Books for Sweden; by IDG Books Australia
Publishing Corporation Pty. Ltd. for Australia and New Zealand; by
TransQuest Publishers Pte Ltd. for Singapore, Malaysia, Thailand,
Indonesia, and Hong Kong; by Gotop Information Inc. for Taiwan; by
ICG Muse, Inc. for Japan; by Intersoft for South Africa; by Eyrolles for
France; by International Thomson Publishing for Germany, Austria and
Switzerland; by Distribuidora Cuspide for Argentina; by LR International
for Brazil; by Galileo Libros for Chile; by Ediciones ZETA S.C.R. Ltda. for
Peru; by WS Computer Publishing Corporation, Inc., for the Philippines;
by Contemporanea de Ediciones for Venezuela; by Express Computer
Distributors for the Caribbean and West Indies; by Micronesia Media
Distributor, Inc. for Micronesia; by Chips Computadoras S.A. de C.V. for
Mexico; by Editorial Norma de Panama S.A. for Panama; by American
Bookshops for Finland.

For general information on IDG Books Worldwide's books in the U.S.,
please call our Consumer Customer Service department at
800-762-2974. For reseller information, including discounts and premium sales, please call our Reseller Customer Service department at
800-434-3422.

For information on where to purchase IDG Books Worldwide's books
outside the U.S., please contact our International Sales department at
317-596-5530 or fax 317-596-5692.

For consumer information on foreign language translations, please contact our Customer Service department at 800-434-3422, fax
317-596-5692, or e-mail rights@idgbooks.com.

For information on licensing foreign or domestic rights, please phone
+1-650-655-3109.

For sales inquiries and special prices for bulk quantities, please contact
our Sales department at 650-655-3200 or write to IDG Books
Worldwide, 919 E. Hillsdale Blvd., Suite 400, Foster City, CA 94404.

For information on using IDG Books Worldwide's books in the classroom or for ordering examination copies, please contact our
Educational Sales department at 800-434-2086 or fax 317-596-5499.

For press review copies, author interviews, or other publicity information, please contact our Public Relations department at 650-655-3000
or fax 650-655-3299.

For authorization to photocopy items for corporate, personal, or educational use, please contact Netscape Communications Corporation,
Copyright Permission, 501 East Middlefield Road, Mountain View, CA
94043 or fax 650-528-4124.

For general information on Netscape Press books in the U.S., including
information on discounts and premiums, contact IDG Books Worldwide
at 800-434-3422 or 650-655-3200. For information on where to purchase Netscape Press books outside the U.S., contact IDG Books
International at 650-655-3021 or fax 650-655-3295.

® is a registered trademark under exclusive license to IDG Books
Worldwide, Inc., from International Data Group, Inc.

John Kilcullen, *CEO, IDG Books Worldwide, Inc.*

Steven Berkowitz, *President, IDG Books Worldwide, Inc.*

Richard Swadley, *Senior Vice President & Group
Publisher, IDG Books Worldwide, Inc.*

**Netscape®
Press**

Netscape Press and the Netscape Press logo are
trademarks of Netscape Communications Corporation.

Credits

Acquisitions Editors
Ann C. Lush
Jim Sumser

Development Editor
Eric Newman

Technical Editor
Ram Navale

Copy Editor
Lauren Kennedy
Julie M. Smith

Project Coordinators
Ritchie Durdin
Linda Marousek

Graphics and Production Specialists
Mario Amador
Stephanie Hollier
Jim Kussow
Jude Levinson
Ramses Ramirez

Quality Control Specialist
Chris Weisbart

Book Designer
Daniel Ziegler Design

Proofreading and Indexing
York Production Services

About the Author

William R. Stanek (`mozilla-fan@tvpress.com`) has an M.S. in information systems and more than a decade of hands-on experience with advanced programming and development. He is a leading network technology expert and an award-winning author. Over the years, his practical advice has helped programmers, developers, and network engineers worldwide. He is also a regular contributor to leading publications such as *PC Magazine*, where you'll often find his work in the "Solutions" section.

The author served in the Persian Gulf War as a combat crewmember on an electronic warfare aircraft. He flew on numerous combat missions into Iraq and was awarded nine medals for his wartime service, including one of the United States' highest flying honors, the Air Force Distinguished Flying Cross.

Preface

*T**he time is right for us to take the bold action of making our client free — and we are going even further by committing to post the source code for free for Communicator 5.0. By giving away the source code for future versions, we can ignite the creative energies of the entire Net community and fuel unprecedented levels of innovation in the browser market. Our customers can benefit from world-class technology advancements; the development community gains access to a whole new market opportunity. . . .*

Jim Barksdale
President and CEO
Netscape Communications Corporation
January 22, 1998

Enter the world of Mozilla and mozilla.org, where thousands of programmers are changing the way the Net is used forever. With the Mozilla source code, programmers can create powerful custom solutions and learn advanced programming techniques from real-life examples. By providing the Communicator source code freely, Netscape follows in the tradition of great freeware success stories such as Apache, Linux, and BSD Unix — all of which are provided freely and have a huge following today.

I first encountered Mozilla in 1994. Back then, I was employed by the U.S. government and worked extensively with Unix/NT networking and cross-platform programming and free software tools and resources were the cornerstones of my projects. But I never expected the great boon that came in 1994 — the year of many firsts. Linus Torvalds released Version 1.0 of the Linux kernel; Rob McCool, the author of the NCSA Web server, left NCSA and went on to help create the Apache Web server; and Netscape Communications Corporation, founded by Marc Andreessen and Jim Clark, took the Web community by storm with the release of Navigator (a.k.a. Mozilla).

Mozilla — the name makes me think of a movie monster à la Godzilla. But Mozilla isn't a mythical monster from the depths; it is a human-made beast that has grown from a simple graphics browser to a mega-application encompassing 50-plus code modules and more than 30 million lines of code. Its sheer size makes it tremendously complex and somewhat intimidating — even for skilled programmers. Still, imagine the lessons you can learn from such an application, and the opportunities it affords.

Dozens of programmers, project managers, and others worked for years to develop the code base. It is the source of thousands of programming techniques and solutions that were previously Netscape's top secrets. And now, not only can you browse the code base freely, you can use the code base freely as well.

What's This Book About?

Netscape Mozilla Source Code Guide is your official guide to Netscape's open source program, mozilla.org, and the Mozilla source code. The book is designed for readers with fairly advanced skills, and you will need a fundamental understanding of programming and Internet technologies. The book is designed to help you:

- Enter the Open Source movement.

- Understand one of the most-complex applications ever freely released to the public.

- Gain insight into large-scale application development.

- Extend Mozilla for your own custom applications.

In the book, you learn how to:

- Obtain and build the Mozilla source code on Windows, Unix, and Macintosh systems.

- Use essential developer tools such as CVS, Bonsai, Tinderbox, and Bugzilla.

- Extend the source using cross-platform programming techniques.

- Customize the code using the library hooks and extensions.

How Is This Book Organized?

The book is divided into five parts.

Part I: Getting Started

Part I teaches you how to take advantage of the Netscape Open Source program. It covers the Open Source program, licensing the Mozilla source code, and mozilla.org. Chapters also detail how hobbyists, programmers, and project managers can get involved in mozilla.org and the Netscape Open Source program.

Part II: Managing the Source Code

Part II helps you work with the source code; chapter by chapter you learn the skills you need to tame Mozilla. Here you gain a background that is essential to understanding the Mozilla source code and its modules, and you gain details about tools and techniques used to develop solutions for Mozilla. You explore the inner workings of Mozilla's user interface and its back-end functionality. This part details key programming concepts you should know up front, and offers detailed instructions for building the source code on your system.

Part III: Working with the Source Code

Part III provides an overview of the Mozilla modules. This section's goal is to provide a module-by-module resource that you can use to aid your development efforts. It includes an analysis of each major module and its key features, designed to help you find what you need to master Mozilla.

Part IV: Developing and Building Mozilla

Part IV first looks at the build systems used by Mozilla, and then looks at developing and building Mozilla in detail. It covers how to set up developer environments for Windows, Macintosh, Unix, and Linux-based systems; how to download and compile source modules; and how to build the beast — Mozilla.

Appendixes

The Appendixes contain reference resources. Included are CVS, a key development tool you'll use when working with the Mozilla source code; insights into the portability lessons Netscape programmers learned through years of developing Netscape Communicator; and a quick reference for Netscape's Open Source forums and discussions. There is also an appendix that provides an overview of the CD-ROM resources and software.

Who Should Read This Book?

When I first started developing the idea for this book, I asked myself this question a lot: Who is the audience? I initially thought that the book would focus solely on those interested in developing solutions using the Mozilla source code. Over the next year though, as I delved deeper and deeper into the source code, I had a startling realization: Every serious C and C++ programmer should read this book.

Mozilla contains extensive libraries of C and C++ functions and modules. Not only can these functions and modules teach you a lot about coding, but also they can be integrated into your development projects, provided you follow the Netscape Public License agreement. Mozilla also offers a first-class case study in developing large-scale, cross-platform applications, and by studying the structure of the code and its management, you can learn more than you ever imagined you could.

Acknowledgments

Incredible as it may seem, *Netscape Mozilla Source Code Guide* has been nearly two years in the making. I worked out the book's concept in January 1998, right after Netscape made its historic announcement about the Open Source program. I am a big supporter of free software and of Linux, and knew that Mozilla would be a great subject to write about. The problem was that the code wasn't available yet; I had to create a proposal based on a few paragraphs posted in a press release. I pitched the proposal to Ann Lush, an acquisitions editor who I knew was looking for Netscape-related books. She loved the idea and wanted to run with it. When the source code was finally released, I quickly realized how incredibly difficult writing a book about it would be. At the time, there wasn't any documentation, and mozilla.org was just getting started. I was on my own. To write this book, I had to become a Mozilla source code guru (or at least try to be), but you don't just jump into 30 million lines of code without a life preserver — and I didn't have one. I told Ann that the timing wasn't right and that I thought it would be better to wait.

Early in 1999 Ann Lush contacted me through my agents, David Rogelberg and Neil Salkind of Studio B Literary Agency. She wondered if I was still interested in writing a book on Mozilla. I was (and wasn't). After a year of working with the source, I still hadn't mastered it, but I had learned many valuable lessons. Eventually I said yes but stated that the book would have to be very different from what I had originally conceived. Ann agreed, and the rest, as they say, is history.

After many twists and turns, a heartfelt thanks to Ann Lush is definitely in order. As I write this, she is at home on maternity leave with her newborn little girl (who was conceived, carried to term, and brought into the world sooner than this book!). I'd also like to thank my agents, David Rogelberg and Neil Salkind. Great agents help make good writers better.

Thanks to Eric Newman for doing the development work on the book. I hope we can work together many more times in the future. Thanks also to a few pinch hitters, such as Amy Barkat, the technical reviewers, and the rest of the editorial team for shepherding the book through the publishing process.

Thanks also to my wife and family, who helped me make it through the long days and nights of writing.

In the end, so many people helped make this book a reality that it is difficult to name them all. But before I forget, I want to offer a Texas-sized "Thank you!" to the following developers, module owners, and others currently working on the Mozilla project: Akkana Peck, Alex Musil, Andrew Volkov, Bill Law, Bob Jung, Brendan Eich, Brian Ostrom, Charles Manske, Chris Karnaze, Chris McAfee, Chris Saari, Chris Toshok, Chris Waterson, Christine Begle, Christopher Blizzard, Christopher Yeh, Chuck Boatwright, Dan Veditz, Daniel (Leaf) Nunes, Daniel Matejka, David Hyatt, David Matiskella, Don Cone, Don Melton, Doug Turner, Eric Bina, Eric Broadbent, Eric Vaughan, Erik van der Poel, Fred Roeber, Gagan Saksena, Gordon Sheridan, Greg Kostello, Greg Roelofs, Harish Dhurvasula, Hubert Shaw, Jamie Zawinski, Jeff Weinstein, Jerry L. Kirk, Jim Everingham, Joaquin Blas, Joe Francis, John Bandhauer, John Giannandrea, John Kristian, John McMullen, Kathleen Brade, Kevin McCluskey, Kipp Hickman, Lawrence Hardiman, Leif Hedstrom, Lisa Repka, Lou Montulli, Mark Welch, Matt Wilson, Michael Judge, Michael Plitkins, Mike McCabe, Mike Pinkerton, Mike Shaver, Miodrag Kekic, Naoki Hotta, Neeti Jain, Nisheeth Ranjan, Norris Boyd, Pam Nunn, Patrick Beard, Peter Linss, Peter Trudelle, Pierre Saslawsky, Radha Kulkarni, Raman Tenneti, Ramanathan Guha, Ramiro Estrugo, Rick Gessner, Rick Potts, Robert Churchill, Scott Collins, Scott Furman, Scott Putterman, Sol Goldfarb, Srinivas Lingutla, Steve Clark, Steve Dagley, Steve Elmer, Steve Lamm, Stuart Parmenter, Sudharshan Srinivasan, Suresh Duddi, Syd Logan, Terry Weissman, Tom Lane, Tom Pixley, Tom Weinstein, Troy Chevalier, Vidur Apparao, Vladimir Livshits, Wan-Teh Chang, Warren Harris, Will Scullin, and Yung-Fong Tang.

Contents at a Glance

Part I

Getting Started

Part II

Managing the Source Code

Part III

Working with the Source Code

Part IV

Developing and Building Mozilla

Contents

Part I

Part II

Part III

Part IV

PART

I

Getting Started

Getting Started

Netscape shocked the development community by announcing that it would release the source code for Communicator 5.0, marking the first time for a major software company to give away the source code to one of the world's most popular applications. Now it's your turn to make a difference. Get involved. Use the Netscape Open Source program. Develop custom solutions. Become a part of history in the making.

Introducing Mozilla and the Netscape Open Source Program

Early in 1998, Netscape announced to the world that it would provide the source code for Netscape Communicator freely to the Internet community and that this free version of Communicator would be known as *Mozilla*. Mozilla is possibly the single most important development in the history of the Open Source movement — and that's saying a lot considering its predecessors are the likes of Linux, BSD Unix, and Apache. Mozilla is so important because it is a cornerstone application for everything the Internet has to offer, from browsing to e-mail to newsgroups and more.

Every day millions of people access the Internet, or Net, using Communicator. As the number of Net users grows, so do the number of people who use browsers, and a large portion of these users will use browsers based on the Mozilla source code. As a programmer, you have an opportunity to be a part of this historic development, writing code for what could become one of the most widely used applications of all time.

Because Mozilla is so large and complex, there are always hundreds of different initiatives ongoing at mozilla.org, the official headquarters of Netscape's Open Source movement. By becoming a member of the Mozilla team, you can help implement projects you find interesting regardless of whether you want to program, track down bugs, or write documentation. You can even go it alone and develop your own custom solutions using Mozilla.

Introducing Mozilla

Mozilla is many things to many people, and this is because the word's meaning has evolved over time. Mozilla was introduced to the world with Netscape Navigator. It is the original code name for the browser and later for Communicator. It is the internal code name that Navigator and Communicator report in the HTTP header request. It is also the name of Netscape's mascot, a friendly, fire-breathing dinosaur. When Netscape released the source code for Netscape Communicator, mozilla.org adopted the term as well, using it as the catchword for both the free software version of Netscape Communicator and any browsers developed from this code.

So What Is Mozilla?

With so many meanings, it is difficult to know what Mozilla is and isn't. In this book, Mozilla is the name for the free software version of Communicator. Mozilla is based on the first developer release of Communicator 5.0. Most of Mozilla's source code is written in C and C++.

Versions of Mozilla are available for many different platforms, including most Unix, Windows, and Macintosh systems. Support for these many different versions are provided in platform-specific builds. For example, a Unix/X build is used on Unix systems such as Solaris, Linux, Irix, HP/UX and DG/UX. A Win32/MFC build is used on 32-bit Windows systems such as Windows 95, Windows 98, and Windows NT 4.0. A Mac build is used on Macintosh Power PC systems.

Since its release, the Mozilla source code has changed dramatically, so much so that the original codebase had to be retired. The old codebase, known as *Mozilla Classic,* uses the original layout engine and platform-dependent GUI interfaces developed by Netscape, and the current codebase uses next generation layout and cross-platform GUI interfaces. The reasons for moving to a new codebase are many, but the primary reason is that the old codebase held developers back. The original layout engine had outlived its usefulness, and the original front-ends were platform specific and difficult to update for the latest features. To move forward, developers needed a clean break.

The codebase for Mozilla is divided into modules. A module is a collection of source files that usually form a library or link as executables. Libraries can be dynamically linked through DLLs, shared objects through DSOs/Sos, or static. Within the codebase, you may find modules that belong to Mozilla Classic, previous versions of Mozilla that are no longer being developed, as well as the current Mozilla development efforts. If you find old modules while working through the source, keep in mind they usually are considered to be obsolete and are maintained primarily for historical purposes.

How Are Mozilla and Communicator Different?

Mozilla and Communicator are different in many ways — some subtle and some not so subtle. First, browsers based on Mozilla do not have the familiar N logo (see Figure 1-1). The N logo can be used only with official releases of Netscape Communicator. But this is not bad news because you'll probably want to use your own logo anyway, and why would you not? You have the source code and can insert graphics as you see fit.

Figure 1-1: Browsers based on Mozilla can't use the N logo.

Mozilla is also missing features that are proprietary or that Netscape couldn't obtain rights to release publicly. Key features that you'll find missing are:

- **Java support:** the Java implementation originally used by Communicator is the property of Sun Microsystems. However, an Open Java Virtual Machine Interface (OJI) is implemented in Mozilla. The OJI enables you to use Java Virtual Machines and plug-ins that can Java-enable Mozilla.

- **Instant Messenger:** An online messaging tool.

- **Cryptographic features:** SSL (Secure Sockets Layer), S/MIME (Secure MIME) and other cryptographic features are removed because of export restrictions. While you could argue that 40-bit encryption code could have been released, this would require a separate export license, which wouldn't have been granted by the U.S. government under existing regulations.

■ **Netscape Messenger for e-mail and Netscape Collabra for discussion groups:** Messenger and Collabra use proprietary database code. However, mail and news clients are available. There's even an all-Java mail and news client code-named Grendel.

Netscape has stated that development work on Communicator will continue. Netscape's goal for Communicator is to ensure it is a quality product for end users. To maintain stability, ease of use, and more, certain features of Mozilla will not be used in official Communicator releases. This means that as Mozilla and Communicator continue to evolve, there will be other features that Communicator has and Mozilla doesn't — and vice versa.

Understanding the Netscape Open Source Program

Although there are many differences between Mozilla and Communicator, there are also many similarities. (Mozilla and Communicator are the two evolving branches of the same root.) Mozilla is based on the first developer release of Communicator 5.0, and, moving forward, innovations developed in the Mozilla codebase may be integrated into future versions of Communicator. What this means for developers is that the code you create may become a part of both Mozilla and Communicator. This philosophy of achieving innovation through co-operation is at the heart of Netscape's Open Source program, though there's much more to this program than a philosophy. To understand why there is more to it, you have to understand what Open Source is all about and where the program is headed.

What Is Open Source?

You may be wondering what Open Source is all about. The phrase carries much more meaning than the words *free software*. While many organizations give away free software, very few organizations give away their source code. Traditionally, source code contains a company's top secrets. Entire companies and billion-dollar businesses have been built around codebases. Such businesses succeed by keeping their code out of the hands of their competitors, or at least this is the rationale behind maintaining proprietary codebases.

Supporters of Open Source put a 180-degree spin on this notion of secrecy. Instead of hiding their codebases from competitors, they peel back the corporate veil of secrecy and give everyone access to their source code. Their beliefs are simple: When you share knowledge with others and allow others to contribute to the whole, the whole is made better. You foster innovation. You allow others to create solutions without reinventing the wheel. Eventually, the innovations come back to you and you can use them to make your original codebase better, faster, and stronger.

As you can probably guess, there is a lot of back and forth banter between Open Source supporters and Open Source opponents. Open Source supporters want more organizations to join them and tear down the walls of secrecy. Open Source opponents want the whole movement to go away. Regardless of which side of the Open Source movement you are on traditionally, it is hard to argue against the tangible benefits of an Open Source program — just ask the folks at mozilla.org.

Hundreds of individuals have joined in the effort to improve and enhance Mozilla. Their efforts have solved problems and introduced innovations that wouldn't have been achieved otherwise. These individuals have identified and fixed countless bugs, refined and streamlined the codebase, and created new modules and new ways of doing things.

One of the greatest achievements to come out of the Open Source program thus far is Mozilla's NGLayout engine (Next Generation HTML Layout engine). NGLayout is a high performance layout engine that supports HTML 4.0, CSS 1.0/2.0, XML 1.0 and the Document Object Model. The layout engine allows for faster and smoother renderings of complex layouts such as the massively nested table shown in Figure 1-2. Although the table shown in the figure is nested eight levels deep, Mozilla displays it instantly. Under the old layout engine, the table rendering would have been noticeably slow — even if the table had been loaded from cache.

NOTE

NGLayout is used in the official release of Communicator 5.0 and in the current Mozilla codebase. If you'd like to try out the stress tests, you can find them online at `www.mozilla.org/newlayout/testcases/stress/`. When I first ran through the stress tests, I was amazed how fast the test cases were rendered.

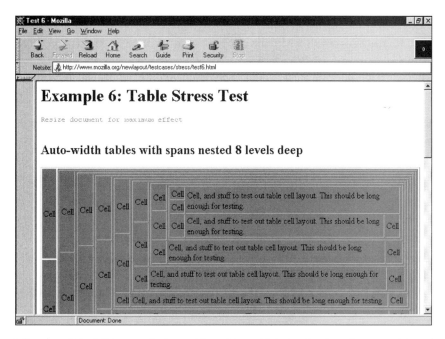

Figure 1-2: NGLayout displays tables with multiple levels of nesting smoothly and quickly.

Where Is Open Source Headed?

While I'd like to say that Netscape's Open Source initiative is headed nowhere but up, many people in the software industry would love to see Mozilla fail. In their eyes, the failure of the Mozilla project would prove that the concepts of openness and innovation through cooperation simply don't work, which is where you and I come into the picture. We have to prove the naysayers wrong. Open Source can and does work; Linux, Apache, and others are a testament and we have witnessed their success.

Netscape has stated publicly that it is behind the Open Source program 100 percent. Netscape shows its support by providing the resources needed to run the Open Source program and by fostering Mozilla's growth in the Net community. Beyond this, Netscape's role in the Open Source program is the same as that of any other participant. Netscape contributes to the codebase and makes use of innovations entered into the codebase. These innovations may or may not appear in future versions of Communicator.

Mozilla is the highest profile Open Source initiative launched in recent years. A resounding success for Mozilla over the long term will benefit the entire Free Software Community. Who knows, we may even see the big guns in the software industry open their vault doors and embrace Open Source.

How to Take Advantage of Netscape's Open Source Program

Taking advantage of Netscape's Open Source program is easy. All you have to do is participate in the program (as discussed in this part of the book) and follow the related licensing agreements. If you do these two things, you can maximize the benefits from the Open Source program.

Licensing Issues

Open Source doesn't mean do as you please. The Mozilla source code is still copyright protected by Netscape, and its use is subject to certain rules and restrictions that are covered in one of two licensing agreements: the Netscape Public License or the Mozilla Public License.

Use subject to a licensing agreement isn't unusual — most free software programs are subject to a licensing agreement such as the GNU General Public License, developed by the Free Software Foundation; or the BSD License, developed by the University of California at Berkeley. What is unusual is that Netscape chose not to use the generic licensing agreements already available. In a moment, you'll understand why, but before we get into the hows and whys of Netscape's licenses, let's look at basic licensing issues.

Licensing Basics

Because the source code is copyright protected by Netscape, you must have Netscape's permission to alter it. The conditions and terms are covered in Netscape's licensing agreements. A key reason for having a licensing agreement is to set the basic rules for use of the original source code as well as for the use of enhancements to this source code.

Free software licensing agreements also tend to foster the growth of the codebase. Netscape's licensing agreements support this by encouraging (and in some cases requiring) programmers to give something back to the codebase. There are many reasons why Netscape chose not to use industry-standard freeware-software licenses; the key reasons are to ensure the following:

- Developers are not able to use the Mozilla source code in both commercial and non-commercial products.

- Enhancements are made available in source code format to the general public.

- If Mozilla is part of a larger work, other code doesn't have to be covered by the Netscape licensing agreement and its source code doesn't have to be revealed to the public.

As stated earlier, Netscape decided to use two different licensing agreements. One agreement covers the use of Netscape's own source code as well as the source code developed by others in conjunction with Mozilla. Because this agreement grants special rights to Netscape, a second agreement was drawn up that doesn't give Netscape special rights. This second agreement can be used only with completely new code and not with modifications to existing Mozilla source code. What this means is that if you develop original code (new code) in conjunction with the Mozilla project, you can use this second agreement.

Netscape Public License

The Netscape Public License (NPL) governs the use of the Mozilla source code and modifications to the source code. The basic premise of the NPL is the same as outlined in licensing basics. You should be able to use the Mozilla source code in both commercial and non-commercial products. If you make enhancements to the source code, those enhancements should be made available in source code format to the general public. However, only your changes need to be published, not the entire source files in changed form. Further, if Mozilla is part of a larger work, the code for this other work doesn't have to be revealed to the public. If you use the Mozilla source code or create enhancements to this source code, you are subject to this licensing agreement.

The sections that follow delve deeper into individual sections of the NPL. However, they aren't legal advice and are meant for descriptive purposes only.

CROSS-REFERENCE
The Netscape Public License and the Mozilla Public License appear in the back of this book.

Modifications to the Source Code

Ordinarily, NPL doesn't cover completely new source code that is developed in conjunction with Mozilla. Because of this, you need to know exactly what a modification is and isn't:

- Renaming and/or combining the contents of source files *is* a modification.

- Changing the content of an existing source file *is* a modification.

- Taking code out of a source file and placing it in a new file *is* a modification.

- Creating a new file that doesn't contain any of the original source code *isn't* a modification.

Code that isn't considered a modification doesn't need to be covered by the NPL. However, the code should be under a compatible license, such as the Mozilla Public License.

Source code modifications must be distributed with executable versions of the product or they must be made available via an electronic distribution method such as FTP. A document that describes your modifications must accompany the source code. The document must also prominently state the origins of the source code.

Other Documentation Requirements

The modification document isn't the only documentation you must distribute or make available with code or products subject to this agreement. If you use code subject to third-party intellectual property claims, you must create a document called LEGAL. This document must describe in complete detail the intellectual property claims and the party making the claim.

Further, source files that use code subject to the license must include Exhibit A from the NPL, if possible, given the structure of the file. Exhibit A provides information on the Netscape Public License and is shown as Listing 1-1. If you've modified the code in the file, be sure to add your name to the list of contributors, as shown in the listing. If you can't include Exhibit A in the file, you must put the notification in a location where users are likely to look for such a file, such as in a separate file in the same directory as the source file.

Printed documentation that accompanies a product must also include the NPL.

LISTING 1-1: EXHIBIT A FROM THE NETSCAPE PUBLIC LICENSE VERSION 1.0

```
"The contents of this file are subject to the Netscape
Public License Version 1.0 (the "License"); you may not use
this file except in compliance with the License. You may
obtain a copy of the License at http://www.mozilla.org/NPL/

Software distributed under the License is distributed on an
"AS IS" basis, WITHOUT WARRANTY OF ANY KIND, either express
or implied. See the License for the specific language
governing rights and limitations under the License.

The Original Code is Mozilla Communicator client code,
released March 31, 1998.

The Initial Developer of the Original Code is Netscape
Communications Corporation. Portions created by Netscape
are Copyright (C) 1998 Netscape Communications Corporation.
All Rights Reserved.

Contributor(s): Brendan Eich (brendan@netscape.com)
William Stanek (mozilla-fan@tvpress.com)."
```

NOTE
The contributor information is added to the example. You would, of course, modify this information to include your name as well as the name of other contributors.

Contributions and Special Rights

Everyone who contributes to the Mozilla project is subject to the NPL, and this includes Netscape. However, because Netscape is the initial developer of the source code, Netscape has special rights to the code that other parties do not. These special rights are defined as follows:

- The right to use code covered by the NPL in other Netscape products without those products' being subject to the NPL.

- The right to license code covered by the NPL to third parties under terms different from those of the NPL.

- The right to revise the license in the future.

Netscape retains these rights to ensure that the company can meet certain product and licensing agreements. If Netscape didn't have these rights, the company couldn't comply with contractual obligations made to third parties that distribute and use Netscape products.

License Grants

NPL grants a worldwide, royalty-free, non-exclusive right to use the source code, subject to third party intellectual property claims. To understand what this means, let's take the clause apart word by word:

- **Worldwide:** You can use and distribute the source code anywhere in the world.

- **Royalty free:** You can use the source code without having to pay for the privilege.

- **Non-exclusive:** You don't have an exclusive right to the source code, meaning you aren't the only authorized user—anyone and everyone can use the code as well.

- **Subject to third party claims:** The rights of third parties are protected and not included in the previous grants. This means that if you use someone else's code (a third party), this person or organization can claim rights to the code as necessary.

Contributions you make to the Mozilla codebase are subject to these grants as well, provided these contributions are considered to be enhancements, meaning modifications to existing code. If you contribute completely new source code, the grants you provide to other developers are spelled out in the applicable license.

Mozilla Public License

The Mozilla Public License is designed to be identical to the NPL with one exception: The license doesn't grant any special rights to Netscape, and this means:

- Netscape can't use code covered by MPL in other Netscape products without the products being covered under MPL.

- Netscape can't license the code to third parties under terms different from those of MPL.

- Netscape can't revise the existing license for code already covered under a specific version of the MPL. (For example, Netscape can't grandfather code under MPL 1.0 and make it fall under MPL 2.0 rules—unless, of course, you do this when you re-release the code.)

If you are developing new source code in conjunction with the Mozilla project, you can (but don't have to) use this license. The key reason to use this license is that code you issue under this license can be used freely with code covered by the NPL.

License Versions

NPL and MPL give Netscape the authority to create new versions of these licenses. Key licenses versions are 1.0 and 1.1. Netscape Public License version 1.0 and Mozilla Public License are provided as separate documents to which you can attach Exhibit A.

With version 1.1 of the public licenses for Mozilla, Netscape adds stricter wording for commercial use and distribution of the source code. You'll also find additional wording for third party claims, particularly in the areas of patents and intellectual property rights. Unlike the previous version 1.0, the version 1.1 licenses are combined into a single legal document. When you want to apply the Mozilla Public License using the version 1.1 document, you:

- Include the Mozilla Public License Version 1.1 and Exhibit A-Mozilla Public License

- Delete the Amendments and Exhibit A-Netscape Public License.

The Netscape Public License Version 1.1, on the other hand, consists of the Mozilla Public License Version 1.1 with the Amendments and Exhibit A-Netscape Public License. This means you include the entire document in the source code.

What License Should You Use?

When you use Netscape's original source code or modify existing code, you must use the Netscape Public License. When you create new code, you can use the Netscape Public License, the Mozilla Public License, or just about any other license of your choosing.

Being able to choose your license is a good thing, but there are some caveats you should be aware of. If you choose to use the NPL with new code, remember that you grant Netscape special rights when you do so. If you choose not to use Netscape's licenses, you can use other publicly available free software licenses. Keep in mind, though, that the GNU General Public License isn't compatible with NPL. Basically, this is because the grants in the GNU License conflict with grants in NPL.

Granting special rights to Netscape may be something you don't want to do. If so, you may want to develop the code in such a way that you always use new source code files. For example, you can modify a file subject to NPL so that it calls or references your source code file. While the changes you make to the original source code are covered by the NPL, the code in the new source files would be covered by the license of your choice.

Exploring mozilla.org

In this chapter you've seen several references to mozilla.org. By now you may have even visited mozilla.org's Web site (`www.mozilla.org`). However, do you really know what mozilla.org is all about?

What Is mozilla.org?

Distributed software projects need a central resource for the coordination of activities and integration of changes. For Mozilla, that central resource is mozilla.org. If you visit mozilla.org's Web site, shown in Figure 1-3, you'll quickly discover that a lot of effort goes into maintaining Mozilla and although the members of mozilla.org are in charge of the effort, the entire Mozilla project depends on contributors like you and me. Without contributors, there wouldn't be a Mozilla project and there wouldn't be a need for mozilla.org.

mozilla.org has many responsibilities. These responsibilities include collecting and distributing changes to the source code, providing tools that help authors work with the code, operating discussion forums that help coordinate development efforts, and publishing bug lists, road maps, and other important documentation. Still, the most important responsibility of the organization is to provide a useful and responsive service for Mozilla developers.

Who Are the Members?

mozilla.org is a Netscape-sponsored organization. Netscape pays for the hardware needed to run the Web site, the discussion forums, and other services. Members of the organization are employees of Netscape. If you want to learn about the current members, follow the Who We Are links in Mozilla's menu, as shown in Figure 1-4.

Figure 1-3: mozilla.org's Web site is a great place to learn about Mozilla.

Figure 1-4: Members of mozilla.org integrate code changes, resolve problems, and coordinate enhancements.

Although members of mozilla.org may write code, they are not the primary programmers of the Mozilla source code. Most of the source code in Mozilla is written by the Netscape Client Engineering team or by programmers like you and me. Rather than write code, mozilla.org members integrate code, resolve problems, and help coordinate future enhancements to the source code.

Summary

Mozilla and Netscape Communicator are evolving together. It is possible that source code you work on today will become a part of both applications in the future. Normally, development of the Mozilla source code falls under one of two licenses, either the Netscape Public License or the Mozilla Public License. As you begin to work with Mozilla, it is important that you understand the difference between these licenses. NPL grants special rights to Netscape and is used in combination with existing code. MPL doesn't grant special rights and can be used only with new code.

A key resource for Mozilla developers is mozilla.org. The mozilla.org Web site is organized into several different areas. You'll find links related to the organization as a whole, the organization's development, and its products. If you want to learn more about mozilla.org, I suggest that you start by reading the mission statement posted online. Afterward, move on to the other organizational links. The information you'll find here will give you a good overview of what mozilla.org is all about.

Getting Involved

You can go it alone and use the Mozilla source code to develop your own custom solutions without ever becoming a part of the goings-on at mozilla.org. However, you'll miss out on a very rewarding experience that involves teamwork, a community, and skills building. Indeed, the best part of Netscape's Open Source efforts is that the program is set up to help anyone get involved with the ongoing development of Mozilla. If you want to become a part of these efforts, all you need is a willingness to be a part of a team effort and the dedication to contribute in whatever area makes sense based on your skill set.

Serious programmers will find that there are hundreds of different ways to contribute. After all, Mozilla is a programming effort, and it revolves around source code. For example, if you specialize in network programming, you'll feel right at home with the folks working on Mozilla's networking libraries. If you want to program front-end interfaces, you'll want to join other developers who are working on Mozilla's cross-platform front-end. And the list goes on and on. While programming is a key focus of the project, Mozilla is a development effort, and no development effort would be complete without project managers, documentation specialists, and all the other people who help the project flow smoothly.

Whether you decide to contribute actively to Mozilla or to develop your own custom solutions, you'll need to stay in touch with where the Mozilla project is heading and what's happening in various development areas. As you'll discover in this chapter, there are many different ways to track Mozilla's progress. You can tune in to status reports from mozilla.org, follow newsgroup postings, and much more.

Joining the Open Source Team

As you learned in the previous chapter, mozilla.org is the main organization that manages Mozilla. mozilla.org does not have paid memberships and is not managed by third parties. Its managers are employees of Netscape. If you want to become a part of mozilla.org, you need to join the open source development team. You do this by learning about the team, following the rules of engagement, and then making contributions when you are ready. Source code and documentation are the key ways to participate in the Mozilla project, but you can contribute in other ways as well.

NOTE
I use the phrases such as "contribute to the team" and "join the team" purposely. Netscape personnel staff mozilla.org. These staff members serve as representatives of Netscape, and their goals are to coordinate activities and integrate source code changes. mozilla.org is not a membership organization, however. No dues or payments of any kind are required to participate.

Before You Contribute

Structure and rules are important to the success of any project, and Mozilla is no exception. The Mozilla project began in early 1998, and many of the current contributors have been with the project from day one. They know Mozilla well and they've been working hard to make it better. These early contributors are the ones who set the pace and direction for the initial development efforts. They also helped shape the structure of the project.

Each day, new contributors join the open source team. They watch what's going on and participate by making real contributions. In time, they make suggestions, and if they've proved themselves through their contributions, those suggestions are considered earnestly; this enables new contributors to help shape the future of the project as well.

With this in mind, don't be in a hurry to suggest changes without first demonstrating know-how through your actions. Accomplishments speak volumes. If you want to be a part of the Open Source team, nothing demonstrates your dedication more than your accomplishments. Don't try to bully your way in by talking a good talk; succeed by doing. Show the current contributors you know your stuff by making real contributions such as source code, documentation, or other essential resources.

Contributing Source Code

Source code is the heart of Mozilla. After all, Mozilla is a software project. This means there are many opportunities for serious programmers. Examples of the types of projects you could work on are:

- Updating Mozilla's graphics libraries to support new types of images
- Helping to port Mozilla to your favorite operating system
- Adding support for new technologies such as ActiveX
- Helping to clean up and modularize APIs
- Improving Mozilla's support for Perl, XML, Java, and other key technologies
- Extending current functions with new features
- Working with others to help make international and localized versions of Mozilla
- Implementation of next generation features such as the cross-platform front-end interface
- Enhancing the networking libraries to support new protocols
- Revamping the preference dialogs to make them more user-friendly

You could also lend a hand in any of the ongoing Mozilla projects. You'll learn more about these projects in the section of this chapter, "Where's Mozilla Headed?"

Contributing Documentation

Mozilla is a huge project and there is always a need for people to help with the documentation. This means there are numerous opportunities for those who want to write documents rather than code. Examples of documentation projects are:

- Writing design specifications
- Creating flow charts for the source code
- Updating the user documentation
- Writing white papers that cover the technical aspects of Mozilla
- Translating existing documents into other languages

Contributing in Other Ways

Just because you're a programmer and want to learn Mozilla's secrets doesn't mean you want to write code or documentation. But you can still contribute, and here's how:

- Get involved with project planning.
- Design new graphics for use in Mozilla interfaces.
- Help with internationalization and localization efforts by offering your linguistic skills.
- Become a champion of Mozilla and the Open Source movement.

How to Contribute

Mozilla is one of the most exciting projects you'll ever be a part of. You'll learn large-scale development skills, get experience creating code for a commercial-grade application, and become a part of an elite developer community. All you have to do is contribute your time and skills.

If you'd like to contribute to the Mozilla project, here are some suggestions:

- Don't try to specialize in many different areas. Mozilla is too complex. Instead, select a specific area, library, or API you'd like to specialize in, such as the networking library, and then familiarize yourself with the related source code.

■ Determine who is in charge of the area you'd like to work in. Introduce yourself to this person and let him or her know you are interested in helping out, but don't make specific suggestions until you are sure you know what's going on. (See "Understanding Modules" later in this chapter.)

■ Check on projects that are underway for this area. If projects are underway, do some investigative work to see what's been done on the project and what hasn't. (Learning about current and future projects is discussed later in the chapter. Look for the section, "Where's Mozilla Headed?")

■ Follow discussion groups. You'll find there are many Mozilla-related discussion groups on Usenet. If there are groups related to your chosen area, keep track of them. (You'll learn about these discussion groups in the section of this chapter, "Staying in Touch with Discussion Groups.")

■ Read this book to learn about Mozilla's source code, development tools, and more. When you finish and have worked on the preceding items, start developing content in your chosen area.

Understanding Modules

The Mozilla source code is organized into modules, which are collections of source files. Each module has a designated owner who manages the module. Module owners decide which improvements to add to a module, which bug fixes to use, and so on. Usually, each module is also assigned peers who can help field questions related to the module.

Meet the Module Owners

If you want to find out who owns a particular module, visit mozilla.org. mozilla.org is responsible for assigning module ownership and keeping a list of module owners. This list is published on the module ownership page, shown in Figure 2-1. The URL for this page is `www.mozilla.org/owners.html`.

You can use this page to learn a lot about modules and their ownership. Module entries are listed alphabetically and provide the following information:

■ **Owner:** The name of the module owner, provided as a clickable mailto link. (The link usually includes courtesy copies for the module's peers as well.)

- **Source:** The location of the module's source code, provided as a clickable link to the module's Mozilla Cross Reference page.

- **Newsgroup:** The names of any newsgroups related to the module.

- **Peers:** A list of people who help coordinate module efforts.

- **Documents:** A list of documents related to the module.

NOTE

All modules in Netscape's Open Source program are listed on this page at the current time. This means that some of the listed modules aren't specific to Mozilla. For example, the Directory SDK module is implemented in Netscape server products and provides tools and SDKs for accessing LDAP Directories. As the program expands, you may see separate pages for other types of modules.

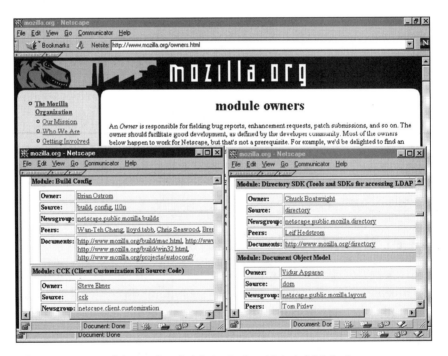

Figure 2-1: Modules are listed alphabetically with helpful links for owners, source files, newsgroups, peers, and documents.

More on Module Owners

Ideally, the module owner is the person who knows the module the best and as such, the person who knows what is the best course for the module. You can think of module owners as project managers who are responsible for all aspects of the module. In this role, they have the right to make decisions related to the module and its future.

Module owners are responsible for submitting module changes to mozilla.org and can delegate the authority to others as necessary. This enables other programmers to submit changes directly to the source code repository, which is kinda cool. You'll learn more about checking code in and out of the source repository in Chapter 4.

Although module owners are responsible for the module, mozilla.org has the final say as to what changes are incorporated into the source distribution. This enables mozilla.org to coordinate and control Mozilla's overall future, and is necessary to ensure that Mozilla meets the necessary usability, compatibility, and quality standards.

Becoming a Module Owner

mozilla.org's module ownership policies are designed to allow ownership to change over time. This means that today's module owners may not be the same module owners six months from now. The key issues driving ownership are who knows the module the best and who can manage the module the best. So if you get to be a module's guru, you may end up being the module owner.

Module ownership changes through one of several different ways. A current module owner who doesn't want the job anymore can give up control of the module. If a module owner isn't doing a good job and refuses to be reasonable, mozilla.org may assign the module to someone else. You can also petition mozilla.org (or the module owner) if you feel you should be the module owner. However, you should have a strong track record as a contributor and sound reasoning to back up such a claim.

Where Is Mozilla Headed?

Mozilla is quite possibly the largest development project you'll ever work on. Worldwide, the project has thousands of contributors who work in hundreds of different areas. So before you dive into the source code, documentation, or whatever else you want to work on, you should take a look at where Mozilla's been and where its headed.

Development Overview

The mozilla.org team has some pretty high goals for making Mozilla the best of its class. These goals focus on reworking existing Mozilla modules so that they are easily enhanced, have cross-platform functionality, are easily accessed from other modules and at the same time ensure that new modules have these same features inherently. These goals gave rise to many major development initiatives. Some of the key initiatives that have global consequences to the Mozilla source code are XPCOM, XP-IDL, NGLayout, and XPFE.

A Quick Look at XPCOM and XP-IDL

Although modules are a key aspect of Mozilla, some of the original libraries weren't designed as modules. During the early development of the Mozilla source code, decisions were made to break existing code into modules as necessary and ensure that new code was created in modules. New Mozilla modules are to be created using principles based on XPCOM, a cross-platform architecture that mimics COM (but is not truly written using the COM architecture).

To specify and query their programmatic interfaces, new modules should use XP-IDL. XP-IDL is a CORBA IDL-based language with extensions to support Mozilla's cross-platform requirements. This enables the modules to be scripted with easy-to-use C++ entry points. The goal is to make it easy to create event hooks and to script key parts of the browser using Netscape's own JavaScript.

CROSS-REFERENCE
You'll find detailed information on XPCOM and XP-IDL in Chapter 3. This chapter details techniques you need to know in order to work with Mozilla's back-end architecture.

A Quick Look at NGLayout and XPFE

When Netscape released the Mozilla source code, the application used a fairly old layout engine and front-end interfaces that were platform-specific. To help developers move forward, this layout engine and the old-style front-end interfaces were set aside in favor of NGLayout (a new layout engine) and XPFE (a cross-platform front-end).

All user interfaces that you develop for NGLayout should be written in HTML or XML with style elements abstracted and expressed in CSS wherever possible. Style elements that can be queried, modified, or superimposed from remote sources should be written as RDF that conforms to proper XML syntax. Additionally, event-based behavior should be separated from the HTML or XML using Action sheets and defined with JavaScript handlers.

CROSS-REFERENCE

You'll find detailed information on NGLayout, XPFE, and Action sheets in Chapter 6; it details techniques you need to know in order to work with Mozilla's user interfaces and front-end functionality.

More Development Initiatives

As you know, Mozilla is changing all the time, and this means that many development initiatives are underway right now. To learn more about current development initiatives, visit the Development Roadmap section of mozilla.org (`www.mozilla.org/roadmap.html`). In the roadmap section, you'll find a brief history of Mozilla, and information on where the project is headed.

Following Current and Future Projects

With so many people working on Mozilla, there are numerous projects ongoing at any given time. To keep pace with key projects, visit mozilla.org's projects list. The URL for this page is `www.mozilla.org/projects.html`.

At the time of this writing, many projects are under development. The following are samples of these projects:

■ **ColorSync:** An initiative to manage color displays so that all viewers see colors as the Web designer intended.

- **Configurable UI:** An initiative that uses RDF to create customizable toolbars. The emphasis is on enabling both users and Web publishers to modify toolbars.

- **ElectricalFire:** An initiative to create a high-performance Java virtual machine that uses Just In Time compiling to speed up the execution of Java code and is portable across multiple architectures.

- **Internationalization (I18N):** An initiative to extend Mozilla's support for other writing systems.

- **JavaScript Debugging:** An initiative to create a cross-platform debugging support module for JavaScript that will include a Java-based GUI debugger, a JavaScript logging tool, and a console debugger.

- **Localization (L10N):** An initiative to extend Mozilla's language support and localize the Mozilla user interface for new languages.

- **Open JVM Integration:** An initiative to extend the plug-in architecture to enable Java virtual machines to be plugged into Mozilla.

- **SilentDownload:** An initiative to enable files to be downloaded without interfering with network performance. This is done by downloading files while Mozilla's networking library isn't being used by the end-user.

Keep in mind that the project list is really for projects that are large in scope. These projects usually revolve around new modules or new functionality that affects multiple modules. If you want to find internal projects that are specific to a particular module, you should contact the module owner.

Other resources you'll want to tap into to stay current with project developments are:

- mozilla.org News (`www.mozilla.org/news.html`): A chronological list of key initiatives and important news for the Mozilla developer community.

- Blue Sky (`www.mozilla.org/blue-sky/`): A wish list for future projects to enhance Mozilla.

Status Reports

Another way to keep track of where Mozilla is headed is to tune in to mozilla.org's weekly status reports. You'll find the status reports page at `www.mozilla.org/status/`. These reports provide a quick summary of development work on key projects and modules. Old reports are archived so that you can go back through reports for previous weeks; this is a great way to catch up with Mozilla happenings.

For daily updates, visit MozillaZine. MozillaZine (`www.mozillazine.org`) provides news and commentary on current Mozilla events. You'll also find useful resources, demos, and more.

Staying in Touch with Other Developers

Developing code in a vacuum isn't fun. You need to be in touch with other developers, and a great way to do this is to use mozilla.org's discussion forums. Mozilla discussion forums are sponsored by mozilla.org and are designed for developers who want to discuss the Mozilla source code. With this in mind, you should discuss only source code and/or development issues. If you want to discuss other issues, this is not the place to do it.

Each discussion forum is provided as both a newsgroup and a mailing list. This allows you to choose you whether you receive messages from news or e-mail.

CROSS-REFERENCE

You'll find a list of newsgroups and mailing lists in Appendix C. Online, you can find an updated list on the mozilla.org community page (`www.mozilla.org/community.html`).

The forums are organized by topics and projects. mozilla.org enables you to participate in discussions related to subjects that interest you, such as discussions on how to improve Mozilla's performance, as well as projects you are working on, such as the XPFE. Before I delve into how you can join the Mozilla newsgroups and mailings lists, let's look at the ground rules for the discussion forums.

What You Should Know Up Front

mozilla.org has set a few ground rules for those who want to participate in the discussion forums. These rules are designed to promote earnest discussion without a lot of the ranting, raving, and incivility that goes on in most other discussion mediums.

Here are the rules:

- Don't cross-post. This means don't send the same message to more than one discussion forum (unless absolutely necessary). You'll make a lot of people angry. If you feel you must cross-post, make sure you set the Followup-To and Reply-To fields to ensure that replies go only to one discussion group.

- Don't post anonymous messages and do ensure that people can reply to your e-mail address. Although you could argue that you want to block your e-mail address so that you can avoid receiving unsolicited email, don't do it. If you want to say something, say it and make sure people can respond to you directly.

- Don't post *flames*. If you haven't spent a lot of time in discussion forums before, angry messages, called flames, may catch you off guard. Remember that while rules are useful, not everyone follows them, and if someone sends out an angry message that attacks you personally, the best course of action is to simply ignore the transgressor. But if you feel you must defend your honor, do so outside the discussion forum.

- Don't send messages with large attachments. You'll find that most people are very bandwidth conscious and if you post a message with a large attachment, expect to receive a lot of flames. A better alternative to posting a large attachment is to create a Web page that links to the file and announce the URL in your message. The only exception to this is that attachments are welcome in the patches/bug fix forum.

- Don't submit off-topic messages. Forums are set up to discuss specific topics, and your messages should relate to that topic. With this in mind, don't use a discussion forum to promote your own agenda, such as your favorite operating system or programming language.

- Do edit your responses. If your newsreader or mail program is set to quote the original message, be sure to edit the quoted text as much as possible. This makes it easier for others to follow the conversation and conserves bandwidth. Don't worry—readers should be able to get to the original message if they want to.

- Do ignore spammers. People who send unsolicited e-mail to the forum should be ignored.

- Do use plain text as your message format of choice. Not everyone has an e-mail program or a newsreader capable of using HTML or rich-text formatted messages, and reading HTML-formatted messages in this type of reader isn't any fun.

Working with Mozilla Newsgroups

All Mozilla newsgroups are provided in the `netscape.public.mozilla.*` Usenet hierarchy. You can subscribe to them as appropriate for your news software. A good way to start is to search for `netscape.public.mozilla` using the news programs search interface. If your news server doesn't carry these newsgroups, you have several options.

You can send e-mail to your ISP or the company news administrator and ask if they can subscribe to the `netscape.public.mozilla.*` Usenet hierarchy. You'll want to mention that all the information needed to do this (including the public key for `news.mozilla.org`) is available at `www.mozilla.org/newsfeeds.html`.

The other option you have is to configure your newsreader to use the Mozilla news server. The news server, `news.mozilla.org`, is available on the standard news port 119. In Netscape Communicator 4.0, you add this server to Netscape Message Center by selecting New Discussion Group Server from the File menu. In Communicator 4.5, you add this server by choosing File ➪ Subscribe, and then clicking the Add Server button in the Subscribe to Newsgroups dialog box.

Once you have access to the Mozilla news server, you need to subscribe to newsgroups you are interested in. In Netscape Message Center, select the entry for `news.mozilla.org`, and then click Subscribe.

The various categories of newsgroups are displayed using a tree structure. Click on the plus sign next to a folder to drill down through the categories. When you find a newsgroup you want to subscribe to, select the newsgroup, and then click on the dot in the Subscribe column next to the newsgroup name or the Subscribe button. You should see a check mark in the Subscribe column. After you find all the newsgroups you want to subscribe to, click OK.

Working with Mozilla Mailing Lists

Some people prefer mailing lists to newsgroups because the messages come to their inbox directly rather than their having to use a separate reader to access messages individually. If you're one of these people, you'll be happy to know that each Mozilla newsgroup has a corresponding mailing list.

Because these mailing lists follow a strict naming structure, you can usually determine the mailing list name from the newsgroup name and vice versa. For example, the newsgroup, `netscape.public.mozilla.announce@mozilla.org` has a corresponding mailing list called mozilla-announce and the newsgroup `netscape.public.mozilla.ui` has a corresponding mailing list called `mozilla-ui@mozilla.org`. Following this, you can determine the name of a mailing list based on the newsgroup name by performing the following steps:

1. Remove the `netscape.public` prefix.

2. Replace any dots (.) in the name with dashes, such as changing mozilla.ui to mozilla-ui.

3. Add @mozilla.org to the result.

CROSS-REFERENCE

You'll find a partial list of newsgroups and mailing lists later in this chapter and in Appendix C. These steps are provided to help you access new discussion forums that you may encounter.

Once you know the name of the list you want to work with, you can subscribe to it, get helpful information, and access its archives. To subscribe to a mailing list, send a message to *thelist*`-request@mozilla.org`, where *thelist* is the actual name of the list, such as mozilla-announce. In the subject line of the message, enter the keyword subscribe. You don't need to enter anything in the body of the message.

Once you subscribe, you can send messages directly to the list or simply reply to messages as they come into your inbox. If you don't want to receive the mailing list anymore, you should unsubscribe. You do this by sending an unsubscribe message to *thelist*`-request@mozilla.org`. In the subject line of the message, enter the keyword unsubscribe.

All other commands you send to a mailing list must be sent to the -request address as well. Other commands you may want to use include info, digest, and archive help:

- An info message tells the mailing list to send you an informational message about using the mailing list. Use the subject line: info.

- A digest message tells the mailing list to send summary messages containing multiple messages rather than individual messages. Use the subject line: set listname digest.

- An archive help message tells the mailing list to send you information on how to access the message archives. Use the subject line: archive help.

More Discussion Opportunities

Although newsgroups and mailing lists are great ways to stay in touch with other developers, they don't give you real-time interaction. For real-time discussions, you'll want to use Internet Relay Chat (IRC).

Conversations on IRC are confined to specific channels, sort of like radio channels. mozilla.org's main channel is #mozilla. To access this channel, you'll need to configure your favorite chat client to connect to mozilla.org's chat server, `irc.mozilla.org`.

TIP

One of the most popular chat clients on Windows systems is mIRC. mIRC is a shareware chat client. You can download a copy of it from IRCHelp.Org using the URL www. irchelp.org/irchelp/mirc/.

If you are using mIRC, you can configure the client to access mozilla.org's chat server as follows:

1. Start mIRC and if necessary, select Options from the File menu to open the mIRC Options dialog box.

2. In the mIRC Options dialog box, select the Connect category, and then click the Add button. This opens the dialog box shown in Figure 2-2.

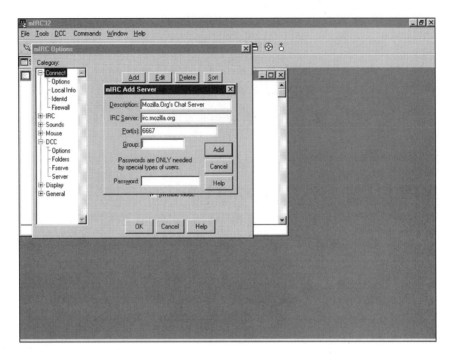

Figure 2-2: Configuring mIRC to access mozilla.org's chat server

3. Add a description for the chat server, such as mozilla.org Chat, and then enter irc.mozilla.org in the IRC Server field.

4. Complete the process by clicking Add.

Once you fill out your personal information, you can connect to mozilla.org's chat server as follows:

1. Start mIRC and, if necessary, select Options from the File menu to open the mIRC Options dialog box.

2. In the mIRC Options dialog box, select Connect category. Using the dialog box shown in Figure 2-3, select mozilla.org's chat server.

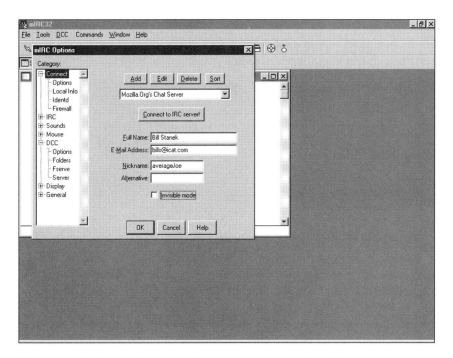

Figure 2-3: Connecting to mozilla.org's chat server with mIRC

3. Click Connect to IRC Server!

4. In a moment, you should see the mIRC Channels Folder dialog box, which prompts you to enter a channel. Enter #mozilla and then click the Add button.

5. Next, with #mozilla selected in the channels list, click the Join button.

6. The next dialog box you see is the chat dialog box, which is divided into two panes. The left pane shows the running conversation and the right pane shows who is in the chat room.

7. An input area is available in the bottom portion of the dialog box. Type in text you want to post to the chat and press Enter. That's all there is to it!

8. When you want to end the session, click the Disconnect button on the toolbar.

Summary

The Netscape Open Source program is designed to help get you involved in the on-going development efforts at mozilla.org. To learn more about current development efforts, use the resources discussed in this chapter. To stay in touch with other developers, use the discussion groups I point out. Additionally, Appendix C provides a more detailed look at discussion groups.

PART

II

Managing the
Source Code

Managing the Source Code

Now that you know all about the Netscape Open Source program and how to join the Open Source movement, it is time to roll up your sleeves and dive into Mozilla. What are you waiting for? This part of the book teaches the techniques you need to get your hands around Mozilla. You learn how to create and manage modules, how to check code in and out using CVS, and more.

IN THIS CHAPTER

—So Much Code, So Little Time
—Modularization: The Process of Creating Modules

Making Sense of the Mozilla Source

With so much code, it is hard to know where or how to get started with Mozilla. Fortunately, I've spent the past year and half learning about Mozilla and its modules. During this time, I've learned many techniques that can help you start programming faster, more easily, and more efficiently. The chapter starts with an overview on how modules are organized, named, and used. Next, you learn about system requirements and obtaining the source code. Afterward, you learn how to find functions and variables using the Mozilla Cross-Reference, an online tool for browsing and searching the Mozilla source code.

So Much Code, So Little Time

Mozilla is a complex application with dozens of modules and millions of lines of code. Finding your way through this maze of modules and code isn't easy. Thus, rather than dive head first into the code, let's take a look at how Mozilla is put together.

Understanding Module Files and Structure

Mozilla source code is organized into modules. A module is a collection of source code and support files. A quick way to access the code for individual modules is from the module owners' page at mozilla.org (`www.mozilla.org/owners .html`). Clicking on the source links takes you to the top of a module's source tree, where you'll usually find one or more of the following subdirectories:

- **src:** Module source files

- **macbuild:** CodeWarrior project files needed for building the source on the Macintosh

- **include:** Included header files

- **public:** Local files which get copied to the Mozilla distribution directory (mozilla:dist) or an appropriate subdirectory of this directory

- **tests:** Files used in testing the module

Most of Mozilla's source files are written in C and C++. Because of this, you'll find C header files with an .h extension, C source files with a .c extension, and C++ source files with a .cpp extension.

Support files can come in a variety of formats. For example, modules can have graphics, such as the images used in toolbars, or property files that are used to set object properties. These files should have extensions that indicate the types of content they contain, such as .GIF for GIF images.

Module files can be written in other programming languages. You'll find files written in Java, JavaScript, and XML, to name a few of these other languages.

Working with Modules

Modules listed on the owners' page and in the Mozilla source tree aren't necessarily a part of Mozilla or the standard Mozilla build. Some modules are actually separate applications that are designed to be used with Mozilla, such as Grendel, which is a Java-based mail and news client. Other modules are completely separate from Mozilla, such as the Directory SDK, which contains tools and SDKs for accessing LDAP directories.

Of the many different ways to access the Mozilla source, one of the best is to use the Mozilla Cross Reference (`lxr.mozilla.org/`). The Mozilla Cross Reference provides a tree-like structure for browsing and searching modules and other related files. The source tree is similar to the directory structure you find when you download and unpack the Mozilla source. However, when you download the source, you normally get only the browser components and not all the additional modules.

CROSS-REFERENCE

If you are working on projects that aren't included in the basic browser build, you'll need to download additional components on a module-by-module basis. For example, if you want to work with the source code for the Directory SDK, you'll need to download the source files for this module or check them out using Concurrent Versions System (CVS). CVS is a version control and source tree management utility that you'll learn all about in Chapter 4.

Modules are organized within the source tree by type or purpose. Usually, you'll find modules that link as executables in `mozilla/source/modules`; DLLs or SOs are in `mozilla/source/libs`, and include files are in `mozilla/source/includes`. Most other modules are organized by project, such as `mozilla/ef` for the Electrical Fire project.

NOTE

Normally, when you obtain additional modules, you'll unpack them in the root of your source tree and in this way, you can grow the source tree structure on your system.

Module and Source Naming Conventions

Naming conventions are extremely important in helping programmers quickly understand the source code and in preventing namespace collisions. When you create new structures or modify current structures within the source code, you'll want to ensure that you follow the current naming conventions. In Mozilla, the naming convention used depends on the structures available in the programming language in use and on the techniques implemented by the original programmers of the module.

CROSS-REFERENCE

The module sections in Part IV outline the naming conventions used on a module-by-module basis.

Module and File Naming

While module names aren't very consistent, key modules do use prefixes and suffixes, such as FE or XP. The module prefixes and suffixes you'll see include:

- **BE:** For modules dealing with Mozilla's back-end structures

- **FE:** For modules dealing with Mozilla's front-end interfaces

- **LIB:** For modules that are created as libraries

- **XP:** For modules that are designed for cross-platform use, such as XPCOM

Naming conventions also apply to source and support files. Key source files are prefixed or suffixed with an abbreviation of the module in which the files reside. Usually this abbreviation is the first few letters of the module name or the initial letter of each keyword in the module name, but it doesn't have to be this specific. For example, key source files in the RDF module include `fs2rdf.c` and `fs2rdf.h`, but key source files in the browser hooks module include `hk_conf.c` and `hk_file.c`.

Structure Naming

Types, functions, and macros usually include an abbreviation of the module in which the function resides. Keywords that follow the name may have their first letter capitalized. For example, the naming of NSPR types, functions, and macros follows these conventions:

- Types exported by NSPR begin with PR and are followed by keywords with initial caps, such as PRInt, PRFileDesc, and PRThread.

- Function definitions begin with PR_ and are followed by keywords with initial caps, such as PR_Cleanup, PR_Read, and PR_WaitCondVar.

- Preprocessor macros begin with PR_ and are followed by all uppercase characters, such as PR_BYTES_PER_SHORT and PR_EXTERN.

Naming conventions may also apply to function calls. Calling conventions are used to support cross-platform declarations of prototypes and implementations. External functions or variables may be prefixed with the module's abbreviation and the keyword EXTERN, such as PR_EXTERN. Declarations for external functions or variables may be prefixed with the module's abbreviation and the keyword IMPLEMENT, such as PR_IMPLEMENT. Definitions and declarations of functions that are called *via function pointers* may be prefixed with the module's abbreviation and the keyword CALLBACK, such as PR_CALLBACK.

If a module is written primarily in C++, classes, structs, and enumerated types usually are prefixed with ns to define a namespace. The reason for this is that the C++ namespace facility isn't available to the entire codebase, and namespaces are created manually. Because of this, the class name `nsTest` is used for the class Test, and its interfaces are named with `nsITest`. Enumerated types are prefixed with `eType_`, such as:

```
enum nsTest { eTest_x ... }
```

Method, Variable, and Data Naming

Depending on the module they are in, methods, variables, and other elements may or may not have a prefix. Still, there are basic rules in place for method and variable naming. Method names use initial caps for keywords, such as MyMethod. Instance variables are prefixed with an *m*, such as mInstanceVariable. Private global variables are prefixed with a *g*, such as gGlobalVariable. Private global constants are prefixed with a *k*, such as kConstant.

The most extensive naming conventions often apply to algebraic types. Signed integer types may be named with a module prefix, the abbreviation Int, and a numeric value that indicates the bit length of the integer, such as PRInt8 for an 8-bit integer type in the NSPR module. For an unsigned 8-bit integer type, the name would be PRUint8. Similarly, a 64-bit floating-point integer would be named PRFloat64, and a Boolean type would be named PRBool. In the source code a type definition using this convention would look like this:

```
#include <prtypes.h>
  typedef PRIntn PRBool
  #define PR_TRUE (PRIntn)1
  #define PR_FALSE (PRIntn)0
```

Code Formatting Conventions

Just as there are naming conventions, there are also formatting conventions for the source code. Although the conventions that apply to the source code you are working on may vary slightly, here's a list of the formatting conventions applicable at the time of this writing:

- Curly braces should be on the same line as if, for, while, and switch statements.

- Curly braces should be on a new line for method implementations.

- Indenting for a source file should be consistent and should be two spaces for each level of indentation.

- White space should not follow a method name and the opening left parenthesis.

- Tabs should not be used in source files.

TIP

Source code created before these formatting conventions were adopted may not follow this syntax. However, if you are working with old modules, you may want to update them to the current standards.

At the top of every source file, you should include comments that help in parsing the file with the Mozilla developer tools. The comment should include the programming language used in the source file and information on the tab/indentation structure used. An example comment follows:

```
/* -*- Mode: C++;    tab-width: 2; indent-tabs-mode: nil; c-
basic-offset: 2 -*-
```

You can break down the elements in the previous comment as follows:

- Mode: the programming language used, such as C or C++

- tab-width: set to 2; the number of spaces for each tab setting

- `indent-tabs-mode:` set to nil; tabs aren't to be used in source files

- `c-basic-offset:` set to 2; the offset for indentation

After this comment, you should include notice of the license that applies to the source file, such as NPL or MPL. With NPL, the notice will look similar to one shown in Listing 3-1.

LISTING 3-1: NETSCAPE PUBLIC LICENSE NOTICE IN SOURCE FILES

```
*The contents of this file are subject to the Netscape
*Public License Version 1.0 (the "NPL"); you may not use
*this file except in compliance with the NPL. You may
*obtain a copy of the NPL at http://www.mozilla.org/NPL/
*Software distributed under the NPL is distributed on an
*"AS IS" basis, WITHOUT WARRANTY OF ANY KIND, either
*express or implied. See the NPL for the specific language
*governing rights and limitations under the NPL.
*
*The Initial Developer of this code under the NPL is
*Netscape Communications Corporation. Portions created by
*Netscape are Copyright (C) 1998 Netscape Communications
*Corporation. All Rights Reserved.
```

Modularization: The Process of Creating Modules

Increasingly, source code is being created using object-oriented techniques — and as you've seen in this chapter, Mozilla is no exception. Mozilla is shifting to a structure in which source code elements are created as standalone code modules. The basic architecture for this modular structure is based on the Component Object Model (COM).

When you work with or create modules, there are many key concepts you need to learn about. These concepts include virtual interfaces, interface identifiers, factories, repositories, and linked libraries. The sections that follow introduce these concepts.

Virtual Interfaces and IIDs

Mozilla modules make extensive use of C++ virtual interfaces. A pure virtual interface is a class that defines all its methods as virtual, which makes it easy to pass function tables between modules.

Each virtual interface is assigned an Interface Identifier (IDD). IIDs are used to dynamically find, load, and bind interfaces. IIDs are unique 128-bit identifiers based on globally unique identifiers (GUIDs). Windows-based systems use GUIDs extensively, especially with ActiveX controls and Web-based applications. The structure for IIDs in source code is:

```
struct nsID {
   PRUint32 m0;
   PRUint16 m1, m2;
   PRUint8 m3[8];
};
```

Following the source code, you'd see that a typical IID looks something like this:

```
{99b42120-6ec7-11cf-a6c7-00aa00a47dd2}
```

And you could initialize the previous IID as follows:

```
ID = {0x99b42120, 0x6ec7, 0x11cf,
        {0xa6, 0xc7, 0x00, 0xaa, 0x00, 0xa4, 0x7d, 0xd2}};
```

TIP

On Windows-based systems, you can use uuidgen and guidgen to create IIDs. These utilities are distributed with Visual C++ and Visual Basic.

The nsISupports Interface

The main interface for modules is nsISupports. From the naming conventions discussed previously, you know that ns sets the namespace manually and I stands for interface. If you are familiar with COM, you can think of nsISupports as Mozilla's answer to IUnknown in COM.

All module interfaces inherit from nsISupports. nsISupports is primarily used to provide interface interrogation and reference counting. Interface interrogation is used to determine which interfaces an object supports. Reference counting is used to track object references. The IID for nsISupports is defined as NS_ISUP-PORTS_IID. In the source code, you'll often see references to this IID, such as:

```
static NS_DEFINE_IID(kISupportsIID, NS_ISUPPORTS_IID);
```

Interface interrogation and reference counting functionality are implemented through three methods: QueryInterface(), AddRef(), and Release(). In the source code, these methods are typically defined as:

```
NS_IMETHOD QueryInterface(const nsIID &aIID,
                                void **aResult);
NS_IMETHOD_(nsrefcnt) AddRef(void);
NS_IMETHOD_(nsrefcnt) Release(void);
```

TIP

The NS_IMETHOD and NS_IMETHOD_(type) macros are quick ways to use virtual nsresult and virtual type. On Windows-based systems, these macros expand to virtual nsresult __std-call and virtual type __stdcall. These extensions are for COM and you have to use the ex-panded macros only when you're concerned with COM compatibility.

Working with QueryInterface()

QueryInterface() is used to determine interface support. When QueryInterface() is called, the caller passes an IID and a pointer to the address where the resulting interface can be placed. If the query is successful, QueryInterface() returns NS_OK. Otherwise, QueryInterface() returns NS_NOINTERFACE. An example using QueryInterface() is shown in Listing 3-2.

LISTING 3-2: WORKING WITH QUERYINTERFACE()

```
NS_IMETHOD nsSample::QueryInterface(const nsIID &aIID,
                                    void **aResult)
 {
   //check for null pointer
   if (aResult == NULL) {
     return NS_ERROR_NULL_POINTER;
   }

   //query interface
   if (aIID.Equals(kISupportsIID)) {
     *aResult = (void *) this;
   } else if (aIID.Equals(kISampleIID)) {
     *aResult = (void *) this;
   }

   //query isn't successful
   if (aResult != NULL) {
     return NS_ERROR_NO_INTERFACE;
   }

   //query is successful
   AddRef();
   return NS_OK;
 }
```

In the source code, you can use the result to ensure the interface exists, as shown in Listing 3-3.

LISTING 3-3: STORING THE RESULTS OF THE QUERY

```
//store instance of result
nsresult result = instanc->QueryInterface(aIID, aResult);

  //if result doesn't equal NS_OK, delete the instance
  if (result != NS_OK) {
    delete instanc;
```

```
  }

  //otherwise return the result
  return result;
  }
```

A key feature of `QueryInterface()` is the capability to determine whether interfaces are implemented by the same object instance. If you use `QueryInterface()` on interfaceX and obtain interfaceZ, you must be able to use `QueryInterface()` on interfaceZ and obtain interfaceX. This means the interfaces are implemented by the same object. Similarly, if interfaces K and L are implemented by the same instance, using `QueryInterface()` on either interface should return the same interface. Again, this means the interfaces are implemented by the same object.

Working with AddRef() and Release()

When you work with interfaces, reference counters are extremely important. Normally, you want to initialize the counter to zero and then update the counter as you work with interfaces and objects. A successful call to `QueryInterface()` should, in turn, call `AddRef()` on the requested interface before returning.

`AddRef()` is used to increment a reference counter that can apply to either an entire object or to each interface of an object. To decrement the counter, you use `Release()`.Generally, if a call to `Release()` causes the counter to reach zero, the object should free itself, which frees up memory used by the object. Additionally, `AddRef()` and `Release()` should always return the resulting reference count. In the source code, these techniques could be implemented as shown in Listing 3-4.

LISTING 3-4: INCREMENTING AND DECREMENTING THE REFERENCE COUNTER

```
//increment counter
nsRefCount nsTest::AddRef()
{
   return ++mReferenceCount;
}

//decrement counter
```

Continued

LISTING 3-4: *(continued)*

```
nsRefCount nsTest::Release()
{
  //if decrementing the counter sets it to zero,
  //delete the reference and reset counter to zero
  if (--mReferenceCount == 0) {
    delete this;
    return 0;
  }
  //otherwise return the decremented counter value
  return mReferenceCount;
}
```

 CAUTION
Static objects shouldn't reference counters. If they do, the `AddRef()` and `Release()` methods may cause problems, such as memory leaks or inadvertent access of freed objects.

As you work with modules, you'll discover there are many different ways to work with `AddRef()` and `Release()`. Key techniques are covered in the sections that follow.

Using Global and Member Variables

Tracking variables in modules is very important, especially when it comes to global and member variables. As you may already know, these variables have scopes that enable them to be changed by many functions, and this can cause problems, such as a memory leak.

To prevent problems, you should always call `AddRef()` on any global or member variable that is being passed to a function, and then, afterward, you should call `Release()`. Calling `Release()` reduces the counter and ensures memory is freed as necessary. In the source code, the variable handling would look something like this:

```
mTest->AddRef();
UpdateTest(mTest);
mTest->Release();
```

Using In Parameters and Local Pointers

When you pass an interface in to a function, local copies of the interface pointer are assumed to be in the scope of the calling function. Because of this, you don't need to use `AddRef()` or `Release()` and could use an interface as follows:

```
nsresult UpdateTest (ITest *aTest1, ITest *aTest2) {
  ITest local = aTest;
  if (aTest->Check() == NS_OK) {
    local = aTest2;
  }
  return local->CheckOff();
}
```

Using Out Parameters

When a function returns a new interface, the function should call `AddRef()` on the interface before returning it. This technique applies to interfaces returned by `CreateInstance()`, `QueryInterface()`, and `NS_NewXYZ()`. Samples of how you could use `AddRef()` with new interfaces are shown in Listing 3-5.

LISTING 3-5: USING ADDREF() WITH FUNCTIONS THAT RETURN A NEW INTERFACE

```
//Example 1
ITest *GetTest()
{
  ITest *result = mTest;
  result->AddRef();
  return result;
}

//Example 2
nsresult GetTest(ITest **aTestResult)
{
  if (aTestResult == NULL) {
    return NS_ERROR_NULL_POINTER;
  }
  *aTestResult = mTest;
```

Continued

LISTING 3-5: *(continued)*

```
    (*aTestResult)->AddRef();

    return NS_OK;
}
```

Don't forget to call `Release()` when you are finished with the interface. Again, this ensures that the counter is decremented and memory is freed as necessary.

Using In-Out Parameters

In-Out parameters present a special case because they are used for both input and output. Anytime a function changes the value of an interface In-Out parameter, it should call `Release()` on the interface passed in and `AddRef()` on the interface passed out. An example of this technique is shown in Listing 3-6.

LISTING 3-6: USING IN-OUT PARAMETERS WITH ADDREF() AND RELEASE()

```
nsresult RefreshTest(ITest **aTest)
{
  if (aTest == NULL || *aTest == NULL) {
     return NS_ERROR_NULL_PARAMETER;
  }
  if ((*aTest)->Stale()) {
    (*aTest)->Release();
    *aTest = mTest;
    (*aTest)->AddRef();
  }
  return NS_OK;
}
```

Factories

Normally when you create instances of a class, you have to access the class declaration. Then if you need to work with classes dynamically, you need to link libraries together. Unfortunately, these compile time and linking dependencies reduce the versatility in your class implementations. To get around the dependency issues, you can use factories.

Factories are special classes that are used to create instances of other classes. With factories you eliminate compile-time and linking dependencies, effectively hiding class declarations and the creation details of objects. Eliminating compile-time dependencies enables you to create objects without having access to the class declarations for the objects. Eliminating linking dependencies enables you to dynamically load objects.

The nsIFactory Interface

The interface used to implement factories is nsIFactory. The nsIFactory interface is the equivalent of IClassFactory in COM. Generally, the nsIFactory interface is implemented as shown in Listing 3-7.

LISTING 3-7: THE NSIFACTORY INTERFACE

```
/*
 * The nsIFactory interface
 */

class nsIFactory: public nsISupports {
public:
    NS_IMETHOD CreateInstance(nsISupports *aOuter,
                              const nsIID &aIID,
                              void **aResult) = 0;
    NS_IMETHOD LockFactory(PRBool aLock) = 0;
};
```

The NSRepository Class

The NSRepository class eliminates linking dependencies by creating a repository for factories. NSRepository does this by mapping sets of IIDs to factories and their associated libraries. NSRepository supports four key methods: `CreateInstance()`, `FindFactory()`, `RegisterFactory()`, and `UnregisterFactory()`. These methods are shown in Listing 3-8.

LISTING 3-8: THE NSREPOSITORY CLASS AS ORIGINALLY IMPLEMENTED

```
class NSRepository {
public:
```

Continued

55

LISTING 3-8: *(continued)*

```
//Find a factory based on its class ID
static nsresult FindFactory(const nsCID &aClass,
                            nsIFactory **aFactory);

//Create an instance of a referenced class based on its
//class ID
static nsresult CreateInstance(const nsCID &aClass,
                               const nsIID &aIID,
                               nsISupports *aDelegate,
                               void **aResult);

//Register a factory for a class using a class ID
//and a pointer
static nsresult RegisterFactory(const nsCID &aClass,
                                nsIFactory *aFactory,
                                PRBool aReplace);

//Register a factory for a class using a class ID
//and the path to a dynamically loadable library
static nsresult RegisterFactory(const nsCID &aClass,
                                const char *aLibrary,
                                PRBool aReplace,
                                PRBool aPersist);

//Remove registration for a factory using a class ID
//and a pointer
static nsresult UnregisterFactory(const nsCID &aClass,
                                  nsIFactory *aFactory);

//Remove registration for a factory using a class ID
//and a dynamically loaded library
static nsresult UnregisterFactory(const nsCID &aClass,
                                  const char *aLibrary);
```

```
    //Unload dynamically loaded libraries that are not in use
    static nsresult FreeLibraries();
  };
```

CreateInstance() is used to create an instance of a referenced class based on its class ID. FindFactory() is used to find a factory based on its class ID.

RegisterFactory() is used to register factories. Because the method is over-loaded, two different techniques for registration are available. You can use a class ID and a pointer to register a factory, or you can use a class ID and the path to register a dynamically loadable library. When you use pointers, you can set the aReplace flag to replace a current class instance. When you use dynamically load-able libraries, you can access a factory and its class instance either at run-time or externally. To do this, you must set the aPersist flag, which tells the repository to store the class ID and library relationship in its permanent store.

UnregisterFactory() is used to remove the registration for factories. As with RegisterFactory(), this method is overloaded so that it supports class IDs with pointers and class IDs with dynamically loadable libraries. When you remove registration for class instances with dynamically loaded libraries, the FreeLibraries() method is called to unload the libraries.

Creating and Registering DLLs

After you've created a factory, moving the factory to a DLL is relatively easy. A DLL that contains a factory must export NSGetFactory() and, optionally, NSCanUnload(). NSGetFactory() is used to verify that the class ID passed in is the correct one for the factory you want to implement. NSCanUnload() enables NSRepository to free up memory by unloading DLLs that are no longer needed by calling FreeLibraries(). If you don't implement NSCanUnload(), the DLL will not be unloaded.

Using NSGetFactory() and NSCanUnload()

Sample implementations for NSGetFactory() and NSCanUnload() are shown in Listing 3-9. The example doesn't take into account the case when multiple fac-tories are used in a DLL, and you'll need additional code to determine which fac-tory to return in a given instance.

LISTING 3-9: WORKING WITH NSGETFACTORY() AND NSCANUNLOAD()

```
//Verify class ID for factory
extern "C" NS_EXPORT nsresult NSGetFactory(const nsCID
&aCID,                                          nsIFactory
**aResult)
 {
   if (aResult == NULL) {
     return NS_ERROR_NULL_POINTER;
   }

   *aResult = NULL;

   nsISupports *instanc;

   //if class ID is valid, create new instance
   //otherwise return error
   if (aCID.Equals(kSampleCID)) {
     instanc = new nsTestFactory();
   } else {
     return NS_ERROR_ILLEGAL_VALUE;
   }

   //if instance isn't set return out of memory error
   //otherwise proceed with interface query
   if (instanc == NULL) {
     return NS_ERROR_OUT_OF_MEMORY;
   }

   nsresult result = instanc->QueryInterface(kIFactoryIID,
       void **) aResult);

   //Incorrect interface; delete the instance
   if (result != NS_OK) {
       delete instanc;
   }
```

```
   return result;
  }

 //Determine if DLLs are no longer needed
 extern "C" NS_EXPORT PRBool NSCanUnload()
 {
   return PRBool(gInstanceCnt == 0 && gLockCnt == 0);
 }
```

Registering the DLL

Once you move a factory to a DLL, you can register it. For manual registration, you can use the NSRepository's `RegisterFactory()` and `UnregisterFactory()` methods. For self-registration, you may want the DLL to export additional functions for self-registration and unregistration. The functions are `NSRegisterSelf()` and `NSUnregisterSelf()`, which enable a DLL to register and unregister all its factories. The basic syntax for these functions is:

```
 extern "C" NS_EXPORT nsresult NSRegisterSelf(const char
 *path);
 extern "C" NS_EXPORT nsresult NSUnregisterSelf(const char
 *path);
```

TIP
On Windows-based systems, you can use RegFactor.exe to work with self-registering DLLs. On Unix, a similar program is regfactory.

Summary

Mozilla is one of the largest applications ever to have its source code released to the public. To help navigate your way through this maze of code, use the tips and techniques discussed in this chapter. Managing source files and modules with CVS is covered in the next chapter.

Managing Source Files and Modules

The Mozilla project is all about contribution. The more the Net community contributes, the better Mozilla will be. With thousands of people potentially working on various projects, controls have to be in place to ensure that things go smoothly. These controls are used both to protect the work of others and so that people are not deterred from contributing. After all, how would you feel if you spent 60 hours working on a source file and someone posted changes that erased your work?

Most of the Mozilla source code and module management is handled through the Concurrent Versions System (CVS), a version control system. You use CVS to check out source modules and to check in code that you've updated. CVS tracks file changes as well, enabling you to obtain the latest versions of files without having to download an entire module each time you want to refresh your code base.

In this chapter, you learn how to use CVS, to set up a CVS client, and work with code modules.

CROSS-REFERENCE

A summary of CVS commands is available in Appendix A.

Understanding the CVS Architecture

CVS is freeware and is available for many different platforms. The basic architecture is a client-only install with a network drive providing file services for developers. A more structured architecture follows a client/server model with a client installed on developers' desktops and a server used for managing the source code. This client/server architecture is implemented at mozilla.org. The CVS server you'll use is `cvs-mirror.mozilla.org`.

The main function of CVS is to track changes in source files and to enable you to review old versions of files as necessary. While CVS tracks changes, it does not have change controls, such as bug tracking. Rather than save each version of source files separately, CVS saves only the modifications and records these modifications in history files.

FTP is an alternative to CVS. However, while FTP can transfer files, the protocol doesn't have version tracking capabilities. As a result, you'll have to transfer all the module files or even the entire code base rather than transfer only the files that have been updated.

Figure 4-1 provides an overview of the CVS architecture. The network drive or server storing the source files is referred to as the *CVS repository*. The CVS repository stores a complete copy of all source files and is organized in a directory tree structure.

Normally, you don't access the source files in the repository directly. Instead, you log in to the CVS server and check out a copy of the source files into a working directory known as your local directory tree. When you are ready to commit your changes, you check the source files back into the repository. The server records your changes in the repository and also notes other key information, such as when the changes were made and who made them.

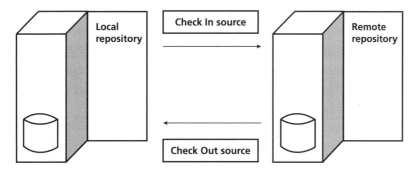

Figure 4-1: CVS uses a source repository and a local directory tree.

Setting Up a Local Directory Tree

Now that you know a bit about CVS, it's time to set up your local directory tree. You do this by installing the Mozilla source code on your system.

Obtaining the Source

You can also use FTP to download the latest source archive. Visit one of the mirror sites listed at www.mozilla.org/mirrors.html. When you access the FTP server, you'll usually want to get the most recent source archive from mozilla/source. The source directory contains archives that have compiled properly on at least one system.

On the FTP Server, you can also obtain the source from mozilla/nightly. The nightly directory contains the snapshots of the source code made each night. However, these snapshots are generated automatically and may not build at all.

ON THE CD-ROM

The easiest way to obtain the source is to extract it from the compressed archives found on the CD-ROM that accompanies this book. On the CD-ROM, you'll find the source code in the source\mozilla directory. If you access the source\mozilla directory, you'll see that the source files are stored separately for Unix\Windows and Mac.

Creating the Tree

Regardless of whether you get the source files from the CD-ROM or via FTP, the latest Unix and Windows source files are archived with GZIP and TAR. The archive will be named something similar to mozilla-*19990408*.tar.gz, where *19990408* is the build date and tar.gz is the extension that indicates the archive method. Mac files are archived in a SIT file, such as mozilla-19990408.sit.

Unpack the source code in a new folder and be sure to preserve the directory structure. The directory you unpack the source into is known as the root of your local directory tree. For example, if you created a new folder called `source` and unpacked Mozilla into this directory, the root of your local directory tree is `source\mozilla`.

When you work with Unix and Windows, you usually want to execute CVS commands at the root of the local directory tree. On the Mac, you set the local directory tree root to a specific value. Once you obtain and unpack the source code, you can use CVS to retrieve additional modules and to periodically update your source tree.

Setting Up the Environment for CVS

Once you've created a local directory tree, you need to install a CVS client and set up your CVS environment.

 ON THE CD-ROM
On the CD-ROM, you'll find the necessary client software in the cvs directory for your respective system, such as `cvs\win32` or `cvs\mac`.

CVS Environment Settings

Unix and Windows systems need to have a specific setup for CVS. The first environment variable you want to check is $HOME. This environment variable should be set so that CVS can create and update files in your home directory. Files CVS may create in your home directory include `.cvspass` (used to record your preferred CVS repository and login) and `.cvsrc` (used to record your CVS preferences).

Next, you need to set the $CVSROOT environment variable and login. $CVS-ROOT specifies the location of the CVS repository, which in this case is `cvs-mir-ror.mozilla.org`; the username for login; and the location for the root of the directory tree. The CVS login tells the CVS server which password to use for the specified user. Platform-specific steps for setting up the environment follow.

NOTE

Although GUI-based clients are available for Windows and Unix, I recommend using the command-line clients and CVS Version 1.10 or later. The command-line clients are easy to use and don't require installation of other components, such as Java or TCL/TK.

Regardless of whether you choose a command-line client or a GUI client, you'll need to enter command arguments when you work with CVS. Generally, these command arguments follow both the syntax I use in this chapter and syntax elsewhere.

CVS Setup on Unix

CVS setup on Unix varies depending on the shell environment you are using. If you are using C shell, you set the $CVSROOT and the CVS server login as follows:

1. Access the root of your local directory tree. If the directory tree is located in /source/mozilla, enter:

   ```
   CD /source/mozilla
   ```

2. Ensure that $HOME is set properly. The corresponding path is where CVS writes its password and configuration files.

   ```
   set HOME=/your/home/dir
   ```

3. At the csh prompt, enter:

   ```
   set CVSROOT=:pserver:anonymous@cvs-mirror.mozilla.org:/cvsroot
   ```

4. And then enter:

   ```
   cvs login
   ```

5. When prompted, enter:

   ```
   anonymous
   ```

65

The $CVSROOT setting and password are recorded in `.cvspass` for future use, and then your CVS client attempts to log in to the CVS server. You need to go through the setup only once. The next time you access CVS, your current settings are used automatically. If you have a problem logging in to the server, simply repeat these steps.

CVS Setup on Windows

On Windows, you set $CVSROOT and the CVS server login as follows:

1. Access the root of your local directory tree. For example, if this directory is D:\source\mozilla, enter:

```
D:
CD \source\mozilla
```

2. Ensure that $HOME is set properly. The corresponding path is where CVS writes its password and configuration files. If it isn't, set it to a working directory such as:

```
set HOME=C:\working
```

3. At the MS-DOS prompt, enter:

```
set CVSROOT=:pserver:anonymous@cvs-mirror.mozilla.org:/
cvsroot
```

4. And then enter:

```
cvs login
```

5. When prompted, enter:

```
anonymous
```

The $CVSROOT setting and password are recorded in `.cvspass` for future use, and then your CVS client attempts to log in to the CVS server. You need to go through the setup only once. The next time you access CVS, your current settings are used automatically. If you have a problem logging in to the server, simply repeat these steps.

NOTE

To use CVS under Windows, you must unpack the source from a TAR file rather than a ZIP file. The ZIP format doesn't store dates with sufficient accuracy for the CVS system. Because of this, CVS can't use the timestamps on source files to determine if files need to be updated, and this causes CVS to transfer entire files to the repository for comparisons.

CVS Setup on Macintosh

Several CVS clients are available for Macintosh, including MacCVS and MacCVS Pro. Although these programs have similar names, they have different developers. Further, MacCVS is a command-line tool and MacCVS Pro is a GUI tool. Throughout this chapter and in Chapter 9, I discuss the MacCVS Pro tool.

To get started, you need to set the options for your CVS session. You do this by selecting Edit ➪ Session. Table 4-1 summarizes the key session options. Once you configure the session options, you can access CVS through the Action menu.

TABLE 4-1: SESSION OPTIONS FOR MACCVS PRO

OPTION TYPE/NAME	DESCRIPTION AND USAGE
Checkout and Update Options	
Local Tree Directory	Sets the location for the source code on your system.
Merge Policy	Sets the file merging policies. You should set Auto Merge Text Files and Update Binary Files.
Default Module	Sets the default module for CVS. Use `mozilla/build/mac`.
Default Revision	Sets the source code revision for checkouts. Leave this blank.
Remote Host Information	
Server Host Name	Sets the CVS server name. Use `cvs-mirror.mozilla.org`.
CVS User Name	Sets the user name for CVS. For anonymous checkouts, use anonymous. If you want to check in code, you'll need to change this.

Continued

TABLE 4-1: *(continued)*

CVS Password	Sets the password for CVS. For anonymous checkouts, use anonymous. If you want to check in code, you'll need to change this.
CVS Root	Sets the root of the CVS directory tree. Use /cvsroot.
Network Time Out	Sets the timeout for periods of inactivity. A recommended setting is 10 minutes.
Encoding and File Mappings	
Add	Enables you to add encoding and file mappings. If you want to be able to start Perl scripts from the Finder, click Add, and then enter:
	Suffix .pl,
	Type TEXT, Creator McPL

Creating Your CVS Sandbox

Before you create source code or modify the existing Mozilla source, you should set up a sandbox. A CVS sandbox is simply a local area for developing Mozilla on your system. By setting up a local directory tree you're most of the way there, although you aren't working with the latest versions of the Mozilla source files. Thus, you should update the source files to ensure you have a fresh start on your sandbox.

To update the source files on Unix and Windows systems, follow these steps:

1. Access the root of your local directory tree from the command or shell prompt.

2. Tell CVS to checkout the current branch of Mozilla by entering the following command:

```
cvs -z3 checkout SeaMonkeyAll
```

The previous CVS command can tell you a lot about how CVS is used. The -z3 flag sets the level of Gzip compression for file transfers. Although you can use level 9 compression (-z9) at a cost to system resources, level 3 compression is usually the best option. SeaMonkey is the name of the Mozilla 5.0 branch. By checking out SeaMonkeyAll, you tell CVS that you want to check out all the Mozilla source files that have changed since the archive for your local directory tree was created.

To update the source files on Macintosh systems, follow these steps:

1. Start MacCVS Pro.

2. Select Action ⇨ Default Mozilla Module.

By checking out the default module, you tell CVS to update your local source tree. CVS will update all the Mozilla source files that have changed since the archive for your local directory tree was created.

CAUTION

Updating the local source tree may destroy changes you've made to the working copies of the source. To prevent this, you will need to copy the source files you are working with to a different directory before updating the tree. Or you need to commit your changes back to CVS.

Checking Out Modules

If you examine the local directory tree, you'll find that it contains the core Mozilla modules only. Therefore, if you want to work with other modules, you'll need to retrieve them. Don't worry — checking out additional modules is easy. All you need to know is the name of the modules you want to work with.

Here's an example of how you could check out the Netscape Directory SDK for C:

1. Access the root of your local directory tree from the command or shell prompt.

2. Tell CVS to checkout the related source module:

```
cvs checkout DirectorySDKSourceC
```

3. Now you can work with the new module's source files. Before you refresh the files (re-check them out), you should create copies of your work. If you don't, any updates you've done may be overwritten.

NOTE

Netscape Directory SDK for C actually has two modules: DirectorySDKSourceC and DirectorySDKSourceBuild. The DirectorySDKSourceBuild module is used to build the module separately from the browser build and as such is needed only when you check out the source into a new sandbox. Creating additional sandboxes is covered in the next section.

Creating Additional Sandboxes

If you are developing modules separately from the Mozilla build, you may want to create a separate sandbox for them. A separate sandbox ensures that the modules are independent from the browser build. A prime example of a module that you may want in its own sandbox is the Netscape Directory SDK, which can be built separately from the browser build.

An example of how you could create a separate sandbox for the Directory SDK follows.

1. Create a new directory that isn't within the current local directory tree, and then access this directory.

2. Configure the tree separately for login. Start by setting $CVSROOT, such as:

   ```
   set CVSROOT=:pserver:anonymous@cvs-mirror.mozilla.org:/
   cvsroot
   ```

3. Next, enter:

   ```
   cvs login
   ```

4. Then when prompted, enter:

   ```
   anonymous
   ```

5. Check out the DirectorySDKSourceC and DirectorySDKSourceBuild modules into this directory using:

   ```
   cvs checkout DirectorySDKSourceC DirectorySDKSourceBuild
   ```

6. You can now manage and build the Netscape Directory SDK separately from the Mozilla browser source.

Checking In Source Files and Modules

While anyone can check out modules, checking in modules is an entirely different matter. To check in source files, you must follow these steps:

1. Obtain permission from the module owner.

2. Get write access to the CVS repository.

3. Ensure that your code is portable (and doesn't break the build on other platforms).

4. Follow the check in and tree rules.

5. Submit your changes.

Getting Permission and Write Access

If you work on a project and want to contribute source files, you should talk with the module owner or project leader and then arrange to submit source files through this person. Once you become a regular contributor, you can ask for permission to check in source files directly. If you get permission, you can get write access to the CVS repository by filling out the CVS Contributor Form (`www.mozilla.org/hacking/form.html`).

The CVS Contributor Form sets out the terms for using mozilla.org's CVS server and making source code contributions. In the form, you'll be asked to enter your business contact information. The e-mail address you use on this form is used to create your CVS user name. Typically, if your e-mail address is `william@tvpress.com`, the user name you'll receive is `william%tvpress.com` (the @ symbol is replaced with a % symbol). You will also receive a password.

Ensuring That Your Code Is Portable

Mozilla is a cross-platform programming project. Regardless of whether or not you are developing for a single platform, your source code shouldn't break the build on other platforms. If it does, you will be responsible for fixing it. To help avoid build problems, your C/C++ code should follow these rules:

- **Avoid assignments in Boolean expressions and if statements if possible.** Assignments in Boolean expressions and if statements may cause warnings with Mac compilers.

- **Avoid complex inline functions.** Instead, call the function and define it outside of the class.

- **Avoid overloaded methods with similar signatures.** You may find that on different compilers and platforms, the methods have the same behavior.

- **Avoid returns statements that have an inline function in the return expression.** Instead, call the function beforehand and resolve the return to a specific value.

- **Do declare iterator variables outside of `for()` loops.** If you don't, the scope of the variable may be other than expected. This is caused by a change in the C++ standard where the iterator variable was original scoped with the outer block of code rather than within the loop.

- **Do declare local initialized aggregates as static or initialize them by hand.** Instead of char* test_int[] = {"A", "B", "C"} you'd either use static char* test_int[] = {"A", "B", "C"} or you would initialize the array by hand.

- **Do turn on warnings for your compiler, and then write code that doesn't generate warnings.** The reason for this is simple. If your compiler issues a warning, a compiler on another platform usually will generate errors.

- **Do use #ifdef __cplusplus code blocks within header files.** C header files with exposed C interfaces should be compatible with both C and C++. Although you may be tempted to extern "C" {} the old header file, don't do this. Instead, create an #ifdef __cplusplus block.

- **Do use .cpp as your extension for C++ files.** This is a standard naming convention used by Netscape for C++ source files. If your compiler doesn't like this extension, you may need to use a compiler wrapper that copies the `.cpp` file to another file with the extension the compiler is looking for. An example of a compiler wrapper is available for STRICT_CPLUS-PLUS_SUFFIX in `ns/config/rules.mk` and `ns/build/*`.

- **Do use a new line character at the end of source files.** Some compilers on Unix systems look for this.

- **Do use C++ style casts with macros.** The macro should detect whether style casts are supported and behave accordingly. An example of style casts used with macros is found in `base/src/nscore.h`.

- **Do use default constructors.** Otherwise, the source code will have problems with some compilers.

- **Do use fully scoped forms.** Types declared inside of another class should be referred to with their fully scoped form. Following this, you would use `Test::kBool` instead of `kBool`.

- **Do use main() at least once in C++ modules.** New modules should use `main()` in a C++ file to ensure compatibility with certain compilers on Unix systems. All you need is a file that calls `main()`, which is then implemented in a C file.

- **Do use the naming conventions for constants and type definitions.** If you don't use the naming conventions, you may get unexpected results on some platforms. Thus, rather than using `Bool`, you would use `XP_Bool` or `RDF_Bool`.

- **Do use the NSPR types for intrinsic integer types.** The exception is when you are writing machine-dependent source code that is called from cross-platform code. Here, you may need to cast from a NSPR type to a native type.

- **Do use virtual declarations with subclass virtual member functions.** When a function is declared as virtual in a class, all subclass member functions must be declared as virtual as well. If you don't do this, you'll get compiler warnings.

- **Don't use multiple return statements with inline functions or if/switch constructs.** Instead, initialize a return variable and then resolve the returns to a single point at the end of the function.

- **Don't wrap include statements with an #ifdef statement.** If the symbol is not defined, other compiler symbols may not be defined and it will be difficult to test the code on multiple platforms. The exception is when you are including different system files for different machines. Here, you may need to have a platform-specific #ifdef statement.

- **Don't block out sections of code with comments.** Instead, use #if 0 and #endif to block out sections of code. This ensures that the code is portable.

- **Don't pass by value when you can pass by reference.** Pass by value can cause problems in the code and should be avoided in favor of pass by reference. When you pass an object by value as a function parameter, a temporary copy is made. This copy gets passed, and is then destroyed on return from the function. If you don't create a copy constructor, the compiler's copy constructor may be invoked implicitly, which can cause problems if you meant to pass by reference. If you truly want to use pass by value, you should create your own copy constructor. Otherwise, you may want to explicitly prohibit pass by value. To do this, declare a copy constructor as private and then don't provide a definition.

- **Don't use C++ templates.** Some compilers don't implement C++ templates. Because of this, you shouldn't use them in your source code. The only exception to this rule is nsCOMPtr, which has been tested for compatibility. You use nsCOMPtr in XPCOM source files.

- **Don't use carriage returns in cross-platform source code.** Some compilers on Unix systems don't understand carriage returns and look instead for the end-of-line character, which is a line-feed or a combined carriage return and line feed.

- **Don't use exceptions.** Exceptions aren't implemented by some compilers and should be avoided. The exception to this rule is machine-specific source code where you catch all exceptions within this code. If you throw an exception outside the machine-specific code, you'll cause serious problems.

- **Don't use large includes or large include depths.** Large include files and large depth of includes can cause problems with the Visual C++ 1.5 compiler. Try to limit the depth and size of your included header files.

- **Don't use run-time type information (RTTI).** RTTI isn't supported in older compilers. Instead, you may want to create a classOf() virtual member function and add it to the base class of your hierarchy, overriding subclass member functions. If this function returns a unique value for each class in the hierarchy, you'll be able to do type comparisons at runtime.

- **Don't use semi-colons where they aren't needed.** For example, don't use a semicolon after {}. If you do, you may break some compilers.

- **Don't use static constructors.** Initializer functions for static constructors aren't implemented reliably by compilers. Instead, you should use a wrapper function that creates a single instance of the needed object and then replace all references to the static object with a call to the wrapper function.

- **Don't use varargs that are inline functions.** Instead, define the function separately to ensure portability.

- **Don't put constructors in header files.** Otherwise, you may cause compiler errors.

- **Don't use C++ comments in C source files or in header files included in C files.** Very few C compilers support C++ style comments. Instead, use the standard C comments /* to start and */ to end.

- **Don't use initializer lists with objects.** Instead, use a wrapper function.

- **Don't use mutable.** Some C++ compilers don't support the mutable keyword. Instead, you use a class instance as you would mutable, such as:

```
void MyClass::MyConstMethod() const
{
  MyClass * notThis = NS_CONST_CAST(MyClass *,this);
  notThis->mFoo = 3;
}
```

▓ **Don't use the C++ namespace facility.** As with RTTI, namespaces aren't implemented in older compilers. To prevent namespace collisions, use the naming conventions discussed in Chapter 3.

▓ **Include only filenames in #include statements.** If you include a path, Mac compilers may not treat the path as expected.

▓ **Watch your placement of variable declarations that require construction or initialization.** These variables need a constructor. They should always be placed at the start of the method rather than inside if/switch statements.

Following the Check In and Tree Rules

Before you check in any code, you should ensure that the code follows the cross-platform programming techniques outlined previously and that the code doesn't break the build on any platform. You test for cross-platform compatibility by compiling the source for different target platforms. The minimum set of target platforms you must test for is Win32, MacPPC, and Linux. If you haven't tested for compatibility on these platforms, do not check in your code.

Code that you plan to check in should be polished and complete. Do not leave sections of the code to be finished later. Also, do not comment out or #ifdef large sections of code.

When you check in source code, you are responsible for following the source tree process and the applicable rules. These processes and rules specify when you can check in code and what you must do after you check in code. The basic tree process works like this:

▓ Everyone who checks in source code is on "the hook" for the next build date. The source tree is closed at 8:00 AM PST Monday through Friday. No source code check ins are allowed when the tree is closed (unless you are working to fix a build problem).

▓ The build team then pulls the tree, and tries to build it on Win32, Linux, and MacPPC systems.

- Everyone who checked in code since previous build is on the hook and must be available at 10 AM PST. If the build breaks, those on hook work to fix the problems and eventually the tree builds.

- Before the tree is re-opened, several things happen. First, Netscape reviews source code that was checked in when the tree was closed. All code checked in should relate to the build. Next, if people were waiting to merge source into the main tree from a branch, they are given the opportunity (if they've coordinated this beforehand by asking for a "car pool lane").

- When the tree is re-opened, the tree status is updated and the hook is cleared.

NOTE
The tree process may change slightly from time to time. Check the current tree rules online at www.mozilla.org/hacking/bonsai.html.

As you can see, if you check in code, you are also responsible for the status of the Mozilla build and must be available to fix problems after check in. Because of this, you should be very familiar with Bonsai and Tinderbox before you check in code.

Bonsai is used to watch the activities related to the source tree. Tinderbox is used to track the status of the tree and whether the source builds on various platforms. If Tinderbox shows that the tree is red, you can't check in code and must wait until later. For more information on Tinderbox, see the section "Tracking Builds with TinderBox" in Chapter 5.

Committing Changes and Adding to the Repository

You check in source code by submitting your changes to the source repository. In CVS, you submit changes to existing source files with the commit command and add new files to the repository with the add command. The CVS server then updates the source files to reflect your changes and also records exactly what you changed, when you changed it, and other key information.

When you commit changes or add new files to the repository, you should enter a log message that provides a brief description of the file or your changes. You can enter a log message interactively or by using the -m option when you submit your changes. If you don't use the -m option, you'll be prompted to enter a log message.

Another option you may want to use when committing or adding files is -kb, which indicates a binary file. Always use this option when you submit binary files.

To commit changes, access the directory in your local source tree containing the file you want to submit to the repository. Then enter the following command for a source file:

```
cvs commit -m "Your log message" <filename.c>
```

Or enter the following command for a binary file:

```
cvs commit -kb -m "Your log message" <filename.c>
```

where *"Your log message"* is the actual message you want to log in the repository and *filename.c* is the actual name of the file.

Adding files to the repository is a two-step process. You add the file to register it for version control and then submit the file to the repository using `commit`. Thus, to add a file, you would change to the directory in your local source tree containing the file you want to submit to the repository and then enter the following commands:

```
cvs add filename.c
cvs commit -m "Your log message" <filename.c>
```

Summary

CVS is an essential tool for Mozilla developers because it helps you manage source files and modules. Once you install CVS, you can set up a sandbox and start working with the code. Other developer tools are discussed in the next chapter.

Developer Tools and Techniques

N ow that you know how to manage the Mozilla source code, it is time to learn about the available developer tools. You'll find a diverse set of tools for source code management and development at mozilla.org. Most of these tools have been customized specifically for use with Mozilla, and you'll need to learn how to use them to successfully develop the source code.

Developer tools include Mozilla Cross Reference, Bonsai, Tinderbox, and Bugzilla. Mozilla Cross Reference is used to find functions, variables, and files within the source code; Bonsai is used to track the source tree; Tinderbox is used to check the status of the build process; and, Bugzilla is used to track and report bugs in the source code.

Using Mozilla Cross Reference

Mozilla Cross Reference is a tool for browsing and searching the Mozilla source code. Browsing with Mozilla Cross Reference enables you to follow the directory tree structure to specific files within source modules. Searching with Mozilla Cross Reference enables you to find specific functions, variables, files, and text.

Another way to think of Mozilla Cross Reference is as a hypertext version of the source code that is indexed for easy searching. Its reference pages are generated with a tool called *Linux Cross Reference* (LXR), which was adapted for use with the Mozilla source code.

Mozilla Cross Reference accesses reference pages on the main CVS server at mozilla.org. These reference pages are updated throughout the day, making Mozilla Cross Reference the best resource to use when you want to find recent changes to the source code. You can access the main page for this utility at `cvs-mirror.mozilla.org/webtools/lxr/`. From this location, you have four options: browse the source tree, search for files, search for identifiers, or search using free flow text. These options are discussed in the sections that follow.

NOTE

LXR was originally used to display the source code of the Linux kernel. LXR was created by Arne Georg Gleditsch and Per Kristian Gjermshus.

Browsing the Tree

Browsing the source tree is a good way to familiarize yourself with Mozilla's structure and the content of its source modules. Browsing is also a good way to find source and support files when you don't have a specific name or resource in mind — sort of the "I'll know it when I see it" approach. For example, if you believe that a support file is in the calendar module but you don't remember its name, you can use Mozilla Cross Reference to browse the contents of this module.

The root of the directory tree is located at `cvs-mirror.mozilla.org/webtools/lxr/source/`. When you access the tree root, you'll find that each module has its own folder. By clicking on these folders, you can drill down to a module's source files. Mozilla Cross Reference provides two ways to track where you are in the source tree. As you drill down through the source tree, the URL becomes more specific, and so does the path reported by Mozilla Cross Reference. Although the URL points to your exact location, the cross-reference path always begins with `mozilla` (which is the root of the directory tree).

TIP

Bookmark modules you commonly use. You'll have quick access to check for updates, such as new files. If you print out a listing from the cross-reference but don't have the URL for later access, simply substitute `lxr.mozilla.org/`*branchname*`/source/` for mozilla in the path, such as `lxr.mozilla.org/seamonkey/source/`.

Listings of file names are clickable. Clicking on a source filename opens the file in your browser where you can read through its contents. (See Figure 5-1.) The entire contents of source files are indexed for quick searches. You can jump to a particular line of a file by adding its anchor location (an anchor identifies a place in an HTML document) to the end of the URL. You can also perform quick searches for other uses of functions, variables, and structures by clicking on their links.

```
mozilla/network/main/mkgeturl.c - Netscape                              _|8|x

File  Edit  View  Go  Communicator  Help

    Bookmarks    Go to: http://cvs-mirror.mozilla.org/webtools/lxr/source/network/main/mkgeturl.c

416         PR_Free(freenode);
417     }
418
419     NETExitCallbackHead = NULL;
420
421     return;
422  }
423
424  /*  Gather manual proxy information from the prefapi. Called from
425      SetupPrefs and SelectProxyStyle */
426  PRIVATE void
427  NET_UpdateManualProxyInfo(const char * prefChanged) {
428
429      XP_Bool bSetupAll=FALSE;
430      char * proxy = NULL;
431      int32 iPort=0;
432      char text[MAXHOSTNAMELEN + 8];
433
434      if (!prefChanged)
435          bSetupAll = TRUE;
436
437      if (bSetupAll || !PL_strcmp(prefChanged, pref_proxyFtpServer) ||
438          !PL_strcmp(prefChanged, pref_proxyFtpPort)) {
439          if( (PREF_OK == PREF_CopyCharPref(pref_proxyFtpServer,&proxy))
440              && proxy && *proxy) {
441              if ( (PREF_OK == PREF_GetIntPref(pref_proxyFtpPort,&iPort)) ) {
442                  sprintf(text,"%s:%d", proxy, iPort);
443                  StrAllocCopy(MKftp_proxy, text);
444                  iPort=0;
445              } else {

Document: Done
```

Figure 5-1: In Mozilla Cross Reference, source files have line-by-line links, and key identifiers are indexed for quick searches.

To find a particular line within a source file, you access the source file in the Mozilla Cross Reference, add the number symbol (#) to the URL and then enter the line number you want to access. For example, if you want to access line 1500 in the source file shown in the figure, you would enter the following URL:

```
cvs-mirror.mozilla.org/webtools/lxr/ source/network/main/
mkgeturl.c#1500
```

To find other uses for a function, variable, or structure listed in a source file, simply click on it. Mozilla Cross Reference then performs an identifier search on the item you select. You'll find more information on identifier searches in the next section.

Searching the Source Code

When you are looking for a specific piece of information, the best way to get it is to search the source code. Mozilla Cross Reference provides three different search techniques that enable you to search for identifiers, text, and files. Although you can perform each of these searches using the main interface at `lxr.mozilla.org/mozilla/`, individual search interfaces are also available:

- For identifier searches, use `lxr.mozilla.org/mozilla/ident`
- For free text searches, use `lxr.mozilla.org/mozilla/search`
- For file and directory searches, use `lxr.mozilla.org/mozilla/find`

Identifier Searches

Identifier searches enable you to quickly determine how and where a structure is used in the source code. While location is important, the answer to how a structure is used is the most important in your coding efforts. Examples of identifiers are:

- Enumerated types
- Function prototypes
- Functions
- Macros
- Structures

■ Type definitions

■ Unions

■ Variables

When you search for identifiers, you must use the exact name of the identifier, keeping in mind that searches are case-sensitive. Following this, a search for xp_bool returns the result of "not used," but a search for XP_Bool returns an extensive set of results (see Figure 5-2). The reason for this is that xp_bool isn't defined in the source code, but XP_Bool is defined.

As you can see from Figure 5-2, the search results go a long way in telling you how and where XP_Bool is used in the source code. You see that XP_Bool is defined as a type, a preprocessor macro, and a variable that is referenced in 954 files. By selecting any of the links shown, you can access these definitions and references directly.

Figure 5-2: Identifier searches tell you how and where an element is used in the source code.

Free-Text Searches

Identifier searches are great if you know the exact name of the element you want to research. Unfortunately, you don't always know the exact name of elements you want to look up, and this is where free-text searches come into the picture.

With a free-text search, you can search the entire text of the source code, including comments, and you can do so using wildcards and regular expressions. Unfortunately, free-text searches don't tell you how an element is used in the text; they tell you only where an element is used. Because of this, you may want to use a free-text search to find an element and then run an identifier search on the element.

Figure 5-3 shows an example of a free-text search. As you can see, the search results tell you the file name and specific line number within the file that contains the reference you are looking for. Additionally, the results contain the entire text of the line.

Figure 5-3: Free-text searches enable you to search the source code using wildcards and pattern matching.

If you are familiar with Unix searches using grep or glimpse, you'll find that free text searches have similar capabilities. You can search for characters within strings, ranges of characters, patterns, and more. Table 5-1 provides a quick summary of special pattern matching symbols and expressions you can use in your searches.

TABLE 5-1: USING PATTERNS AND BOOLEAN OPERATIONS IN YOUR SEARCHES

SPECIAL SYMBOLS	DESCRIPTION	EXAMPLE
^	Beginning of a line designator	Search at the beginning of a line for pattern: ^if(AB_UseExtended*
$	End of line designator	Search at the end of a line for pattern: Selection(m_pane))$
#	Match multiple characters	Search for words beginning with: XP_B#
*	Match multiple characters	Search for words beginning with: XP_B*
.	Match single character	Search for this 7 character string: XP_B...
\\	Escape special characters if they are to be used as regular characters. Special characters include $ ^ * [	( ) ! \ ; , # > < - .	Search for XP*XP finds occurrences of XP*XP
[]	Match a single character in a range, such as [a-zA-Z] to match the characters a-z and A-Z but not numerical values or symbols.	Search for X[a-zA-Z]_Bool finds XP_Bool but not X1_Bool
[^]	Match the compliment of a single character in a range, such as [^a-zA-Z] to match the characters numerical values or symbols but not the letters a-z or A-Z.	Search for XP[^a-zA-Z]Bool finds XP_Bool but not XPEBool
;	Search with logical AND.	Search for XP_Bool and #Value using XP_Bool;#Value
,	Search with logical OR.	Search for XP_Bool or boolValue using XP_Bool,boolValue

TIP

Multiple character searches can have different behaviors with # (the glimpse symbol) and * (the grep symbol). The grep symbol (*) is designed to be used as part of a regular expression and not used with symbols specific to glimpse. Because of this, when you use ; or , and want to also match multiple characters, you should use # instead of *.

File and Directory Searches

The final type of search you can perform is a file and directory search. Use this type of search when you want to find a file or directory and don't know its full path. As with free text searches, you can use wildcards and regular expressions in your file and directory searches.

A search returns a directory path and file name for matching entries. You'll find that this is the fastest way to find files and to determine the contents of directories.

CAUTION

Generally, you don't want to use # with file name searches. If you do, you may not get the results you expected. Instead, use * to match multiple characters.

Controlling the Tree with Bonsai

Bonsai is used to track activities related to the CVS repository. Using Bonsai, you can:

- View the status of the source tree
- Get a list of changes for modules
- View the check-in logs
- Track the revision history of source files
- Create scripts to back off changes on your local directory tree

Each of these tasks is examined in detail in the sections that follow.

Viewing Tree Status

Before you check code in or out, you should check the status of the source code base you are working with. For Mozilla 5.0, the key code base is called *SeaMonkey*. You can access the SeaMonkey status page online using `cvs-mirror.mozilla .org/webtools/bonsai/toplevel.cgi?treeid=SeaMonkey`. You'll also find code bases for other branches or for projects being developed, such as the Mozilla Classic Source Code, New Layout, and Grendel code bases.

The tree control page tells you many things about the tree. You can determine the tree status, the date and time of the last known good tree, who is on the hook for the next build, and more.

The status of the tree is either open or closed. Generally, the tree is closed when the build team is trying to build the tree on the test platforms. During this time, you can check in source files that relate to the ongoing build, but you cannot check in new source files.

Another key piece of information the tree control page tells you is who is on the hook for the next build and what changes they've made. Being on hook means that you must be available to answer questions or solve problems during the next build. To check changes developers on hook have made, simply click on the changes link next to their CVS user name.

Getting Lists of Changes

CVS keeps a change history for files. The history is useful in tracking who made changes, what resources were changed, and how those changes were made. The easiest way to get a list of changes is to use the CVS query form shown in Figure 5-4. The URL for this form is `cvs-mirror.mozilla.org/webtools/bonsai/ cvsqueryform.cgi?cvsroot=/cvsroot`.

The menu on this form provides a quick way to perform common queries and lookups. Simply click on one of the query links and then submit the form using the Run Query button. Still, you'll find that for most queries, all you need to do is select a module, enter the Branch as HEAD, and then run the query using default values for other fields. Either method should give you a list of source code that was checked in.

NOTE

HEAD is the designator for the main code base for a tree. If you know of a different branch, you can enter the branch name.

Figure 5-4: Querying the CVS archive enables you to track the change history for modules and source files.

Once you submit the query form, you'll get a list of CVS checkins to the module you've selected. A sample query result is shown in Figure 5-5. As you can see, the query results tell you many things about source code that was checked in to the repository, including:

■ **When:** The date and time the checkin was made.

■ **Who:** The person who made the checkin based on their CVS user name.

■ **File:** The name of the file checked in.

■ **Rev:** The revision number of the file.

■ **+/-:** The number of changes shown as the number of lines with additions and deletions.

■ **Description:** The log message for the checkin, which should summarize the changes that were made in the source file

Options and links on the result page are very useful in providing a better understanding of changes. Clicking on the Show me ALL the Diffs button reveals a summary of all changes made on the listed files. Clicking on a file name enables you to make a query on the file and to examine differences between this submission and the last submission. Clicking on the revision number of a file enables you to track the revision history of the file.

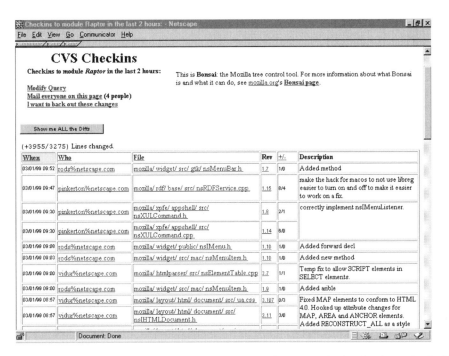

Figure 5-5: Query results provide an overview of source code that has been checked in to the selected module.

Viewing Check in Logs

Each source file in the CVS repository has a log associated with it. Reading through these logs can help you keep pace with the source file's development. An example log is shown in Figure 5-6. The log shows the revision history for nsCSSBlockFrame.h, and includes the revision number, the name of the person who made the log entry, the date of the log entry, and the text of the entry.

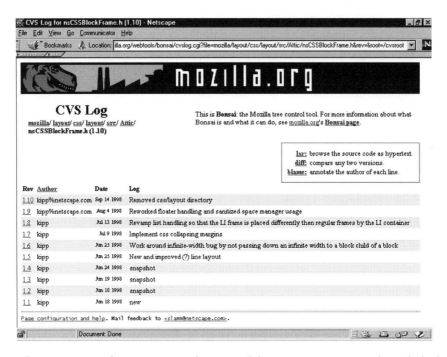

Figure 5-6: Before you start work on a module, you may want to go through the logs for key source files.

You can access source logs in several different ways. One way is to use the browse option of the CVS query form. When you browse, you drill down through modules and directories to specific files. You then select a file you want to work with and choose View Logs when given the option.

Another way to access source logs is to use the CVS log script directly (`cvs-mirror.mozilla.org/webtools/bonsai/cvslog.cgi`). Using the script, you can designate source files you want to research without having to browse with Bonsai.

Tracking Revision History

CVS tracks a revision history for all source files, provided that developers remember to update the version number when making submissions. The revision history lets you compare different versions of the source file line by line as shown in Figure 5-7. This feature is one of the most powerful and useful aspects of CVS.

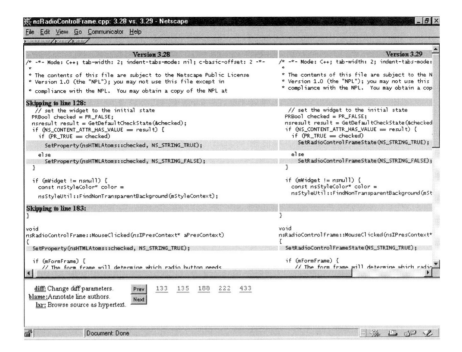

Figure 5-7: The revision history is a powerful feature that enables you to track differences in source files.

Sections of code that have been changed are listed in blocks. Although this may not be clear in the figure, these blocks have annotations that are color-coded based on the type of change. In the example, several lines of code have been changed in the latest revision. You'll also see highlighted annotations for additions and deletions.

The easiest way to access the revision history for a file is to perform a CVS query in Bonsai, click on a file you want to track, and then select the version of the file you want to examine on the CVS Differences page.

The revision history page also gives you access to other options. These options are in a separate frame at the bottom of the page and are used as follows:

- **diff:** Enables you to track differences in source file revisions

- **blame:** Enables you to see who made changes to the source file

- **lxr:** Enables you to access the file in Mozilla Cross Reference

TIP

Source changes are handled with a script called *CVS blame.* This script tracks changes to source files by making line-by-line annotations. These annotations show who made the change and in what revision the change was made. You can also access the script directly at `cvs-mirror.mozilla.org/webtools/bonsai/cvsblame.cgi`.

Creating Scripts to Back Off Changes

The results of CVS queries can be used to back off (undo) changes in your local directory tree. Being able to back off change is extremely important, especially if you refreshed your tree with a broken build and you need to continue developing your source files. Backing off changes is a three-step process:

1. Run a very specific query in the CVS query form, ensuring that the results of the query contain the files for which you need to back off changes.

2. On the result page, select I want to back out these changes. This generates a script that enables you to back off changes. Save the script to a file so you can run it as a shell script or batch file (if possible).

3. Access the root of your local directory tree. Execute the script or enter the necessary CVS commands manually.

CROSS-REFERENCE

If you know the date and time of the last good build for your system, you can also back off changes by date. Learn more in the section of this chapter, "Tracking Builds with TinderBox."

Tracking Builds with Tinderbox

Tinderbox lets you track the status of the source tree and the build process. Using Tinderbox, you can determine which platforms have built successfully and which platforms haven't. You can also determine who submitted changes and how those changes broke the build. Because of this, it is extremely important that you regularly check Tinderbox.

Tinderbox Basics

As you know, the source tree is built daily on a variety of test platforms, and the developers who have submitted changes are on the hook for those changes during the next official build process. What you may not know is that the build process actually runs continuously throughout the day (and night) on a group of dedicated build systems.

When one of these systems finishes a build, the system sends a build log to the Tinderbox server. The Tinderbox server, in turn, records the build log in its database and runs a Bonsai query to determine whose changes went into the build. The build log and the query results are then compiled and made accessible via Tinderbox.

The "on hook" rules for Bonsai state that you are responsible for being available to fix problems during the next official build. However, there's no reason you can't check for problems before this — in fact, you should. If a build is broken, you can't check in code except to fix the build. Thus, after you check in source code, you should check the builds on all platforms and ensure that they work. If necessary, use the build logs to determine what went wrong and fix the problem.

Working with Tinderbox

The main Tinderbox page is available online at `www.mozilla.org/tinderbox.html`. From this page, you can run predefined queries for current projects such as SeaMonkey. If you want to create your own queries, you can use the showbuilds script (`cvs-mirror.mozilla.org/webtools/tinderbox/showbuilds.cgi`).

The showbuilds script accepts several parameters including tree (the code base you want to examine) and hours (the number of hours you want to see in the Tinderbox history). The key tree you'll work with is SeaMonkey. Following these perimeters, you'll get a 24-hour history for SeaMonkey using the following URL:

```
cvs-mirror.mozilla.org/webtools/tinderbox/showbuilds
.cgi?tree=SeaMonkey&hours=24
```

The results of a query are shown in Figure 5-8. As you can see, Tinderbox packs a lot of information into the result table. Timestamps in the Build Time column indicate the time of the build and are listed in reverse chronological order, meaning that the most recent entries are first. The Guilty column shows the CVS user name for the person who checked in source code at the specified time. The remaining column headers indicate systems in the build group.

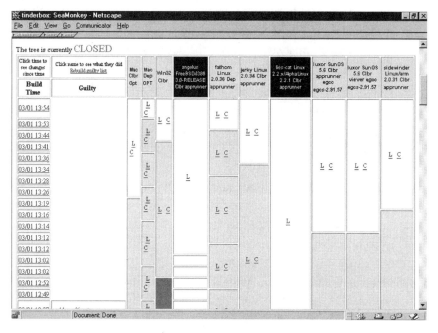

Figure 5-8: Tinderbox packs a lot of information into the result table. Be sure to use the links provided to dig deeper for clues on how to resolve build problems.

Build systems are organized by platform and build type. You'll see many different types of platforms, including Mac, Win32, Linux, SunOS, and FreeBSD. These are the primary build systems. Secondary build systems set up by developers are available as well. To see the builds on these systems, you should use the MozillaTest tree (`cvs-mirror.mozilla.org/webtools/tinderbox/showbuilds.cgi ?tree=MozillaTest`). Generally, you are responsible for proper builds on primary systems and not on secondary systems.

Build types are indicated by the system name. The keyword Clobber or the abbreviation Clbr indicates that builds are checked out and compiled from scratch. The keyword Depend or the abbreviation Dep indicates that builds are updated and rebuilt in the same directory, and incrementally rebuilt.

Cell colors indicate the status of the build at a particular time. Entries in the table cells enable you to access logs and comments related to the build. Click on L entries to display a menu that enables you to view the build logs or add comments to the build logs. Click on star entries to display comments that have been added to the build logs. Click on C entries to show changes that occurred since the last build.

Understanding Tree Status

As you set out to work with Tinderbox, don't forget that Tinderbox results are shown in reverse chronological order, with the most recent entries shown first. The following sections provide tips for working with the tree in various states.

Green Tree

A green tree occurs when the primary builds are green at the current time, which means that the most recent build process was successful. If you just checked in your code, the code probably wasn't a part of this build, and you should check back to ensure that the tree stays green.

Yellow Tree

When a build is in process on a system, the tree is yellow. If you checked in code when the tree was green, you should watch the progress of the build and ensure that the tree goes back to green.

Build logs are updated throughout the build process. If you want, you can view the build logs and add comments to the logs during the build process.

Orange Tree

An orange tree means that the build process on the primary systems was successful but that the build process on the secondary systems wasn't. If this occurs and your name appears in the Guilty column, you should check the MozillaTest tree to determine what went wrong with the build, and, if possible, you should try to fix the problems in your source code.

Generally, you want to examine the logs for the first build to break because this should give you the best indicator of what went wrong. Click on an L in the first orange box above a green box to view the build log. Afterward, you can click on the C in the same box to see what code was checked in at this time.

Red Tree

A red tree means that the build broke on a primary system. If this occurs and your name appears in the Guilty column, you are responsible for fixing the problem. Generally, you want to examine the logs for the first build to break because this should give you the best indicator of what went wrong. Click on an L in the first red box above a green box to view the build log. Afterward, you can click on the C in the same box to see what code was checked in at this time.

A red tree also means that you can't check in new code (unless you are fixing a problem). When the tree is red, you shouldn't update your local directory tree either. If you do, you may find that you need to back off changes to get back to where you can develop and build your source. One way to back off changes was covered previously in "Creating Scripts to Back Off Changes." Another way to back off changes is to follow these steps:

1. Go backward through the Tinderbox entries until you find one where the tree is green and then note the date and time.

2. Access the root of your local directory tree.

3. Update your local directory tree using the following command:

   ```
   cvs update -D date
   ```

   where *date* is the date and time stamp you want to use.

4. When the tree turns back to green, update your local directory tree using the command:

   ```
   cvs update -A
   ```

CAUTION

If you forget to run update -A, all your CVS commands will continue to use the date and time stamp you set above, which can cause your local directory tree to become stale. You can solve this problem by updating the tree with the -A option.

Using Bugzilla

Bugzilla is a bug tracking and reporting system developed by Netscape. You can use Bugzilla to report bugs in the Mozilla source releases and to browse currently reported bugs.

Reporting Bugs with Bugzilla

Bugzilla has a sophisticated system for bug reporting that enables you to provide a lot of details without a lot of effort. You can access the bug reporting system online at `bugzilla.mozilla.org/enter_bug.cgi`. From this page, select the product that the bug affects, such as the Calendar module. This takes you to a page where you can log in to Bugzilla.

If you've never reported a bug before, you need to obtain a password. Enter your e-mail address in the field provided and then click on Email me a password. You should get an e-mail message that has your password in a few minutes. If you ever need to change your password, use the form at `bugzilla.mozilla.org/changepassword.cgi`.

After logging in, you should see a bug reporting form similar to the one shown in Figure 5-9. Key fields in this form are used as follows:

- **Version:** The current build version you are working with.

- **Component:** The module or library the bug relates to.

- **Platform:** The hardware platform the bug relates to. If this is a cross-platform bug, select All.

- **OS:** The operating system the bug relates to. If this is a cross-platform bug, select All.

- **Priority:** The importance of the bug and the order in which a bug should be fixed. Priorities from highest to lowest are P1, P2, P3, P4, and P5.

- **Severity:** The severity of the bug. Critical bugs cause crashes, data loss, and severe memory leaks. Major bugs cause major loss of functionality. Minor bugs cause less severe problems or represent a bug with an easy workaround. Most trivial bugs relate to tweaks or spelling/positioning corrections. Enhancement bugs are requests for enhancements to the component.

- **Assign to:** The developer you want to assign to fix the big. Generally, you should leave this blank to assign the bug to the component owner.

After you fill out a bug report, you have two options. You can submit the bug using Commit or you can save the bug report as a template for future use. To save the report, bookmark the link provided and don't forget to actually submit the report using Commit afterward.

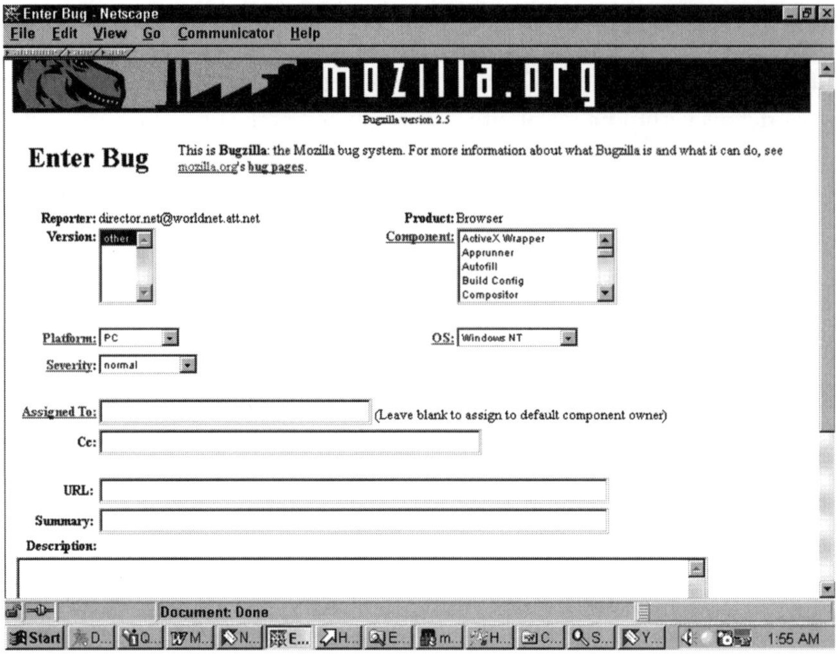

Figure 5-9: Report bugs with this form.

Bug Tracking in Mozilla

Bugzilla provides two ways to track bugs. You can query the bug database for specific instances of a bug, or you can run a bug report for a particular project.

Querying Bugzilla

Bug queries are handled with the form shown in Figure 5-10. This form is accessible online at `bugzilla.mozilla.org/query.cgi`. As you can see, the form enables you to fine-tune the query in a wide variety of ways. You can enter parameters based on bug status, resolution, operating system, priority, severity, and more. Rather than go into every feature of this form, I focus on running and remembering queries.

To get the most out of Bugzilla, you should tailor your queries for the modules you use and then save the queries for future use. Begin by configuring the query options and then running the query to test the results. When you find a query that you want to use regularly, you have two options. You can elect to remember the query as the default query or to remember the query by assigning it a name.

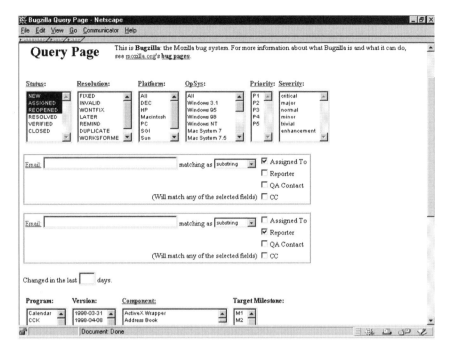

Figure 5-10: Tailor your Bugzilla queries for the modules you use and then save the queries for future use.

If you want it to be your default query:

1. Scroll down to the bottom of the form, and then select Remember this as the default query.

2. Click Submit query.

NOTE

Bugzilla remembers your reports using cookies. If you clean out your cookie file or disallow cookies, you won't be able to store queries for future use.

If you want to remember the query by name:

1. Scroll down to the bottom of the form, select Remember this query, and name it.

2. Enter a name for the query, and then click Submit query.

3. Reload the query form, and then you can use the remembered query.

4. To run the query, select Run remembered query, and then choose the query from the corresponding selection menu. Afterward, click Submit query.

A sample query result is shown in Figure 5-11. As you can see, queries are summarized by:

- **ID:** The bug's ID number in Bugzilla

- **Sev:** The severity of the bug, from critical to trivial

- **Pri:** The priority of the bug—its importance and the order in which it should be fixed

- **Plt:** The platform the bug occurs on

- **Owner:** The person in charge of resolving the bug

- **State:** The status of the bug, such as new, opened, resolved, or re-opened

- **Result:** The resolution for a bug that been resolved. If the bug has not been resolved, Result is blank.

- **Summary:** A summary description of the bug

If you want a more descriptive result, click on the Long Format button at the bottom of the result page. The long format gives you detailed descriptions and additional comments submitted by those who have encountered the bug.

Generating Bug Reports

If you want to generate bug reports by project, the easiest way to do this is to use the bug report form (`bugzilla.mozilla.org/reports.cgi`). Using this form, you can select the product you want to work with, such as the Calendar module, and the output format, which is either a bug count or a chart.

A bug count report provides a summary of bug occurrences, a bug count by engineer, and a quick overview of individual bugs by engineer. These summaries are listed by totals and status (new, open, reassigned). A chart report shows a time history for bug reporting by status.

TIP
With bug count reports, be sure to select the Links to Bugs switch. This will add links to the report that enable you to view individual bugs.

Figure 5-11: The results of a bug query can provide insight into problems you are experiencing.

Summary

As you learned in this chapter, several different tools are available to Mozilla developers. You'll use Mozilla Cross Reference anytime you need to find something in the source code, Bonsai to examine the source tree, Tinderbox to track builds, and Bugzilla to find and report bugs. Trust me, the more you use these tools, the more you'll appreciate them.

PART

III

Working with the Source Code

III

Working with the Source Code

Learn the skills you need to tame Mozilla. All the key concepts, techniques, and tasks are covered. Explore the user interface. Dive into program interface internals. Create windows, menus, and toolbars. Manage threading and synchronization. Create directories and files. Allocate memory and handle errors.

User Interface Design Concepts

When you work with Mozilla's user interfaces, you are no longer doing behind-the-scenes work. You are working in a high-visibility development area, and everyone who uses Mozilla may one day see your work. To help get your development efforts on track more quickly and more smoothly, you need to know how the user interfaces are put together, and this is exactly what you'll find in this chapter. Still, no single chapter can explore every facet of the Mozilla user interface (UI). Thus, rather than explore every possible design technique, this chapter focuses on the most valuable key techniques and concepts.

The user interface in the classic version of Mozilla is platform specific and defined in platform-specific modules, such as WinFE and MacFE. The next generation user interface is defined in the XPToolkit and XPApps modules. XPToolkit defines a set of cross-platform user interfaces. XPApps is an application layer built on top of XPToolkit.

Many design principles went into creating Mozilla's user interface. These principles detail what colors are used for toolbars and buttons, how the menus and toolbars are designed, and much more. Understanding these design principles is the key to being able to enhance and extend the user interface.

Understanding Mozilla Color Palettes

Mozilla is a cross-platform application that runs on many different platforms and configurations. Before you create any user interface elements, you should be sure that you are using compatible colors and a standard color palette if possible. Color palettes affect everything you do with the user interface. If you use too many colors, you can cause color conflicts. Color conflicts can cause the browser to map the wrong color for display, resulting in both distorted images and possible future problems with images when users browse the Web.

To avoid color conflicts, you need a strong understanding of how color palettes are used in applications. One of the strictest scenarios is designing a color palette for 8-bit displays. On an 8-bit display, you have only 256 colors to work with and if you use all 256 colors in the user interface, the user may experience frequent problems with color mapping.

If you're a graphic designer as well as a programmer, you've probably heard all about browser color palettes. The browser color palette contains a set of safe colors for displaying Web pages and graphics. On Windows systems with 8-bit displays, this palette contains 226 colors and is supported in most modern graphics programs as the Web or browser palette.

What you may not know about is what happened to the other 30 colors allocated in the normal 256-color palette. Well, these colors are allocated to Mozilla itself as its internal color palette. And as you might imagine, color palettes for implementations specific to Windows, Unix, and Mac systems are slightly different; I'll examine these differences in a moment. Afterward, I'll take a look at how color palettes are implemented in the cross-platform UI and enhanced color palettes.

Windows Color Palette

If you can't use the PhotoShop palette on the CD-ROM, create your own palette using the RGB values shown in Table 6-1. These colors should be placed in the palette in the order shown. Note that color 23 is the reserved transparent color for Windows. This color should be used only for the transparent mask in your images and should not be used otherwise.

TIP

I recommend opening the color palette in PhotoShop or re-creating it in your favorite drawing application so that you can work with it to create sample icons. After you've worked in a restricted environment, you'll have a better understanding of color usage.

ON THE CD-ROM

On 8-bit displays, the Windows color palette has 30 colors and is designed to provide a strong color mix for Mozilla's toolbar icons, buttons, and logos. On the CD-ROM, you'll find the color palette in the file `/colors/win32/netscape_w.act`. This is a PhotoShop color palette file.

TABLE 6-1: COLOR PALETTE SUMMARY FOR WINDOWS

COLOR NUMBER	RED	GREEN	BLUE
1	255	255	204
2	255	255	0
3	204	153	102
4	255	102	51
5	128	128	0
6	51	255	153
7	0	255	0
8	0	128	0

Continued

TABLE 6-1: *(continued)*

COLOR NUMBER	RED	GREEN	BLUE
9	66	154	167
10	0	128	128
11	0	55	60
12	0	255	255
13	0	153	255
14	0	0	255
15	0	0	128
16	204	204	255
17	153	153	255
18	102	102	204
19	51	51	102
20	255	0	0
21	128	0	0
22	255	102	204
23	255	0	255
24	153	0	102
25	153	102	153
26	255	255	255
27	192	192	192
28	128	128	128
29	34	34	34
30	0	0	0

Macintosh Color Palette

The Macintosh color palette is based on the Macintosh system color palette. The system palette is designed to be used for icon creation on the Mac and can be accessed in the Mac resource program.

Color Palette for Unix X Systems

If you can't use the PhotoShop palette on the CD-ROM, start your favorite drawing application and create your own palette using the RGB values shown in Table 6-2. Note that color 23 is the reserved transparent color for Unix. This color should be used only for the transparent mask in your images and should not be used otherwise.

ON THE CD-ROM

Color palettes on Unix X systems are slightly different from those on Windows and the Macintosh. Unix X systems have icon colors, Motif UI colors, and image colors. The result is that Unix X systems with 8-bit displays have 24 colors for Mozilla, 16 colors Motif UI colors, and 216 colors for Web pages and graphics. On the CD-ROM, you'll find the color palette in the file /colors/unix/netscape_x.act. This is a PhotoShop color palette file.

TABLE 6-2: COLOR PALETTE SUMMARY FOR UNIX

COLOR NUMBER	RED	GREEN	BLUE
1	255	255	0
2	255	102	51
3	128	128	0
4	0	255	0
5	0	128	0
6	66	154	167
7	0	128	128
8	0	55	60

Continued

TABLE 6-2: *(continued)*

COLOR NUMBER	RED	GREEN	BLUE
9	0	255	255
10	0	0	255
11	0	0	128
12	153	153	255
13	102	102	204
14	51	51	102
15	255	0	0
16	128	0	0
17	255	102	204
18	153	0	102
19	255	255	255
20	192	192	192
21	128	128	128
22	34	34	34
23	255	0	255
24	0	0	0

Enhanced Color Palettes

Creating icons with 24 or 30 colors isn't easy and doesn't allow for a lot of variance in your user interface. Still, the environment limitations can teach important lessons about the use of color in user interfaces. These limitations also provide a better understanding of why it is so important to avoid color conflicts if at all possible.

By working with such a limited environment, you'll have a greater appreciation for why it's so important to limit your use of colors, even when you are developing for systems that support 16-bit or 24-bit color. With 16-bit displays, you have

65,536 colors to work with. With 24-bit color displays, you have 16.7 million colors to work with. Color palettes you develop for these display modes can be enhanced considerably compared with their 8-bit counterparts.

Still, when you move on to these enhanced color palettes, you'll find that most icons use a color palette with 152 colors and that these color palettes are independent of one another. For example, the Personal icon could have a different palette from that of the Bookmarks icon. However, an initiative is underway to standardize icons, like Back, Forward and Print, on the same palette. Each icon would then have a standard color palette of 152 colors with each color carefully selected to allow for a wide variation of color usage.

If you're wondering why saving a few colors matters when you have 65,536 or 16.7 million colors available, consider a case where users have multiple applications open on the desktop and each of these applications is using different color palettes. Or consider a case where users have accessed a Web page that uses true color 24-bit images. These situations can easily result in color conflicts if you aren't careful in your UI development.

The standard Mozilla browser interface uses about 20 different icons — give or take a few depending on the setup. If each icon uses 152 different colors, Mozilla alone will use over 3,000 colors. To compound matters, the standard Mozilla editor interface uses even more icons because of its extensive toolbar. In the end, you'll be much happier if you plan to restrict your use of color from the beginning and create a standard color policy for all your user interface endeavors.

ON THE CD-ROM

On the CD-ROM, you'll find a sample 152-color palette in the file `/colors/update/netscape_xpfe.aco`. This is a PhotoShop color swatch file.

Designing Windows and Widgets

Mozilla's windows and widgets are a key part of the user interface. Windows are used to set preferences, open file locations, print documents, and more. Widgets are general-purpose user interface elements, such as radio buttons and text boxes.

Windows and Window Design

Windows are containers for widgets and come in several varieties. The most common window types are browser windows and dialog windows. Browser windows contain menu bars, toolboxes, and widgets. Dialog windows contain form widgets, dialog widgets, and other types of widgets.

Mozilla's windows can be specified in HTML but usually are designed in XUL (XML-based User Interface Language). XUL is an XML-based language that uses HTML/CSS and the DOM. Using XUL, you can create a window and add widgets to it. While commands and actions for the window are handled with JavaScript in most instances, you can hook to C/C++ if necessary.

To understand how Mozilla's windows are created, let's take a closer look at the design of the Preferences dialog box. Preferences are designed to help users quickly find options they are looking for. Because of this, the organization of the dialog box is extremely important.

Categories and Subcategories

The Preferences dialog box has four main areas: category, message banner, preferences panel, and command buttons. The category area is organized as a tree view, enabling users to easily browse through the various preference categories. Categories are organized according to the feature or application component to which they relate and are also broken down into subcategories to ensure that preference sets are more manageable. For example, you use the Appearance category to change the appearance of the display. Subcategories of Appearance include Fonts and Colors, which are related to the display but have too many options to be integrated into the main category dialog box.

Figure 6-1 shows the original Preferences dialog box implemented in Communicator and Mozilla.

Preference categories tend to change based on the type of product and its components. Standard Communicator categories include Appearance, Navigator, Mail & Groups, Composer, Offline, and Advanced. Typically in the Mozilla browser and editor build, you'll find that the categories are Appearance, Navigator, Composer, and Advanced. As you can see, the first and last categories are the same, but the middle categories have changed to reflect the available components.

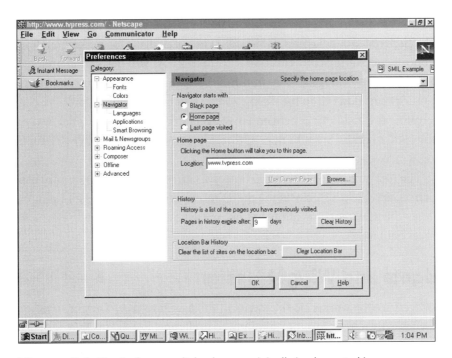

Figure 6-1: The Preferences dialog box as originally implemented in Communicator/Mozilla.

If you integrate other applications into Mozilla, you want to add preferences for these applications. Following the precedent set by Netscape, you probably want to add new categories before the Advanced category. For example, if you add a personal information manager component to Mozilla, you could have the following categories: Appearance, Navigator, Composer, Calendar, and Advanced.

Message Banner, Preferences, and Commands

Each category and subcategory has a corresponding message banner. The *message banner* contains a title on the left and a section of right-aligned text that describe the currently selected category or subcategory. As you add categories and subcategories, you'll need to create new message banners. The message banner area is displayed to the left of the category area, but it doesn't have to be arranged this way. For example, you may want to center the message banner at the top of the dialog window.

Beneath the message banner is the preferences panel for the selected category. The preference panel contains various types of widgets for making preference selections and adding configuration information. As you design the preferences panel for a new category, keep in mind that you have a finite area to work with. If your options don't fit in the dialog window, you'll need to use pull-down menus, scrolling text fields, or other similar widgets to make the additional options available. You may also want to have a More Options button that accesses another dialog window.

The final area is for command buttons. Currently, three buttons are used: OK, Cancel, and Help. OK closes the preferences window and saves all changes. Cancel closes the preferences window but doesn't save any changes. Help opens the preferences help window.

Widgets and Widget Design

Widgets are the worker bee elements in the user interface. They are used to handle key tasks from user input to scrolling to preference selection. Two main categories of widgets are widely used: *general* and *form*.

As the name implies, general widgets are used to perform general UI tasks and include slider controls, progress bars, and tab controls. Form widgets are used to display input elements normally associated with HTML forms but are also widely used in the Mozilla UI. These widgets include push buttons, radio buttons, check boxes, and edit fields.

As you design interface components, such as dialog windows, you should keep in mind how certain types of widgets are used and use them accordingly. Table 6-3 provides a quick summary for the most commonly used widgets.

TABLE 6-3: COMMONLY USED WIDGETS

WIDGET	USAGE
Check box	Chooses one or more selections from a group
Color picker	Selects colors for preferences and dialog settings
Combobox	Combines a pull-down with a popup menu for displaying a list of options

WIDGET	USAGE
Disclosure triangle	Accesses additional items in a tree or make selection to display additional items
Edit field	Inputs a single line of text or a password
File picker	Inputs filenames or select a file to open
Font picker	Selects font family, typeface, and size for preferences and dialog settings
Grippy pane	Shows, hides, or manipulates toolbars
List box	Displays multiple selection and enables user to make a selection
Progress bar	Shows progress in file access, downloads, and so on
Push button	Makes selections
Radio button	Chooses one selection from a group
Scrolling text field	Inputs multiple lines of text
Slider control	Selects a value in a specific range
Tab control	Organizes multiple selections with tabs
Tree control	Accesses items and options in a menu tree
Up/Down arrow	Moves up or down

Designing Menus

The Mozilla browser is one component of a larger application that can include other components for mail, news, HTML editing, and so forth. To give the application a consistent feel in different components, the menu system follows a specific design, and you should understand this design if you want to build your own menus or add components.

Mozilla's Menu System

Menu systems are made up of menu bars, menu lists, and menu items. As in most applications, Mozilla's menu bar extends across the top of the application window. The menu bar contains clear and concise keywords that serve as the title of each menu. Clicking the mouse while over a menu title displays a menu list and its options, which can include menu items and submenus. Separator lines are used to organize long menus and make them easier to use. Technically, a separator is a special type of menu item.

Mozilla's menus are designed in XUL. Using XUL, you can define individual menus and the menu items they contain. You can also use XUL to set commands to execute when menu items are selected. These commands are handled with COM and C++.

In Communicator, the menus follow a specific order, and new menus are added for various components. The normal order for menus is File, Edit, View, Communicator, and Help; additional menus are added between View and Communicator. Such menus include Insert, Format, Table, Tools, Message, and Go.

The Mozilla menu system follows the original design for Netscape Communicator with some slight variations. In the typical Mozilla build, the standard browser menus are File, Edit, View, Go, Window, and Help. Go is an additional menu specific to Mozilla, and the original Communicator menu may be renamed as Window to reflect that this isn't a part of the standard Communicator build.

If you build the editor with the browser component, you'll find that the standard menus in Mozilla Composer usually are File, Edit, View, Insert, Format, Table, Tools, Window, and Help. Here, the Insert, Format, Table, and Tools menus are added for Composer, and Window is again renamed.

Several other features are built into the menu system for the New submenu and for the Communicator/Window menu. The New submenu's design for integration is such that you can create a new Navigator window or a new page for editing regardless of which application you use. New commands specific to the current component follow the standard commands. A separator line separates the standard commands from the component-specific commands.

The Communicator/Window menu also has integration features with sets of commands separated by separator lines. The first set of commands opens new windows for components. The second set of commands opens component tools, such as bookmarks or history. The final set of commands accesses currently open application windows. In Mozilla builds, you may find variations on this theme, and of course you can create your own variations as well.

Menu Access Features and Options

If you plan on adding new menus or menu items to existing menus, you need to know how menus are controlled. You can access the menu system using the mouse or an access key combination, and it's these access key combinations to which you need to pay particular attention to.

Access keys are different for Windows, Unix, and Macintosh. For example, on Windows, you use Alt in combination with an access key to activate menus and options. Generally, the access key is the first letter of the menu or the menu item name, with the exception of when a letter is already used; in this case you can use any available letter.

On Windows, for example, you press Alt+F to activate the File menu. Once the menu is activated, subsequent uses of Alt and an access key are context sensitive for the active menu. Pressing Alt by itself cancels all menus. An alternative is to use the Esc key to cancel the current menu without deactivating all menus.

Typically, you can also activate menu options directly. You do this using a modifier key in combination with an accelerator key. For example, on Macintosh, the Command key is the modifier and it's used in conjunction with accelerator keys to access menu options directly.

If you plan on adding menus or menu options, you need to ensure that new menus and options don't conflict with existing access keys. Further, you should also ensure that your new accelerators don't cause any conflicts. Here are some basic rules to help you make key selections:

- Try to use the first letter of the menu or option name if possible.

- If the first option is not possible, try to use a key consonant in the menu or option name.

- If neither of the previous options works, use a vowel in the menu or option name.

Designing Toolbars

A toolbox is a container for toolbars, and it's within a toolbox that you'll find Mozilla's toolbars. Mozilla's standard toolbars include the Navigation toolbar, the Personal toolbar, and the Location toolbar. These toolbars contain several UI elements, including buttons and tool tips. The sections that follow examine these elements.

Toolbar Basics

Before you work with the toolbox and toolbars, you need to know how toolbars are used in Mozilla. As with menus, Mozilla's toolbox is designed in XUL. In XUL you define a toolbox element and then add toolbars to it. Afterward, you add buttons to the individual toolbars. These buttons have actions that are usually handled via JavaScript.

On the left edge of a standard toolbar, you'll find a grippy pane. A grippy pane is a UI for manipulating the toolbar. Clicking on the grippy pane expands or collapses the toolbar depending on its state. Dragging the grippy pane moves the toolbar to a new location. The shape of the grippy pane changes when it is collapsed, which gives users a visual cue that the toolbar is closed.

Toolbars defined in the XPToolkit module can be customized using style sheets and modified at runtime through the DOM. Specific behaviors you can control with style sheets include colors, backgrounds, toolbar styles, and the tab style for grippy panes. Because markup is used instead of source code #ifdefs, you don't have to recompile when you want to change the look and feel of your toolbars. In fact, you can make runtime modifications to toolbars without having to recompile Mozilla. Runtime modification of toolbars enables you to show/hide toolbars and to change their appearance without having to recompile Mozilla.

Toolbar Buttons

Toolbars contain two key types of buttons: image buttons and menu buttons. Image buttons are standard buttons capable of displaying an image and descriptive text. Menu buttons extend image buttons so that pop-down menus or pop-down trees can be displayed beneath the button. After examining the basic types of buttons, I'll examine button display modes and positioning.

Image Buttons

Home and Reload are examples of image buttons. Image buttons support four states:

- Disabled
- Normal
- Rollover
- Depressed

Disabled buttons cannot be selected and are "grayed out" on the toolbar. Normal buttons are selectable and are displayed on the toolbar without any special highlighting. The state of a normal button changes to rollover when the mouse pointer is over the button. In the rollover state, buttons have a distinctive border. This border is a dark outer color and a light inner color to give the button dimension and the appearance that it has popped up, or is raised.

Clicking on a button selects it and changes its state to depressed; this gives a visual cue that the button has been selected. Typically, selected buttons have a light outer color and a dark inner color to suggest that the button has been pushed in.

The state of an image button usually is handled through JavaScript event handlers. Because of this, image buttons support the following JavaScript event handlers:

- `onClick`
- `onMouseOver`
- `onBlur`
- `onChange`
- `onFocus`

Image buttons also need to support text positioning and manipulation. Button text may need to be aligned to the left or right of an image. Text positioning modes are:

- Text right image left
- Text left image right
- Text bottom image top
- Text top image top

Text may also need to be truncated if it doesn't fit on the button. Text truncation modes are:

- Right truncation
- Left truncation
- Center truncation

Figure 6-2 provides a summary of image button features.

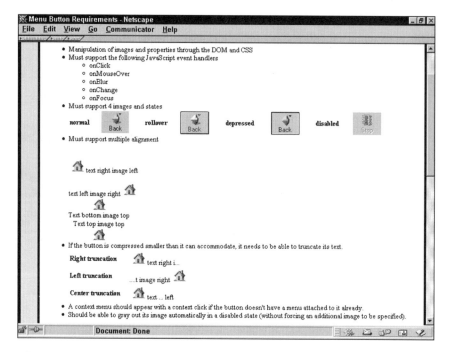

Figure 6-2: A graphical summary of image button states and text positioning

Menu Buttons

Back and Forward are examples of menu buttons. Menu buttons support all the features of image buttons and add support for popdown menus and popdown trees. Popdowns are displayed when you click and hold a menu button.

A popdown tree is a tree view, such as you see when you work with folders and subfolders in Windows Explorer. When users work with tree views, they need to be able to expand or collapse folders without the pop-down trees disappearing. Thus once a tree view is activated it goes away only when the user clicks outside of the tree or on a top-level element. Figure 6-3 shows a popdown menu and a popdown tree view.

Button Display Modes

Buttons also have several different display modes. The display mode determines whether the button is displayed with a graphic, with text, or with a combination of the two. These display modes correspond to the Show toolbar preferences:

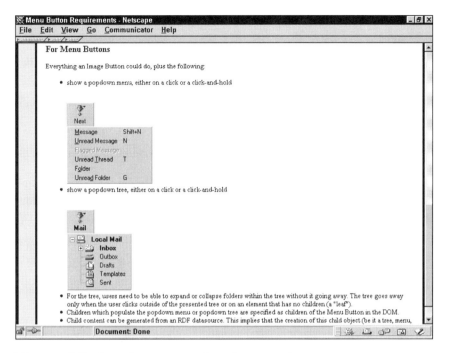

Figure 6-3: A popdown menu and popdown tree view

- Pictures & text
- Pictures only
- Text only

Toolbars are designed to meet a wide range of display modes, including 640×480, which is the minimum supported display size. Because of this, you should design toolbars to support users who meet the minimum requirements. Otherwise, buttons may be truncated or not displayed at all on their system.

The Navigation toolbar is the toolbar most affected by the minimum display size. At 640 × 480, you can fit nine to ten buttons with pictures and text on this toolbar. Using the default font type and size, you can fit eight to ten characters on a button. With Text only and Pictures & text buttons, ensure that you limit the number of characters for text labels accordingly.

NOTE
With image-only buttons, the standard icon size is 23 × 21, with a button size of 27 × 25. With Pictures & text buttons, the standard icon size is 23 × 21, with a button size of 48 × 41. The standard icon sizes aren't etched in stone. You can change icon sizes at any time. However, you should standardize with a particular size and consider resizing based on the user's display settings as necessary.

When the state of a button changes, so does its appearance. Normal buttons are displayed without borders. When the mouse is over a button, dark borders are displayed and the image is highlighted. The image highlighting is rather subtle, and it usually consists of an image with lighter/brighter tones rather than an image with darker/bolder tones. Usually, the image position is also shifted up and to the left 1 pixel when the mouse pointer is over it.

NOTE
In the next-generation UI, a single image may be used to create these different states. Here, you would highlight the image using an effect.

Text in a button changes on mouse over as well. By default, the button text changes from black to blue, but you can customize this behavior.

You'll find button icons and other types of user interface icons in the XPFE module's `AppCores\xul\resources` folder. Icon prefixes specify the UI component with which the icon is associated. The prefixes you'll see include:

- **Dialog:** Dialog window icon for the browser, address book, mail, editor, and so on

- **ED:** Editor toolbar icon

- **Mail:** Mail toolbar icon

- **StatusBar:** Status bar icon

- **TB:** Browser toolbar icon

TIP

Button icons may be stored in different formats. These formats support the button states as normal, rollover, or disabled. The icon suffix specifies the state support. Icons for the normal state have no suffix. Icons for rollover end with mo (mouseover). Icons for disabled end with dis.

Button Positioning

The position of buttons on the toolbar is important. Before you rearrange the buttons, you should consider how the change affects the user experience. For example, Back, Forward, and Stop are the three most used buttons. If you were to change the location of these buttons on the toolbar, you might confuse users.

Back and Forward are next to each other because they represent actions you may use in sequence. Stop, on the other hand, is the last button on the toolbar, and the primary reason is that you don't want to accidentally hit stop when you meant to perform another task.

TIP

I've always wished that the toolbar weren't so busy. I rarely use Search, Guide, or Security, but I'm always changing my preferences. So I've modified the toolbar to add a Prefs button and remove Search, Guide, and Security.

Tool Tips

All buttons on the toolbar have tool tips associated with them. Tool tips are displayed when the pointer remains over a button for a short period of time (about 1 second). After being activated, tool tips are displayed until the user presses the button or moves off the button. Tool tips are also displayed when a button is disabled (unless OS constraints prevent this).

Generally, you should use short, descriptive tool tips. A good length for a tip is 15–35 characters, which is usually 3–5 words. With a tool tip of this size, users get a quick preview of the button's purpose. Some examples of tool tips currently in use include:

- Go to next page

- Go to previous page

- Reload this page from the server

- Search on the Internet

- Interesting places on the Internet

- Print this page

- Show security information

- Stop loading this page

- Drag this to create a link

A key characteristic of the previous tool tips is that they all answer the question "What does this button do?" or "What is this button for?" To answer these questions, you usually need a verb, such as "print," "show," or "search."

Summary

User interface design is one of the most important aspects of application programming, and you can learn many valuable lessons from past and present Mozilla interfaces. These lessons can help you design user interfaces that work on a wide variety of platforms and display resolutions. An area of design that application programmers often don't think about is color. As you've seen in this chapter, color palettes play an important role in helping you create cross-platform interfaces. Beyond color palettes are windows, toolbars, menus, and all the other GUI elements that make interface design one of the most exciting aspects of application programming.

Programming the User Interface

In this chapter, you'll learn more about the inner workings of the user interface. As you work with XPToolkit and XPApps, you'll discover that the core functionality for the user interface revolves around XUL (pronounced "zuul" and short for "XML-based User Interface Language"). XUL is an XML-based language for describing the layout and components of user interfaces. The chapter first looks at the XUL architecture and building application windows, and then moves on to cover the key components of this architecture.

Understanding the XUL Architecture

Let's explore how you can use XUL with C++ and other technologies. I'll start with an overview of XUL and then describe the architecture.

XUL Basics

XUL is used to describe windows and their contents. With application windows, such as the Mozilla browser window, you use XUL to define every aspect of the window's user interface, from its menus to its toolbars to its status bar. Because the user interface is configurable through markup, it isn't hard coded in the source; instead, it is loaded at runtime, enabling programmers to tweak the interface without having to recompile the source code. The capability to dynamically configure the user interface is what makes XUL such a useful resource.

Interactions and events related to the UI flow through JavaScript and are handled either in source code or in a script. With menu options, you normally specify command handlers, which flow through JavaScript to C++. From C++, the handlers may drop through directly to C. With other types of UI elements, such as push buttons, you use JavaScript event handlers, such as onClick or onMouseOver to handle user interaction.

Services are added to handle key tasks such as copying to the clipboard and drag and drop. To implement the necessary UI elements and access services, you'll use XUL markup, which looks very similar to HTML and XML markup. However, while HTML markup is used to describe the contents of a document, XUL markup is used to describe the contents of an entire window, which can include multiple HTML documents. HTML, XML, and XUL achieve flexibility through an object model called *DOM*. Interfaces into the DOM are defined in *Interface Definition Language* (IDL). These interfaces serve as the glue between JavaScript and C/C++ source code.

XUL isn't as complex as it sounds — trust me. In fact, XUL markup looks very similar to plain old HTML. To see how much they are alike, consider the following example that creates a sample pull-down menu called Edit:

```
<window>
<menubar>
<menu name="Edit">
```

```
        <menuitem name="Undo" onclick="EditorUndo()"/>
        <menuitem name="Redo" onclick="EditorRedo()"/>
        <separator />
        <menuitem name="Cut" onclick="EditorCut()"/>
        <menuitem name="Copy" onclick="EditorCopy()"/>
        <menuitem name="Paste" onclick="EditorPaste()"/>
        <menuitem name="Clear" onclick="EditorClear()"/>
        <separator />
        <menuitem name="Select All" onclick="EditorSelectAll()"/>
        <separator />
        <menuitem name="Insert" onclick="EditorInsertText()"/>
    </menu>
  </menubar>
</window>
```

From the example, you can see that XUL makes extensive use of markup tags, such as WINDOW, MENUBAR, MENU and MENUITEM. You can also see that XUL tags have attributes such as NAME and ONCLICK. These tags and attributes are very similar to HTML tags and attributes.

The Architecture

The architecture for XUL is much like what you see in Figure 7-1. C/C++ source code serves as the basis for an object class, which defines core functionality and services. Application core implements the core functionality for an application component. Application services process XUL. Both of these are written in C/C++.

Beyond this, you have documents that describe the layout and contents of application windows. These documents are defined as XML documents, which can combine HTML, XUL, CSS, and JavaScript. HTML is used mostly for layout and it is used because it has established interfaces for JavaScript and CSS; XUL is used to describe windows; CSS is used to set the look and style of windows; and, JavaScript handles events and commands.

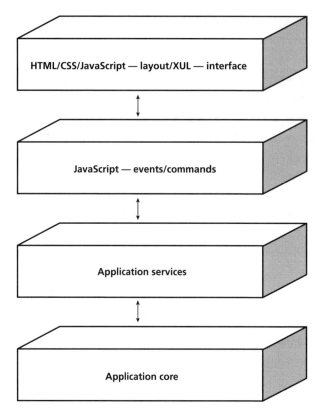

Figure 7-1: The architecture for XUL

Working with Application Services

Application services are processes. They process XUL, initialize the environment, and create window instances. To do this, application services need access to user interface elements and the source code for handling core functions.

Working with AppRunner and AppShell

Currently, the Mozilla application service is implemented in AppRunner (`nsApp Runner`) and AppShell (`nsAppShell`). AppRunner has no application-specific knowledge and is merely a go-between. It loads a XUL file and an application core, and then hooks them together through the application shell, AppShell. The `main()` function of AppRunner sets up the application shell and handles tasks for initializing the shell, running the shell, and shutting down the shell:

```
// Execute the shell.
AppShell()->Initialize();

// Run the shell.
AppShell()->Run();

// Shut it down.
AppShell()->Shutdown();
```

If you examine AppShell, you'll find that it provides key services for the application shell and XUL as well as controllers for widgets and window callbacks. These features are implemented through nsAppShellService, nsCommandLineService, nsWebShellWindow, and nsXULCommand.

Creating Window Instances

AppShell creates window instances using the nsIAppShellService interface. Top-level window instances (application windows) are created with CreateTop LevelWindow(). Dialog window instances are created with CreateDialog Window(). When CreateTopLevelWindow() is called, the parameters passed in are used to initialize the window. If initialization is successful, widgets are added to the window. The window is registered, and then the URL passed into the window is displayed. Following this, the basic structure for CreateTopLevelWindow() is:

```
NS_IMETHODIMP
nsAppShellService::CreateTopLevelWindow(nsIWebShellWindow
                          *aParent,
                          nsIURL* aUrl,
                          PRBool showWindow,
                          nsIWebShellWindow*& aResult,
                          nsIStreamObserver* anObserver,
                    nsIXULWindowCallbacks *aCallbacks,
                          PRInt32 aInitialWidth,
                          PRInt32 aInitialHeight)
{
  nsresult rv;
  nsWebShellWindow* window;
```

```
window = new nsWebShellWindow();
if (nsnull == window) {
  rv = NS_ERROR_OUT_OF_MEMORY;
} else {
  rv = window->Initialize((nsIWebShellWindow *) nsnull,
  mAppShell, aUrl, anObserver, aCallbacks,
  aInitialWidth, aInitialHeight);
  if (NS_SUCCEEDED(rv)) {
    rv = window->QueryInterface(kIWebShellWindowIID,
                                   (void **) &aResult);
    RegisterTopLevelWindow(window);
    if (showWindow)
      window->Show(PR_TRUE);
  }
}

return rv;
}
```

The function parameters are used as follows:

- aParent: The parent for the window to be created. This is included for compatibility with dialog windows and is generally null.

- aURL: The location of the window's contents description, which is displayed within the window. The contents description is written in XUL and interfaced with an IDL definition.

- aResult: The error code or result returned.

- anObserver: A stream observer to give to the new window.

- aCallbacks: Methods that will be called during window construction. This parameter can be null.

- aInitialWidth: The width of the window in pixels.

- aInitialHeight: The height of window in pixels.

Two key details you should pick up on for CreateTopLevelWindow() are the use of observers and callbacks. Windows use observer streams to watch for changes. Windows can then handle changes and issue callbacks as appropriate. (You'll see a more detailed example of this process in the next section.)

The key difference between `CreateTopLevelWindow()` and `CreateDialog Window()` is the fact that dialog windows are created with dialog borders rather than window borders. Other than this, the functions are essentially the same. They even have the same signature:

```
NS_IMETHODIMP   nsAppShellService::CreateDialogWindow(
                        nsIWebShellWindow * aParent,
                        nsIURL* aUrl,
                        PRBool showWindow,
                        nsIWebShellWindow*& aResult,
                        nsIStreamObserver* anObserver,
                        nsIXULWindowCallbacks *aCallbacks,
                        PRInt32 aInitialWidth,
                        PRInt32 aInitialHeight)
```

`CreateTopLevelWindow()` and `CreateDialogWindow()` are implemented in nsAppShellService.cpp. You can access the most current source online at `lxr.mozilla.org/mozilla/source/xpfe/appshell/src /nsAppShellService.cpp`.

To see how these structures are implemented elsewhere in the source, check these URLs:

- `http://lxr.mozilla.org/mozilla/ident?i=nsIAppShellService`

- `http://lxr.mozilla.org/mozilla/ident?i=CreateTopLevelWindow`

- `http://lxr.mozilla.org/mozilla/ident?i=CreateDialogWindow`

Other AppShell interfaces include `nsICmdLineService`, `nsIWebShell Window`, `nsIWidgetController`, and `nsIXULWindowCallbacks`. To obtain the latest implementation of these interfaces, use these URLs:

- `http://lxr.mozilla.org/mozilla/ident?i=nsICmdLineService`

- `http://lxr.mozilla.org/mozilla/ident?i=nsIWebShellWindow`

- `http://lxr.mozilla.org/mozilla/ident?i=nsIWidgetController`

- `http://lxr.mozilla.org/mozilla/ident?i=nsIXULWindowCallbacks`

Programming the Application Core

While the application shell provides services and hooks, it doesn't provide the core functionality for user interfaces. These functions are implemented in the application core and in application-specific classes. The application core is defined in nsAppCores. Application cores for the browser and editor components are defined in nsBrowserAppCore and nsEditorAppCore, respectively.

NOTE
As you set out to work with the application cores, keep in mind that nsBrowser AppCore and nsEditorAppCore detail the XUL way of doing things and contain only core functionality. The remaining functionality is defined in XPViewer. XPViewer contains the original windowing code that is being transitioned to the XUL architecture. As stated in Chapter 6, nsBrowserMain instantiates main and sets up the console and browser windows, nsBrowserWindow creates browser windows, and nsXPBaseWindow handles core windowing tasks.

Working with nsAppCores

nsAppCores is used to register factories, unregister factories, and instantiate class object instances from a factory. Listing 7-1 shows one way in which these methods could be implemented in nsAppCores. For the most current source code examples, use these URLs:

- http://lxr.mozilla.org/mozilla/ident?i=NSRegisterSelf

- http://lxr.mozilla.org/mozilla/ident?i=NSUnRegisterSelf

- http://lxr.mozilla.org/mozilla/ident?i=NSGetFactory

As you examine the listing, note that many different application cores can be instantiated from nsAppCores. These application cores provide the core functionality for the browser, mail, and editor components as well as RDF, toolkit, and toolbar components. Note also the use of NSRegisterSelf(), NSUnregisterSelf(), and NSGetFactory(). These functions were first discussed in Chapter 3, which covers virtual interfaces and factories.

NOTE

In the future, COMConnect may be used to register external DLLs. And if COMConnect is implemented, the way you register objects may change.

LISTING 7-1: SAMPLE FUNCTIONS FOR REGISTERING, UNREGISTERING, AND INSTANTIATING THE CLASS OBJECT INSTANCES

```
//register components
extern "C" NS_EXPORT nsresult
NSRegisterSelf(nsISupports* serviceMgr, const char *path)
{
   nsRepository::RegisterComponent(kAppCoresManagerCID,
     NULL, NULL, path, PR_TRUE, PR_TRUE);
     nsRepository::RegisterComponent(kMailCoreCID, NULL,
     NULL, path, PR_TRUE, PR_TRUE);
     nsRepository::RegisterComponent(kRDFCoreCID, NULL,
     NULL, path, PR_TRUE, PR_TRUE);
     nsRepository::RegisterComponent(kToolbarCoreCID, NULL,
     NULL, path, PR_TRUE, PR_TRUE);
     nsRepository::RegisterComponent(kToolkitCoreCID, NULL,
     NULL, path, PR_TRUE, PR_TRUE);
     nsRepository::RegisterComponent(kBrowserAppCoreCID,
     NULL, NULL, path, PR_TRUE, PR_TRUE);
     nsRepository::RegisterComponent(kEditorAppCoreCID,
     NULL, NULL, path, PR_TRUE, PR_TRUE);
     return NS_OK;
}

//unregister components
extern "C" NS_EXPORT nsresult
NSUnregisterSelf(nsISupports* serviceMgr, const char *path)
{
     nsRepository::UnregisterFactory(kAppCoresManagerCID,
     path);
     nsRepository::UnregisterFactory(kMailCoreCID, path);
     nsRepository::UnregisterFactory(kRDFCoreCID, path);
```

Continued

LISTING 7-1: *(continued)*

```
        nsRepository::UnregisterFactory(kToolbarCoreCID, path);
        nsRepository::UnregisterFactory(kToolkitCoreCID, path);
        nsRepository::UnregisterFactory(kBrowserAppCoreCID,
        path);
        nsRepository::UnregisterFactory(kEditorAppCoreCID,
        path);

        return NS_OK;
}

//create factory class instance
extern "C" NS_EXPORT nsresult
NSGetFactory(nsISupports* serviceMgr,
             const nsCID &aClass,
             const char *aClassName,
             const char *aProgID,
             nsIFactory **aFactory)
{

    if (aFactory == NULL)
    {
        return NS_ERROR_NULL_POINTER;
    }

    *aFactory = NULL;
    nsISupports *inst;

    if ( aClass.Equals(kAppCoresManagerCID) )
    {
        inst = new nsAppCoresManagerFactory();
    }
    else if ( aClass.Equals(kMailCoreCID) )
    {
        inst = new nsMailCoreFactory();
    }
    else if ( aClass.Equals(kRDFCoreCID) )
```

CHAPTER 7: PROGRAMMING THE USER INTERFACE

```
{
    inst = new nsRDFCoreFactory();
}
else if ( aClass.Equals(kToolbarCoreCID) )
{
    inst = new nsToolbarCoreFactory();
}
else if ( aClass.Equals(kToolkitCoreCID) )
{
    inst = new nsToolkitCoreFactory();
}
else if ( aClass.Equals(kBrowserAppCoreCID) )
{
    inst = new nsBrowserAppCoreFactory();
}
else if ( aClass.Equals(kEditorAppCoreCID) )
{
    inst = new nsEditorAppCoreFactory();
}
else
{
    return NS_ERROR_ILLEGAL_VALUE;
}

if (inst == NULL)
{
    return NS_ERROR_OUT_OF_MEMORY;
}

nsresult res = inst->QueryInterface(kIFactoryIID,
(void**) aFactory);

if (res != NS_OK)
{
    delete inst;
}
```

Continued

LISTING 7-1: *(continued)*

```
   return res;


}
```

Management of the application core is handled through `nsAppCoresManager`. Global names are managed through `nsAppCoresNameSet`. Each component also has its own application core and factory. For example, the browser component uses `nsBrowserAppCore` and `nsBrowserAppCoreFactory`. `nsBrowserAppCore` contains the implementation for the core browser functions; `nsBrowserApp CoreFactory` is its corresponding factory.

Working with nsBrowserAppCore

When examining `nsBrowserAppCore`, you can see step by step how the browser application core is created and handled. The key window services are initialized in a function appropriately named `nsBrowserAppCore()`. The basic structure for this function is shown as Listing 7-2. For additional examples, visit `http://lxr.mozilla.org/mozilla/ident?i=nsBrowserAppCore`.

As you can see from the code, three windows are set up with the main window: toolbar, content, and Web shell. These subwindows are defined later as internal frames of the main window.

LISTING 7-2: INITIALIZING THE BROWSER APPLICATION CORE

```
nsBrowserAppCore::nsBrowserAppCore()
{
  //prep script object
  mScriptObject        = nsnull;

  //prep toolbar window
  mToolbarWindow       = nsnull;

  //prep toolbar script context
  mToolbarScriptContext = nsnull;

  //prep content window
```

```
mContentWindow          = nsnull;

//prep content window's script context
mContentScriptContext = nsnull;

//prep web shell window
mWebShellWin            = nsnull;

//prep the web shell
mWebShell               = nsnull;

//increase instance counter and initialize reference count
IncInstanceCount();
NS_INIT_REFCNT();
}
```

After the application core services are readied, the actual instances are initialized and then key functions are defined. Most of these functions handle tasks for toolbar buttons that are passed from JavaScript to C++ using IDL interfaces. Listing 7-3 shows how the basic structure for the `Back()`, `Forward()`, and `ExecuteScript()` functions might look. These functions correspond to the Back and Forward buttons on the browser toolbar.

The code shown for `Back()` and `Forward()` is very similar. Basically, the function makes calls to `ExecuteScript()` that temporarily disable callbacks to the toolbar context, execute a JavaScript `window.back()` or `window.forward()` as appropriate, and then re-enable callbacks to the toolbar context. What you don't see are the `SetEnableCallback()` and the `SetDisableCallback()` functions that enable and disable the context.

LISTING 7-3: IMPLEMENTING BACK AND FORWARD FROM THE BROWSER TOOLBAR

```
NS_IMETHODIMP
nsBrowserAppCore::Back()
{
  ExecuteScript(mToolbarScriptContext, mDisableScript);
  ExecuteScript(mContentScriptContext, "window.back();");
  ExecuteScript(mToolbarScriptContext, mEnableScript);
```

Continued

LISTING 7-3: (continued)

```
    return NS_OK;
  }


NS_IMETHODIMP
nsBrowserAppCore::Forward()
{
    ExecuteScript(mToolbarScriptContext, mDisableScript);
    ExecuteScript(mContentScriptContext, "window.forward();");
    ExecuteScript(mToolbarScriptContext, mEnableScript);
    return NS_OK;
  }


NS_IMETHODIMP
nsBrowserAppCore::ExecuteScript(nsIScriptContext * aContext,
const nsString& aScript)
{
    if (nsnull != aContext) {
      const char* url = "";
      PRBool isUndefined = PR_FALSE;
      nsString rVal;
      aContext->EvaluateString(aScript, url, 0, rVal,
      &isUndefined);
    }
    return NS_OK;
  }
```

Functions defined in the source may have corresponding IDL interfaces. As stated earlier, these interfaces provide the glue necessary for interaction between JavaScript and C/C++.

Creating an Application Core

Now that you know how the pieces of the XUL architecture fit together, you can use this knowledge to create your own application core. The steps to create an application core are:

1. Implement a JavaScript object in your native C/C++ code.

2. Create a factory for the native object.

3. Define the scriptable interface for the object in IDL.

4. Use an IDL compiler to generate the interface and stub functions.

5. Add the object to the name space registry for external JavaScript objects.

6. Add the object to the factory for a DLL.

Implementing the Objects and Interfaces

As you've seen, creating an application core is a lengthy process. You start by implementing a JavaScript object in your native C/C++ code, and then you create a factory for the native object. The JavaScript object for the browser component is described in `nsBrowserAppCore`, and its associated factory is described in `nsBrowserAppCoreFactory`.

The browser application core is created as a single object with a JavaScript interface. The interface is defined in IDL or cross-platform IDL. IDL defines language-neutral interfaces for interaction between distributed objects. Bindings to the document object model are used to map language-specific information to language-neutral information that can be passed from a structured document to a script/program and vice versa. HTML, XML, and XUL have different sets of interface definitions. These definitions represent related objects in the object model.

Because the interface definitions are written in IDL, they are language and platform neutral. This means the interfaces do not require specific operating systems, platforms, or programming languages. The only requirements are that the application implements the document object model and that the objects accessing this model are programmed in a language that has bindings to the document object model, such as JavaScript.

The objects within the document object model follow a specific tree-like structure. Flowing from the base of the object tree are objects called *nodes*. The root node represents the root of the document object hierarchy and has child nodes that represent the components of a document. These child nodes include the elements defined in a document, attributes of these elements, processing instructions within a document, comments within a document, and the actual text within a document.

To examine specific nodes, the document object model uses iterator objects, such as a node iterator or a tree iterator. Node iterators are used to move back and forth between nodes according to their position, such as the next node or the nth node. Tree iterators are a subtype of node iterators and are used to move to various nodes using the parent-child structure of the object tree. For example, tree iterators can move to a parent node or to specific child and sibling nodes.

IDL objects can have methods, attributes, and constants associated with them. Object methods are used to perform specific functions, such as setting a value for an attribute of an HTML or a XUL element. On the other hand, constants and attributes contain information about an object. While constants have fixed values, you can manipulate the values of most attributes. Generally, object attributes correspond to like-named attributes for the associated markup element.

Listing 7-4 shows the basic interface for the browser application core. The interface is used to pass calls back and forth between C++ and JavaScript. To do this, each method defined in the interface must have a corresponding C++ function that can be called from JavaScript. If you examine the source code for nsBrowserAppCore, you'll find the definitions for these functions. For the most current source code examples, use this URL: `http://lxr.mozilla.org/mozilla/ident?i=nsBrowserAppCore`.

LISTING 7-4: IDL INTERFACES FOR THE BROWSER APPLICATION CORE

```
interface BrowserAppCore : BaseAppCore
{
/* IID: { 0xb0ffb697, 0xbab4, 0x11d2, \
{0x96, 0xc4, 0x0, 0x60, 0xb0, 0xfb, 0x99, 0x56}} */

void BrowserAppCore();

void back();
void forward();
void stop();
void loadUrl(in wstring url);
void loadInitialPage();

void walletEditor();
void walletChangePassword();
```

```
void walletQuickFillin(in Window win);
void walletSamples();

void setToolbarWindow(in Window win);
void setContentWindow(in Window win);
void setWebShellWindow(in Window win);

void newWindow();
void openWindow();
void printPreview();
void copy();
void print();
void close();
void exit();

void find();
void findNext();


};
```

Table 7-1 provides an overview of the C++ functions related to the methods defined in the interface. As you examine the table, keep in mind that function calls are usually triggered by elements in the browser's user interface. For example, if a user clicks on the browser's forward button, JavaScript passes a call through IDL to the C++ function `Forward()`.

TABLE 7-1: BROWSER APPLICATION CORE FUNCTIONS WITH INTERFACES

FUNCTION	DESCRIPTION
Back	Used to go to the previous page
BrowserAppCore	Creates the browser application core
Copy	Copies selected items
Close	Closes a window
Exit	Exits the browser
Find	Opens the find dialog

Continued

TABLE 7-1: *(continued)*

findNext	Finds the next choice
Forward	Used to go to the next page
loadURL	Gets a reference URL and loads it into a window
loadInitialPage	Loads the default browser page
newWindow	Creates a new window
openWindow	Opens a window
printPreview	Previews a page loaded into the content window before printing
setContentWindow	Creates the content window
setToolbarWindow	Creates the toolbar window
setWebShellWindow	Creates the Web shell window for the status bar
walletEditor	Starts the wallet editor
walletChangePassword	Prompts to change wallet password

Creating the DOM Interface and Stub Functions

Once you create an interface, you can compile it using an IDL compiler. This creates the DOM interface and stub functions that are used to hook into the actual C++ implementation of the object. For the browser component, the DOM interface, nsIDOMBrowserAppCore, and the related stub functions are contained in nsBrowserAppCore.h.

The C++ implementation of the object is also derived from the DOM interface. Listing 7-5 shows the implementation for nsBrowserAppCore with the nsIDOMBrowserAppCore interface added to it. See Table 7-1 for a description of key functions. For the most current source code examples, use this URL: http://lxr.mozilla.org/mozilla/ident?i=nsBrowserAppCore.

LISTING 7-5: THE BASIC STRUCTURE OF THE NSBROWSERAPPCORE CLASS WITH A DOM INTERFACE

```
class nsBrowserAppCore : public nsBaseAppCore,
                         public nsIDOMBrowserAppCore,
                         public nsINetSupport,
```

```
                       public nsIDocumentLoaderObserver
{
  public:

    nsBrowserAppCore();
    virtual ~nsBrowserAppCore();

    NS_DECL_ISUPPORTS_INHERITED

    NS_IMETHOD      GetScriptObject(nsIScriptContext
                    *aContext, void** aScriptObject);
    NS_IMETHOD      Init(const nsString& aId);
    NS_IMETHOD      GetId(nsString& aId) { return
                    nsBaseAppCore::GetId(aId); }

    NS_IMETHOD      Back();
    NS_IMETHOD      Forward();
    NS_IMETHOD      Stop();

    NS_IMETHOD      WalletEditor();
    NS_IMETHOD      WalletChangePassword();
    NS_IMETHOD      WalletQuickFillin(nsIDOMWindow* aWin);
    NS_IMETHOD      WalletSamples();

    NS_IMETHOD      LoadUrl(const nsString& aUrl);
    NS_IMETHOD      SetToolbarWindow(nsIDOMWindow* aWin);
    NS_IMETHOD      SetContentWindow(nsIDOMWindow* aWin);
    NS_IMETHOD      SetWebShellWindow(nsIDOMWindow* aWin);
    NS_IMETHOD      NewWindow();
    NS_IMETHOD      OpenWindow();
    NS_IMETHOD      PrintPreview();
    NS_IMETHOD      Print();
    NS_IMETHOD      Copy();
    NS_IMETHOD      Close();
    NS_IMETHOD      Exit();
    NS_IMETHOD      Find();
```

Continued

LISTING 7-5: *(continued)*

```
NS_IMETHOD    FindNext();
NS_IMETHOD    SetDocumentCharset(const nsString&
                                     aCharset);
NS_IMETHOD    LoadInitialPage();

// nsIDocumentLoaderObserver
NS_IMETHOD OnStartDocumentLoad(nsIDocumentLoader*
       loader, nsIURL* aURL, const char* aCommand);
NS_IMETHOD OnEndDocumentLoad(nsIDocumentLoader*
       loader, nsIURL *aUrl, PRInt32 aStatus);
NS_IMETHOD OnStartURLLoad(nsIDocumentLoader* loader,
       nsIURL* aURL, const char* aContentType,
       nsIContentViewer* aViewer);
NS_IMETHOD OnProgressURLLoad(nsIDocumentLoader*
       loader, nsIURL* aURL, PRUint32 aProgress,
       PRUint32 aProgressMax);
NS_IMETHOD OnStatusURLLoad(nsIDocumentLoader* loader,
       nsIURL* aURL, nsString& aMsg);
NS_IMETHOD OnEndURLLoad(nsIDocumentLoader* loader,
       nsIURL* aURL, PRInt32 aStatus);
NS_IMETHOD HandleUnknownContentType(nsIDocumentLoader*
       loader, nsIURL *aURL, const char *aContentType,
       const char *aCommand );

// nsINetSupport
NS_IMETHOD_(void) Alert(const nsString &aText);

NS_IMETHOD_(PRBool) Confirm(const nsString &aText);


NS_IMETHOD_(PRBool) Prompt(const nsString &aText,
                           const nsString &aDefault,
                           nsString &aResult);

NS_IMETHOD_(PRBool) PromptUserAndPassword(const nsString
```

```
                                           &aText,
                                     nsString &aUser,
                                     nsString &aPassword);


      NS_IMETHOD_(PRBool) PromptPassword(const nsString
                              &aText, nsString &aPassword);


   protected:
     NS_IMETHOD DoDialog();
     NS_IMETHOD ExecuteScript(nsIScriptContext * aContext,
                              const nsString& aScript);
     void SetButtonImage(nsIDOMNode * aParentNode, PRInt32
                    aBtnNum, const nsString &aResName);
     void        InitializeSearch(nsIFindComponent*);

     nsIScriptContext    *mToolbarScriptContext;
     nsIScriptContext    *mContentScriptContext;

     nsIDOMWindow        *mToolbarWindow;
     nsIDOMWindow        *mContentWindow;

     nsIWebShellWindow  *mWebShellWin;
     nsIWebShell *       mWebShell;
     nsIWebShell *        mContentAreaWebShell;

     nsIGlobalHistory* mGHistory;

     nsISupports *       mSearchContext;
};
```

Registering the Objects and Adding Them to a DLL

After you generate the interface and stub functions, you need to add the object to the name space registry for external JavaScript objects and then add the object to the factory for your DLL. You register an object in the JavaScript name space using the Mozilla service manager. In the service manager, you'll find an object called the nsAppCoresNameSet object. This object implements the nsIScript

ExternalNameSet interface. A brief example of how you could use nsAppCores
NameSet to get the service and register an object in the JavaScript name space
follows:

```
nsIScriptNameSetRegistry *registry;
nsresult result =
nsServiceManager::GetService(kCScriptNameSetRegistryCID,
                             kIScriptNameSetRegistryIID,
                             (nsISupports **)&registry);
if (NS_OK == result)
 {
    nsAppCoresNameSet* nameSet = new nsAppCoresNameSet();
    registry->AddExternalNameSet(nameSet);
}
```

The key methods of nsAppCoresNameSet that you'll use are AddNameSet
and InitializeClasses. AddNameSet registers objects into the name space.
InitializeClasses initializes the object classes at start up. A partial example
of adding the browser application core to the name space and initializing its
external class follows:

```
NS_IMETHODIMP
nsAppCoresNameSet::AddNameSet(nsIScriptContext*
aScriptContext)
{
  nsresult result = NS_OK;
  nsIScriptNameSpaceManager* manager;
  result = aScriptContext->GetNameSpaceManager(&manager);
  if (NS_OK == result) {
    result = manager->RegisterGlobalName("BrowserCore",
                                         kBrowserCoreCID,
                                         PR_TRUE);
    //insert code to finish registration then release the
    //manager when finished
    }
    return result;
}
```

```
NS_IMETHODIMP
nsAppCoresNameSet::InitializeClasses(nsIScriptContext*
aScriptContext)
{
  nsresult result = NS_OK;
  result = NS_InitBrowserCoreClass(aScriptContext, nsnull);

  //complete the initialization process

  return result;
}
```

Next, you need to set up a DLL for the external object. Because the object is scriptable, it needs its related factory. Use NSGetFactory() to pass in a CID and return the object's factory, such as:

```
extern "C" NS_EXPORT nsresult
NSGetFactory(const nsCID &aClass, nsISupports* serviceMgr,
nsIFactory **aFactory)
{
  if (aFactory == NULL) {
    return NS_ERROR_NULL_POINTER;
  }

  *aFactory = NULL;
  nsISupports *inst;

  if ( aClass.Equals(kBrowserCoreCID) ) {
    inst = new nsBrowserCoreFactory();
  } else {
    return NS_ERROR_ILLEGAL_VALUE;
  }

  if (inst == NULL) {
    return NS_ERROR_OUT_OF_MEMORY;
  }

  nsresult res = inst->QueryInterface(kIFactoryIID,
```

```
                                         (void**) aFactory);

    if (res != NS_OK){
      delete inst;
    }
    return res;
  }
```

To complete the process, register the DLL in `nsRespository` and then add BrowserAppCore's `NameSet` object to the `ScriptNameSetRegistry` service. Now when the application initializes the JavaScript environment, the object is available in the registry, and its class is initialized as all other classes are. When JavaScript encounters the `BrowserAppCore` object in the script, it looks it up in the external name registry and it is then able to create its associated object.

For the additional examples, use these URLs:

- `http://lxr.mozilla.org/mozilla/ident?i=GetService`

- `http://lxr.mozilla.org/mozilla/ident?i=AddNameSet`

- `http://lxr.mozilla.org/mozilla/ident?i=InitializeClasses`

- `http://lxr.mozilla.org/mozilla/ident?i=NSGetFactory`

Summary

Mozilla's user interface is fairly complex. The core functionality is implemented in the application core and in application-specific classes. To connect the core to the graphical elements of the user interface, you have an application shell that provides services and interface hooks. Then at the top level, you have XUL definitions that describe windows, menus, toolbars, and other graphical interface components. Use the concepts discussed in this chapter as a starting point and then build on this discussion by browsing the source and visiting mozilla.org.

Defining Windows, Menus, and Toolbars with XUL

Mozilla's cross-platform user interface (UI) is one of the most advanced areas of the application. So far everything I've discussed concerning the UI has been at a low level. You've examined application services, application cores, and IDL interfaces. Now it's time to look at top-level structured documents that describe application windows.

As you'll learn in this chapter, windows can be defined with HTML, XML, CSS, and XUL. Because you should be fairly familiar with standard Web technologies, the chapter focuses on the intricacies of XUL rather than on the structure of HTML, XML, and CSS. The power of XUL is in its simplicity. You use standard markup to define a window and to describe its layout and contents. These contents can include menu bars and toolboxes, which in turn have their own components.

Initializing a Window

When an application window is initialized, the application retrieves an initialization document. The initialization document defines the window's top-level structure and style elements. Typically, top-level structures are defined using internal frames, and style elements are defined in style sheets.

As Figure 8-1 shows, most application windows have three internal frames: a Toolbar frame, a Content frame, and a Status bar frame. An example of how these frames can be implemented is shown in Listing 8-1. Although the frame height and width is hard coded in the example, windows should be sized dynamically based on the user's screen size.

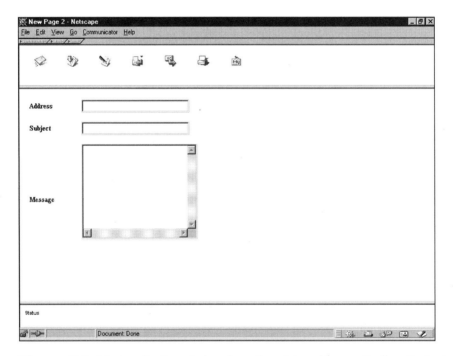

Figure 8-1: Most application windows have three internal frames: Toolbar, Content, and Status bar.

From the listing, you can see that one of the frames is defined in an XML document and the other two frames are defined in HTML documents. The XML document provides the most insight into the inner workings of XUL, and I examine this document in the next section.

LISTING 8-1: INITIALIZING THE APPLICATION WINDOW

```
<html>
<head>
<title>Mozilla Mail</title>
<meta http-equiv="Content-Type" content="text/html;
charset=iso-8859-1">
<LINK REL=stylesheet HREF="mail.css">
</head>
<body bgcolor="#C0C0C0">
<iframe src="MailToolbar.xml" name="mail.toolbar"
width="100%" height="80" >
<iframe src="MailFrame.html" name="mail.content"
width="100%" height="500" >
<iframe src="status.html" name="mail.status" width="100%"
height="34" >
</body>
</html>
```

Creating a Toolbar Window

The Toolbar window is defined as an internal frame of the main window. The document containing the contents of the Toolbar window is shown as Listing 8-2. In the sections that follow, I'll go through the source listing step by step. By examining this source you can learn a lot about the way XUL and HTML are used together in an XML document.

The toolbar created from this source looks much like the example shown in Figure 8-2. The only exception is that text is not shown with the toolbar.

Figure 8-2: In the XUL architecture, toolbars are created in internal frames using XUL, HTML, and CSS.

NOTE

At the time of this writing, the XUL specification wasn't fully defined yet and as with HTML, enhancements to the specification may change the way you use XUL. With this in mind, the examples in the sections that follow are meant to help you get started and are not meant to be all-inclusive or 100 percent syntactically correct.

LISTING 8-2: THE TOOLBAR WINDOW COMBINES XUL AND HTML

```
<?xml version="1.0"?>
<?xml-stylesheet href="xul.css" type="text/css"?>
<!DOCTYPE window>

<xul:window xmlns:html="http://www.w3.org/TR/REC-html40"
 xmlns:xul ="http://www.mozilla.org/keymaster/gatekeeper/
 there.is.only.xul">

<html:script language="JavaScript">
function StartUp()
{
   //set startup functions
}

function SendMailMessage()
{
 //send mail messages
}

function MailSent()
{
 //clean up after send
}

</html:script>

<xul:commands>
   <xul:command name="nsCmd:StartUp" onCommand="StartUp();"/>
   <xul:command name="nsCmd:MailSendMsg"
```

```
          onCommand="SendMailMessage();"/>
    </xul:commands>

    <xul:toolbox>

      <xul:toolbar>
        <html:button cmd="nsCmd:MailSendMsg" style="background-
          color:rgb(192,192,192);">
          <html:img src="resource:Mail_SendMsg.gif"/>
          <html:br/>Send
        </html:button>

        <html:button cmd="nsCmd:MailGetMsg" style="background-
          color:rgb(192,192,192);">
          <html:img src="resource:Mail_GetMsg.gif"/>
          <html:br/>GetMsg
        </html:button>

        <html:button cmd="nsCmd:MailNewMsg" style="background-
          color:rgb(192,192,192);">
          <html:img src="resource: Mail_NewMsg.gif"/>
          <html:br/>New Msg
          </html:button>

        <html:button cmd="nsCmd:MailReply" style="background-
          color:rgb(192,192,192);">
          <html:img src="resource:Mail_Reply.gif"/>
          <html:br/>Reply
          </html:button>

        <html:button cmd="nsCmd:MailForward" style="background-
          color:rgb(192,192,192);">
          <html:img src="resource:Mail_Forward.gif"/>
          <html:br/>Forward
            </html:button>
```

Continued

LISTING 8-2: *(continued)*

```
    <html:button cmd="nsCmd:BrowserPrint" style="background-
        color:rgb(192,192,192);">
        <html:img src="resource:TB_Print.gif"/>
        <html:br/>Print
        </html:button>

    <html:a style="position:relative; direction:rtl; right:3;
        top: 2px;" href="http://www.netscape.com">
        <html:img alt="Throbber!" border=0 src="resource:
        anims00.gif"/>
        </html:a>
    </xul:toolbar>

</xul:toolbox>
</xul:window>
```

Defining the Namespace and Setting up the Window

In XML, parameters are defined by setting processing instructions. Processing instructions always begin with <? and end with ?> and are used to set the XML version, style sheet references, and other key parameters. Once you tell the processor how to handle the document, you declare a document type, and then define the elements associated with the document type. The DOCTYPE assignment is the most basic element in an XML document and is a container for all other elements. In the sample XML document, the instructions and assignments come together as:

```
<?xml version="1.0"?>
<?xml-stylesheet href="xul.css" type="text/css"?>
<!DOCTYPE window>
<window>

//insert the document body

</window>
```

Here, the processing instructions set the XML version to 1.0 and also set a CSS style sheet reference. Afterward, the document type is declared as a window type with the window element forming the base of the document tree. If the document contained only XUL, you could use the window element as shown previously. However, because the document combines XUL and HTML, XML namespaces are set up to avoid namespace collisions. You set up XML namespaces using the syntax:

```
xmlns:type="location of the related specification"
```

such as:

```
xmlns:html="http://www.w3.org/TR/REC-html40"
```

In the toolbar document, the namespaces and the window element are defined as:

```
<xul:window xmlns:html="http://www.w3.org/TR/REC-html40"
 xmlns:xul ="http://www.mozilla.org/keymaster/gatekeeper/
 there.is.only.xul">

//insert the document body

</xul:window>
```

When you use XML namespaces, you can specify the specific namespace type for each element or only for elements where you are concerned about a possible conflict. In the sample document, use the strict application of namespace rules; this is why you see `<xul:` and `<html:` used with all elements names. Other than this, you can use all elements available in the HTML and XUL name space much as you normally would.

Setting up the Toolbox and Its Toolbars

Once you set up a window container, you can add a toolbox to it. As you learned in Chapter 6, a toolbox is a container for toolbars. You set up the toolbox with the TOOLBOX element and then define its toolbars with the TOOLBAR element. Normally, these elements would come together as:

```
<window>
  <toolbox>
```

```
        <toolbar> toolbar definition </toolbar>
        <toolbar> toolbar definition </toolbar>
    </toolbox>
</window>
```

However, the toolbar document uses namespaces, and the proper namespace should be referenced. Because of this, these elements are defined as:

```
<xul:window>
  <xul:toolbox>
    <xul:toolbar> toolbar definition </xul:toolbar>
    <xul:toolbar> toolbar definition </xul:toolbar>
  </xul:toolbox>
</xul:window>
```

Adding Elements to the Toolbar

You can add just about any HTML element to a toolbar, and buttons and forms are the elements most commonly used. Rather than using standard push buttons, you can use HTML 4.0 BUTTON elements, which enable you to add images, text, and other markup to buttons. The following definitions create SendMsg, GetMsg, NewMsg, Reply, Forward, and Print buttons for the toolbar:

```
<xul:toolbar>
    <html:button>
      <html:img src="resource:Mail_SendMsg.gif"/>
      <html:br/>Send
    </html:button>

    <html:button>
      <html:img src="resource:Mail_GetMsg.gif"/>
      <html:br/>GetMsg
    </html:button>

    <html:button>
      <html:img src="resource:Mail_NewMsg.gif"/>
      <html:br/>New Msg
    </html:button>
```

```
<html:button>
  <html:img src="resource:Mail_Reply.gif"/>
  <html:br/>Reply
  </html:button>

<html:button>
  <html:img src="resource:Mail_Forward.gif"/>
  <html:br/>Forward
   </html:button>

<html:button>
  <html:img src="resource:TB_Print.gif"/>
  <html:br/>Print
  </html:button>
</xul:toolbar>
```

NOTE

In the example, note the use of the tag `<html:br/>`. In HTML, you would normally write this tag as `<br>` rather than `<br/>`, so you may be wondering why the slash is needed here. In XML, the slash must be used with elements that have one tag rather than a begin and an end tag.

As you examine the button definitions, note that image files are referenced as resources in the IMG SRC attribute. The addition of `resource:` is necessary because you are using XML namespaces.

Adding Interactivity to the Toolbar

As you've seen, creating windows, toolboxes, and toolbars is fairly easy — as long as you know the markup techniques to use. Adding interactivity to these elements is a bit more difficult. The reason for this is that the XUL command structure has several layers that start with the element definition, go through command nodes, and then go to the JavaScript function calls.

At the top of this structure, you specify the state of an element and how its events are handled. For example, the default state of most buttons is normal. If a button is disabled, a disabled attribute is set in the button element, such as:

```
<button disabled>
  <img src="Mail_GetMsg.gif">
  <br>GetMsg
</button>
```

On the other hand, the rollover and depressed states are normally supported with JavaScript event handlers. You could use onMouseOver to handle the rollover state and onClick to handle the depressed state, such as:

```
<button onMouseOver="MouseOver()" onClick="clickIt()">
  <img src="Mail_GetMsg.gif">
  <br>GetMsg
</button>
```

Through XUL, you can set up a command structure to pass commands or a broadcaster/observer structure to handle state changes. To use a command structure, you assign a command to an element and then specify what happens when the command is executed. You assign commands using the cmd attribute, such as:

```
<html:button cmd="nsCmd:MailSendMsg">
 <html:img src="resource:Mail_SendMsg.gif"/>
 <html:br/>Send
</html:button>
```

The corresponding command definition is set in a commands container, such as:

```
<xul:commands>
  <xul:command name="nsCmd:MailSendMsg"
  onCommand="SendMailMessage();"/>
</xul:commands>
```

As you can see, XUL defines a commands element and a command element. Think toolbox and toolbar. The commands element is a container, and the individual commands defined within it set commands for the document.

In the previous example, the XUL command `nsCmd:MailSendMsg` specifies a function that is to be executed when the button is pressed; in this case, it is `SendMailMessage()`. `SendMailMessage()` asks `AppCoreManager` for a `MailAppCore` instance by a unique name. If the `MailAppCore` doesn't exist yet, `AppCoreManager` creates one. Otherwise, `AppCoreManager` simply gets the data out of the content frame and invokes `SendMailMessage()` on the `MailAppCore` instance.

Creating the Content and Status Frames

Compared with the toolbar frame, the content and status frames are rather ordinary. You don't need to define a subwindow, a toolbox, or toolbars, so you don't really need XUL. Because of this, these frames are defined in standard HTML and don't offer a lot of surprises. Listing 8-3 shows how the source for the content frame could be written. The status frame contains similar markup structures for displaying browser status codes.

LISTING 8-3: THE CONTENT WINDOW CAN BE WRITTEN ENTIRELY IN HTML

```html
<html>
<head>
<meta http-equiv="content-type" content="text/html;
charset=iso-8859-1">
<link rel=stylesheet href="mailcontent.css">
</head>
<body>
<div align="center">
<form enctype="text/plain" onsubmit="return submitforms()">
 <table bgcolor="#c0c0c0">
 <tr><td>
  <fieldset width="100%" height="100%" >
   <legend align=left> Message </legend>
   <table width="100%" height="100%">
   <tr><td>To:</td>
     <td width="100%">
     <input type="text" name="addrto" ></td>
   </tr>
```

Continued

LISTING 8-3: *(continued)*

```
<tr><td>Cc:</td>
  <td width="100%">
  <input type="text" name="addrcc" ></td>
</tr>
<tr><td>Subject:</td>
  <td>
  <input type="text" name="subject" id="subject">
  </td>
</tr>
</table>
</fieldset>
</td></tr>
<tr><td>
 <fieldset width="100%" height="100%" >
  <legend align=left> Text </legend>
  <textarea cols=40 rows=20 name="mailbody"></textarea>
 </fieldset>
</td></tr>
</table>
</form>
</div>
</body>
</html>
```

Using Menu Bars, Broadcasters, and Observers

So far I've just scratched the surface of the features available in XUL. Other features you'll want to examine are menu bars, broadcasters, and observers. You use menu bars to define an application's menus, and you use broadcasters and observers as alternatives to command nodes.

Listing 8-4 shows a document that defines a window for the Mozilla editor. For brevity, the example's menus and toolbars aren't completely defined. I'll go through the source listing step by step in the sections that follow.

LISTING 8-4: WORKING WITH MENU BARS, BROADCASTERS, AND OBSERVERS

```
<?xml version="1.0"?>
<?xml-stylesheet href="xul.css" type="text/css"?>
<!DOCTYPE window>
<window xmlns:html="http://www.w3.org/TR/REC-html40"
  xmlns="http://www.mozilla.org/keymaster/
  gatekeeper/there.is.only.xul">

<html:script>

//insert functions for handling calls.

</html:script>

<broadcaster id="cantUndo"/>
<broadcaster id="cantRedo"/>
<broadcaster id="cantCut"/>
<broadcaster id="cantCopy"/>
<broadcaster id="cantPaste"/>

<menubar>
 <!-- Sample menu -->
  <menu name="File">
   <menuitem name="New Window" onclick="EditorNewWindow()"/>
   <menuitem name="Change Icons" onclick="EditorChange()"/>
   <separator />
   <menuitem name="Print Setup" onclick="PrintSetup()"/>
   <menuitem name="Print Preview"
   onclick="EditorPrintPreview()"/>
   <menuitem name="Print" onclick="EditorPrint()"/>
   <separator />
   <menuitem name="Close" onclick="EditorClose()"/>
   <menuitem name="Exit" onclick="EditorExit()"/>
  </menu>
```

Continued

LISTING 8-4: *(continued)*

```
    <menu name="Edit">
     <menuitem name="Undo" onclick="EditorUndo()"/>
     <menuitem name="Redo" onclick="EditorRedo()"/>
     <separator />
     <menuitem name="Cut" onclick="EditorCut()"/>
     <menuitem name="Copy" onclick="EditorCopy()"/>
     <menuitem name="Paste" onclick="EditorPaste()"/>
     <menuitem name="Clear" onclick="EditorClear()"/>
     <separator />
     <menuitem name="Select All" onclick="EditorSelectAll()"/>
     <separator />
     <menuitem name="Insert" onclick="EditorInsertText()"/>
    </menu>
  </menubar>

  <html:div html:id="header">
  <toolbox>
    <toolbar>
      <!-- Sample toolbar -->

      <titledbutton src="resource:/res/toolbar/ED_Undo.gif"
        align="bottom" value="Undo" onclick="EditorUndo()">
       <observes element="cantUndo" attribute="disabled"
        onchange="undoToggle()" />
      </titledbutton>

      <titledbutton src="resource:/res/toolbar/ED_Redo.gif"
        align="bottom" value="Redo" onclick="EditorRedo()">
       <observes element="cantRedo" attribute="disabled"
        onchange="redoToggle()" />
      </titledbutton>

      <titledbutton src="resource:/res/toolbar/ED_Cut.gif"
        align="bottom" value="Cut" onclick="EditorCut()">
       <observes element="cantCut" attribute="disabled"
```

```
            onchange="cutToggle()"/>
        </titledbutton>

        <titledbutton src="resource:/res/toolbar/ED_Copy.gif"
          align="bottom" value="Copy" onclick="EditorCopy()">
         <observes element="cantCopy" attribute="disabled"
          onchange="copyToggle()"/>
        </titledbutton>

        <titledbutton src="resource:/res/toolbar/ED_Paste.gif"
          align="bottom" value="Paste" onclick="EditorPaste()">
         <observes element="cantPaste" attribute="disabled"
          onchange="pasteToggle()"/>
        </titledbutton>
    </toolbar>
    </toolbox>
    </html:div>

    <html:div html:id="main">
      <html:iframe html:name="content" html:src="Editor.html"
       html:width="100%" html:height="450"></html:iframe>
    </html:div>

    <html:div html:id="footer">
      <html:iframe html:name="status" html:src="status.html"
       html:width="100%" html:height="34"></html:iframe>
    </html:div>
    </window>
```

A Different Approach to Window Creation

Listing 8-4 follows a different approach from that of Listing 8-3, especially when it comes to the use of markup tags and windows. Although the namespace for HTML and XUL is defined, the HTML namespace is the only one referenced in element definitions. Basically, the example assumes that there are no namespace collisions for XUL elements.

As the following code snippet highlights, the window definition is also different from that of the previous window example, Listing 8-3:

```
<window>
<menubar> The menu bar </menubar>

<html:div html:id="header">
 <toolbox> </toolbox>
</html:div>

<html:div html:id="main">
  <html:iframe html:name="content" html:src="Editor.html"
   html:width="100%" html:height="450"></html:iframe>
</html:div>

<html:div html:id="footer">
  <html:iframe html:name="status" html:src="status.html"
   html:width="100%" html:height="34"></html:iframe>
  </html:div>
</window>
```

As you can see, the code sample doesn't use a top-level HTML document; instead, it uses HTML divisions to separate areas of the application window with the menu bar being placed above these divisions. The first division contains the toolbox and its toolbars. The second division defines an internal frame for the main content. The final division creates an internal frame for the status bar.

The toolbar for the second window example also contains a different type of button element called TITLEDBUTTON:

```
<titledbutton src="resource:/res/toolbar/ED_Redo.gif"
 align="bottom" value="Redo" onclick="EditorRedo()">
</titledbutton>
```

TITLEDBUTTON is a XUL element for creating the image buttons and menu buttons discussed in Chapter 6. You use XUL titled buttons much as you use HTML buttons. The key attributes you'll use with titled buttons are:

■ SRC: The source URL for the buttons icon.

■ `ALIGN`: The position of text relative to the button icon.

■ `VALUE`: The button label.

You can also assign event handlers to titled buttons, such as the `onClick` event.

Setting up a Menu System

You can create an entire menu system by combining XUL and JavaScript. While XUL markup describes the menu, JavaScript handles interaction with the menu's components.

As you learned in Chapter 6, menu systems are made up of menu bars, menu lists, and menu items. A menu bar is a container for menu lists, much as a toolbox is a container for toolbars. You set up a menu bar with the `MENUBAR` element and then define its menu lists with the `MENU` element. Normally, these elements would come together as:

```
<window>
  <menubar>
    <menu> menu list definition </menu>
    <menu> menu list definition </menu>
  </menubar>
</window>
```

Menu lists, in turn, contain menu items and often a special type of menu item known as a separator. A separator creates a line to separate menu sections. You define menu items with the `MENUITEM` element, and separators with the `SEPARATOR` element. In a sample menu, these elements come together as:

```
<window>
  <menubar>
    <menu>
      <menuitem />
      <menuitem />
      <menuitem />
      <menuitem />
      <separator />
      <menuitem />
      <menuitem />
    </menu>
```

```
        </menubar>
    </window>
```

As with toolbars, you can add just about any HTML element to a menu bar. The catch is that you have to be careful when it comes to the placement of these additional elements. For example, you don't want to insert an icon in between menus.

Unlike toolbar buttons, which can have multiple events associated with them, menu items usually have only the onClick event associated with them, such as:

```
<menu name="Edit">
    <menuitem name="Undo" onclick="EditorUndo()"/>
    <menuitem name="Redo" onclick="EditorRedo()"/>
    <separator />
    <menuitem name="Cut" onclick="EditorCut()"/>
    <menuitem name="Copy" onclick="EditorCopy()"/>
    <menuitem name="Paste" onclick="EditorPaste()"/>
    <menuitem name="Clear" onclick="EditorClear()"/>
    <separator />
    <menuitem name="Select All" onclick="EditorSelectAll()"/>
    <separator />
    <menuitem name="Insert" onclick="EditorInsertText()"/>
</menu>
```

Using Broadcasters and Observers

As discussed previously, broadcasters and observers are an alternative to command structures that define cmd attributes in elements and use commands containers. The broadcaster/observer structure is built on a fairly basic concept. Broadcasters define flags/states that you want to track, and observers watch object nodes for changes in these flags/states. When a change occurs, the observer can call a function defined in the onchange event handler.

The use of observers and broadcasters implies a persistent state, such as enabled or disabled, which can be expressed to object model nodes. If the state of the broadcaster changes, the observer can notify other objects of the state change. For example, a button's state can change from disabled to enabled in response to a user's interaction with other elements. Here, the user may not directly interact with a button, but when the user makes a change in a document the state of the button may change from disabled to enabled.

When you use the broadcaster/observer structure, you start by setting up your broadcasters, such as:

```
<broadcaster id="cantCopy"/>
<broadcaster id="cantRedo"/>
```

Then you define the observers for the broadcaster, such as:

```
<titledbutton>
 <observes element="cantCopy"/>
</titledbutton>
<titledbutton>
 <observes element="cantRedo"/>
</titledbutton>
```

The broadcaster id attribute must match the observer's element attribute. In the example, the attribute values are set to cantCopy, cantRedo, cantCut, cantCopy, and cantPaste, respectively.

Other attributes used with the OBSERVES element include attribute and onchange. Attribute specifies the attribute of the parent object that should be updated when a broadcaster's attribute changes. For example, if a broadcaster is disabled and the state is changed to enabled, the parent object's state should change as well. To handle the change, you use the onchange event handler. In a sample button, this could come together as:

```
<titledbutton src="resource:/res/toolbar/ED_Copy.gif"
 align="bottom" value="Copy" onclick="EditorCopy()">
 <observes element="cantCopy" attribute="disabled"
  onchange="undoToggle()"/>
</titledbutton>
```

When you use broadcasters and observers, the component's application core must be exposed as a JavaScript object with its method configured for JavaScript reflection. The application core for the editor component is EditorAppCore. Once JavaScript reflection is set up, you can use the broadcaster/observer structure at any time.

In the following example, AppCoreManager has been reflected into JavaScript and as a result, its methods can be used to find EditorAppCore and execute the copy function:

```
function EditorCopy()
  {
    appCore = XPAppCoresManager.Find("EditorAppCore");
    if (appCore != null) {
     appCore.copy();
    } else {
      //appCore hasn't been created yet.
      //set up code to handle this.
    }
  }
```

If you want to trace the call to find from JavaScript to C++, you must do so through the IDL interface. The basic structure of AppCore Manager's IDL interface is:

```
interface AppCoresManager
{
  void Startup();
  void Shutdown();

  void Add(in BaseAppCore appcore);
   void Remove(in BaseAppCore appcore);

  BaseAppCore Find(in wstring id);
};
```

In C++, the corresponding find() function is written as:

```
nsAppCoresManager::Find(const nsString& aId,
nsIDOMBaseAppCore** aReturn)
{
  *aReturn=nsnull;

  nsString nodeIDString;

  PRInt32 i;
  for (i=0;i<mList.Count();i++) {
    nsIDOMBaseAppCore * appCore = (nsIDOMBaseAppCore
*)mList.ElementAt(i);
```

```
    appCore->GetId(nodeIDString);
    if (nodeIDString == aId) {
      NS_ADDREF(appCore);
      *aReturn = appCore;
      return NS_OK;
    }
  }

  return NS_OK;
}
```

For the copy() function, you can follow the flow from JavaScript to C++ in a similar manner. The basic structure of EditorAppCore's IDL interface is:

```
interface EditorAppCore : BaseAppCore
{
  void EditorAppCore();

  void setAttribute(in wstring attr, in wstring value);
  void undo();
  void redo();
  void cut();
  void copy();
  void paste();

};
```

In C++, the corresponding copy() function is written as:

```
NS_IMETHODIMP
nsEditorAppCore::Copy()
{
  if (mEditor) {
    mEditor->Copy();
  }

  return NS_OK;
}
```

Summary

Now that you've had a chance to see how XUL is used to define user interfaces, you can probably understand why other programmers are so excited about the possibilities the technology offers. With XUL, you can change the user interface on the fly and you don't have to recompile the source. This enables you to perfect and tailor the user interface in ways that simply weren't practical with old-style applications. Use the discussion in this chapter as a starting point and then head out to the mozilla.org Web site, `www.mozilla.org`, for the latest details.

IN THIS CHAPTER

— Working with NSPR Integer Types

— Working with NSPR Objects and Pointers

— Using NSPR Boolean Types

— Checking Status Codes and Defining External Functions

— Accessing System Information and the Environment

Core Types and Variables

ozilla modules make extensive use of the Netscape Portable Runtime (NSPR) API. NSPR provides system facilities and low-level services that are platform independent. Core facilities supported include I/O, threading, memory management, and error handling. NSPR is designed to support a wide range of operating systems, including Mac PowerPC, Win32, and nearly two dozen versions of Unix. To provide robust solutions, NSPR attempts to make use of the best features of supported operating systems and is primarily designed to be used with clients written in C or C++.

In this chapter, you learn about the core types and variables provided by NSPR. Types are used in external function declarations, integer algebra, and more. Variables are used for examining system information and checking the environment.

Working with Core Types

You'll find that NSPR types are used extensively in modules. Accordingly, a strong understanding of NSPR types can go a long way in making it easier to work with the Mozilla source code.

The most common NSPR types you'll work with are those used with algebraic operations. These types include 8-, 16-, 32-, and 64-bit integer types, floating-point integer types, and native O/S integer types. While native O/S integer types have platform-dependent implementations, other integer types aren't specific to a particular platform. Beyond this, you'll also work with Boolean and calling operations types.

Working with Integer Types

Most integer types are guaranteed to be a specific bit-length on all platforms and have signed and unsigned implementations. Signed integer types are named `PRIntN` where N is the bit length, such as PRInt8 for a signed 8-bit integer. Unsigned integer types are named `PRUintN` where N is the bit length, such as `PRUint16` for an unsigned 16-bit integer.

With 32- and 64-bit integer types, you find some variation depending on the platform (and sometimes between compilers). On some platforms, 32-bit integers are implemented as `int`, while on other platforms, they are implemented as `long`; and 64-bit integers may be emulated on some platforms using two 32-bit numeric values. Because `long long` and `struct LONGLONG` are not compatible, NSPR defines a set of macros to handle 64-bit values. These macros are defined in the header file `prlong.h` and must be used to ensure cross-platform portability for 64-bit values.

Table 9-1 provides an overview of the 8-, 16-, 32-, and 64-bit integer types. When you use NSPR integer types, you should include the NSPR header file `prtypes.h`. This gives these types a syntax of:

```
#include <prtypes.h>
typedef definition PRIntN;
```

such as:

```
#include <prtypes.h>
typedef short PRInt16;
```

TABLE 9-1: 8-, 16-, 32-, AND 64-BIT SIGNED AND UNSIGNED INTEGER TYPES

INTEGER TYPE	DESCRIPTION
PRInt8	Signed 8-bit integer. Normally implemented as a signed char.
PRUint8	Unsigned 8-bit integer. Normally implemented as an unsigned char.
PrInt16	Signed 16-bit integer. Normally implemented as a signed short.
PRUint16	Unsigned 16-bit integer. Normally implemented as an unsigned short.
PRInt32	Signed 32-bit integer that may be implemented as an int or a long depending on the platform.
PRUint32	Unsigned 32-bit integer that may be implemented as an int or a long depending on the platform.
PRInt64	Signed 64-bit integer that may be implemented as long long or struct LONGLONG on some platforms.
PRUint64	Unsigned 64-bit integer that may be implemented as long long or struct LONGLONG on some platforms.

You can use integer types in many different ways. Listing 9-1 shows examples of how PRInt32 is used in the source file nsVersionInfo.cpp.

LISTING 9-1: USING INTEGER TYPES IN THE SOURCE CODE

```
nsVersionInfo::nsVersionInfo(PRInt32 maj, PRInt32 min,
PRInt32 rel, PRInt32 bld)
{
  major   = maj;
  minor   = min;
  release = rel;
  build   = bld;
}

nsVersionInfo::nsVersionInfo(char* versionArg)
 {
  PRInt32 errorCode;
...
 }
```

Using Native O/S Integer Types

Beyond the standard integer types, NSPR also implements two native integer types: PRIntn, a signed native integer, and PRUIntn, an unsigned native integer. These types are designed to be used for automatic variables and are guaranteed to be at least 16 bits. However, on some platforms native O/S types may be implemented as 32- or 64-bit integers.

When you use native O/S types, follow this syntax:

```
#include <prtypes.h>
typedef int PRIntn;
typedef unsigned int PRUintn;
```

Native O/S types should never be used for fields of a structure and can otherwise be used in a wide variety of circumstances, such as:

```
PRIntn tell()
{
  PRIntn result = -1;
  if (mStore)
    mResult = mStore->Tell(&result);
  return result;
}
```

Using Floating-Point Integer Types

For floating-point operations, you'll want to use a floating-point integer type, and NSPR defines PRFloat64 for this purpose. When you use PRFloat64, follow this syntax:

```
#include <prtypes.h>
typedef double PRFloat64;
```

Listing 9-2 shows examples of how PRFloat64 can be used.

LISTING 9-2: USING FLOATING-POINT INTEGERS IN THE SOURCE CODE

```
static PRIntervalTime pr_PredictNextNotifyTime(PRAlarmID
*id)
{
PRIntervalTime delta;
PRFloat64 baseRate = (PRFloat64)id->period / (PRFloat64)id-
>rate;
PRFloat64 offsetFromEpoch = (PRFloat64)id->accumulator *
baseRate;

id->accumulator += 1;   /* every call advances to next period
*/
id->lastNotify = id->nextNotify;   /* just keeping track of
things */
id->nextNotify = (PRIntervalTime)(offsetFromEpoch + 0.5);

delta = id->nextNotify - id->nextNotify;

return delta;
}
```

Working with Objects and Pointers

When you're working with objects and pointers, types that'll come in handy are
PRSize, PRPtrdiff, and PRUptrdiff. PRSize is used to represent the size of an
object and not the size of a pointer. On the other hand, PRPtrdiff and PRUptrdiff
are used to store pointers or pointer subtraction. PRPtrdiff is for signed pointer differences and PRUptrdiff is for unsigned pointer differences.

Two examples of how you might use PRSize follow:

```
PRInt32 RCFileIO::Write(const void *buf, PRSize amount)
{ return fd->methods->write(fd, buf, amount); }

PRInt32 RCFileIO::Writev(const PRIOVec *iov, PRSize size,
const RCInterval& timeout)
{ return fd->methods->writev(fd, iov, size, timeout); }
```

PRSize, PRPtrdiff, and PRUptrdiff have corresponding types in libc. With PRSize, the syntax is:

```
#include <prtypes.h>
typedef size_t PRSize;
```

With PRPtrdiff and PRUptrdiff, the syntax is:

```
#include <prtypes.h>
typedef ptrdiff_t PRPtrdiff;
typedef unsigned long PRUptrdiff;
```

Using Boolean Types

In NSPR, the standard Boolean type is PRBool. You use Boolean values to test for true/false conditions, and, as such, Boolean values have a wide range of uses in the source code. Two constants are also defined with this type: PR_TRUE and PR_FALSE. You can use these constants when you need to set or check for specific values in assignments or arguments. For example, while you may use PRBool to set up a test, you use PR_TRUE and PR_FALSE to set a specific return value, such as:

```
static PRBool endsWith(nsString* str, char* string_to_find);
static PRBool endsWith(nsString* str, char* string_to_find)
{
 PRBool found = PR_FALSE;
 if (str) {
  int len = strlen(".zip");
  int size = str->Length();
  int offset = str->RFind(string_to_find, PR_FALSE);
  if (offset == (size - len))
  found = PR_TRUE;
 }
 return found;
 }
```

Sometimes you may want to use PRPackedBool, a packed Boolean value, rather than the standard Boolean value. Packed Boolean types are defined as unsigned 8-bit integers and are designed to be used in structures where you wouldn't want to use bit fields but you do want a consistent overhead.

The syntax for `PRBool` is:

```
#include <prtypes.h>
typedef PRIntn PRBool
#define PR_TRUE (PRIntn)1
#define PR_FALSE (PRIntn)0
```

The syntax for `PRPackedBool` is:

```
#include <prtypes.h>
typedef PRUint8 PRPackedBool;
```

Checking Status Codes

Some NSPR functions return a status code, and you can use `PRStatus` to determine the status. Basically, the status is either `PR_FAILURE` for failure or `PR_SUCCESS` for success, giving this type a syntax of:

```
#include <prtypes.h>
typedef enum { PR_FAILURE = -1, PR_SUCCESS = 0 } PRStatus;
```

An example using `PRStatus` is shown below:

```
NS_METHOD
nsJVMManager::NotifyAll(void* address)
{
return (PR_CNotifyAll(address) == PR_SUCCESS ? NS_OK :
NS_ERROR_FAILURE);
}
```

Defining, Declaring, and Calling External Functions

In a module, any time you want to define, declare, or call external functions you'll want to use the preprocessor macros: `PR_EXTERN`, `PR_IMPLEMENT`, and `PR_CALLBACK`. By using these macros with externally visible routines and globals, you ensure that internal cross-files and forward-declared symbols are exported when needed. If a routine or global isn't externally visible, you shouldn't use these macros. Although these macros have platform-specific implementations, the general syntax is:

```
#include <prtypes.h>
PR_EXTERN(type) prototype
PR_IMPLEMENT(type) implementation
type PR_CALLBACK implementation
```

For details on actual implementation for your platform, examine the header file `prtypes.h`.

Functions and variables that are to be exported from shared libraries must be declared with the `PR_EXTERN` attribute. Use `PR_EXTERN` when the prototype for a method is declared, such as:

```
PR_EXTERN(void *)
nsCapsNewPrincipalArray(PRUint32 count)
{
 nsPrincipalArray *prinArray = new nsPrincipalArray();
 prinArray->SetSize(count, 1);
 return prinArray;
}
```

Implementations of symbols that are to be exported from shared libraries must be declared with the `PR_IMPLEMENT` attribute. Use `PR_IMPLEMENT` for the implementation of a method, such as:

```
PR_IMPLEMENT(PRBool)
JVM_IsLiveConnectEnabled(void)
{
 PRBool result = PR_FALSE;
 nsJVMManager* mgr = JVM_GetJVMMgr();
 if (mgr) {
  result = mgr->IsLiveConnectEnabled();
 }
 return result;
}
```

When a function is implemented in one shared library and called from another shared library, the function must be declared with the `PR_CALLBACK` attribute. Typically, this type of function is passed by reference, and `PR_CALLBACK` is included as part of the function definition, such as:

```
void PR_CALLBACK
init_source (j_decompress_ptr jd) { }

boolean PR_CALLBACK
fill_input_buffer (j_decompress_ptr jd) { }

static PR_CALLBACK PRIntn _hashValueCompare(const void
*value1,
const void *value2) { }
```

Accessing System Information and the Environment

Modules can use NSPR to access system information and to obtain the values of environment variables. While system information provides host name, system name, system release, and system architecture as well as system page size, environment variables provide detailed information about the system's environment and setup, provided you know the name of the variable you want to examine.

Getting System Information

To examine system information, you use `PR_GetSystemInfo`. The function expects to be passed three parameters: `cmd`, `buf`, and `buflen`. The `cmd` parameter sets the system information you want to examine. The `buf` parameter is a pointer to a buffer that will hold the null terminated string containing the desired system information. The `buflen` parameter is the size of the buffer in bytes. Additionally, when you use this function, you should include the header `prsystem.h`, giving the function a syntax of:

```
#include <prsystem.h>
PRStatus PR_GetSystemInfo(PRSysInfo cmd, char *buf, PRUint32
buflen);
```

As you can see from the syntax, `cmd` is of type `PRSysInfo`. `PRSysInfo` is an enumerated type that sets the types of information available through `PR_GetSystemInfo`. Its values are:

- PR_SI_HOSTNAME: the host name

- PR_SI_SYSNAME: the system name

- PR_SI_RELEASE: the release number of the system (only used with Unix systems)

- PR_SI_ARCHITECTURE: the system architecture

You'll use these values in the cmd parameter when you call PR_GetSystemInfo. After you set the cmd parameter, you should set the buffer and the buffer length. The minimum size you should use for the buffer is determined by the value of SYS_INFO_BUFFER_LENGTH. If the call is successful, the function returns a status of PR_SUCCESS, signaling that the buffer contains the specified system information. If the call fails, the function returns a status of PR_FAILURE and the buffer is undefined.

Listing 9-3 shows how you could use PR_GetSystemInfo to obtain session information. Note the use of a platform-specific ifdef to ensure that system release is obtained on Unix systems only.

LISTING 9-3: GETTING SYSTEM INFORMATION

```
/* Dump the session info */
char hostname[SYS_INFO_BUFFER_LENGTH];
char sysname[SYS_INFO_BUFFER_LENGTH];
char release[SYS_INFO_BUFFER_LENGTH];
char arch[SYS_INFO_BUFFER_LENGTH];

if (PR_GetSystemInfo(PR_SI_HOSTNAME, hostname,
sizeof(hostname)) != PR_SUCCESS)
hostname[0] = '\0';

if (PR_GetSystemInfo(PR_SI_SYSNAME, sysname,
sizeof(sysname)) != PR_SUCCESS)
sysname[0] = '\0';

#ifdef XP_UNIX
if (PR_GetSystemInfo(PR_SI_RELEASE, release,
sizeof(release)) != PR_SUCCESS)
release[0] = '\0';
#else
```

```
release[0] = '\0';
#endif

if (PR_GetSystemInfo(PR_SI_ARCHITECTURE, arch, sizeof(arch))
!= PR_SUCCESS)
arch[0] = '\0';
```

If you want to determine the system page size, you'll use PR_GetPageSize and/or PR_GetPageShift. PR_GetPageSize returns the number of bytes in a system page. PR_GetPageShift returns the log2 value of the number of bytes in a system page. These values are returned as 32-bit integers.

Neither function accepts a parameter, and the syntax is simply:

```
#include <prsystem.h>
PRInt32 PR_GetPageSize(void);
PRInt32 PR_GetPageShift(void);
```

Getting Environment Variables

If you want to examine environment variables, you can use PR_GetEnv. This function expects to be passed a pointer to a null terminated string that contains the environment variable name and returns a pointer to value of the specified environment variable if it is defined in the system. If the variable isn't defined, the function returns NULL.

The syntax for PR_GetEnv is:

```
#include <prenv.h>
char* PR_GetEnv(const char *name);
```

NOTE
The function returns a pointer to a value. This pointer should be treated as a constant.

You'll find that having access to environment variables is handy, especially if you want to log module activity. A partial example of using environment variables with module logging is shown as Listing 9-4.

LISTING 9-4: ACCESSING ENVIRONMENT VARIABLES

```
#ifdef DEBUG
GC = PR_NewLogModule("GC");
{
 char *ev = PR_GetEnv("GC_SEGMENT_SIZE");
 if (ev && ev[0]) {
  PRInt32 newSegmentSize = atoi(ev);
  if (0 != newSegmentSize) segmentSize = newSegmentSize;
}
ev = PR_GetEnv("GC_INITIAL_HEAP_SIZE");
if (ev && ev[0]) {
 PRInt32 newInitialHeapSize = atoi(ev);
 if (0 != newInitialHeapSize) initialHeapSize =
newInitialHeapSize;
}
ev = PR_GetEnv("GC_FLAGS");
if (ev && ev[0]) {
 flags |= atoi(ev);
}

...

}
#endif
```

Summary

NSPR provides many system facilities and low-level services that are used throughout Mozilla. Core facilities and services support I/O, threading, memory management, error handling, and more. Over time, NSPR will evolve as Mozilla evolves, but what won't change is the importance of its APIs. These APIs ensure that Mozilla source code can run on a wide range of operating systems.

Thread Handling and Synchronization

Implementing threads in a cross-platform application is a significant undertaking. Rather than trying to implement your own processes and structures for thread handling, you should use Netscape Portable Runtime (NSPR) threads. NSPR threads are designed to be lightweight yet robust enough to handle tasks such as initialization, scheduling, and synchronization efficiently.

Threads are created by specific client requests and remain active until they return from their root function or are terminated abnormally, such as when an occur occurs. During initialization, NSPR threads are created as independent execution entities but share address space with other threads in the same process. Because NSPR threads aren't implemented as separate processes, they reduce overhead and can often rely on their containing process to manage key resources for them.

In the sections that follow, you'll find detailed coverage of the key thread handling topics, including:

- Thread handling essentials: types, scopes, states, and priorities

- Thread creation and management

- Thread synchronization with locks, condition variables, and monitors

Thread Handling Essentials

NSPR threads can be scheduled independently of the host operating system and are represented by a pointer to a structure of type PRThread. When you use this structure, you should include the header file prthread.h. The syntax for this structure is:

```
#include <prthread.h>
typedef struct PRThread PRThread;
```

When you successfully create a new thread, you'll have a PRThread that remains valid until the thread returns from its root function, is abnormally terminated, or is joined (provided the thread is created as joinable). Thread resources are limited to the thread stack and the CPU register set. Other resources are borrowed from the containing process.

Threads have scopes, types, states, and priorities assigned to them. The sections that follow examine the various types of threads you can work with, such as user and system threads. Afterward, you'll find hands-on sections for creating, managing, and synchronizing threads.

Working with User and System Threads

NSPR supports both user and system threads as well as threads with global and local scope. Thread type is set with the enumerated type, PRThreadType, which specifies the enumerator PR_USER_THREAD as a user thread and PR_SYSTEM_THREAD as a system thread. The definition for this type is:

```
#include <prthread.h>
typedef enum PRThreadType {
PR_USER_THREAD,
```

```
PR_SYSTEM_THREAD
} PRThreadType;
```

User and system threads are fundamentally different in the way they are used and handled in source code. Generally, user threads are created to handle user-initiated or -oriented tasks, and system threads are created to handle system-level tasks. Because of the way NSPR handles user and system threads, most threads are created as user threads.

The NSPR function that handles cleanup is `PR_Cleanup`. Creating a user thread rather than a system thread ensures that the thread is cleaned up when its related process is terminated. System threads, on the other hand, may not be cleaned up before their related process is terminated. The reason for this is that while cleanup for user threads is synchronized with the related process, system threads are ignored by the cleanup function.

The NSPR function that handles cleanup is `PR_Cleanup`. While `PR_Cleanup` waits for user threads to exit before returning, the function does not wait for system threads. Because of this, you shouldn't use system threads with sensitive data that you may need to store when the containing process terminates.

Using Local and Global Threads

Threads with global scope, also referred to as *native threads*, are handled by the operating system and can be scheduled within a process or across processes. Threads with local scope, on the other hand, are handled by NSPR and are scheduled within an existing process. In many cases, NSPR can schedule and manage local threads without system intervention, which improves performance considerably. On systems that don't support threads, local threads are created through emulation. On other systems, local threads are implemented using the thread-handling features of the client's operating system.

TIP
When you have a choice between using local or global threads, it is usually better to use a local thread and let NSPR handle the thread as necessary for the client's operating system. In this way, you let NSPR deal with the platform-dependent details. Create global threads only when the thread executes code that might directly call blocking OS functions or when you plan on using the application on a specific platform and you know that platform's threading services.

Thread scope is set with the enumerated type `PRThreadScope`. `PRThreadScope` specifies the enumerator `PR_LOCAL_THREAD` as a local thread, `PR_GLOBAL_THREAD` as a global thread, and `PR_GLOBAL_BOUND_THREAD` as a global bound (kernel) thread. The definition for this type is:

```
#include <prthread.h>

typedef enum PRThreadScope {
                 PR_LOCAL_THREAD,
                 PR_GLOBAL_THREAD,
                 PR_GLOBAL_BOUND_THREAD
            } PRThreadScope;
```

Using Joinable and Unjoinable Threads

In addition to having type and scope, threads also have state and priority. Thread state controls what happens to a thread when it returns from the root function. You set thread state with the enumerated type, `PRThreadState`, which specifies the enumerators `PR_JOINABLE_THREAD` for *joinable* threads and `PR_UNJOINABLE_THREAD` for *unjoinable* threads. The key reason for creating a joinable rather than an unjoinable thread is control. If you want to synchronize thread termination and want to have more control over when a thread releases its resources, use a joinable thread.

The definition for PRThreadState is:

```
#include <prthread.h>
typedef enum PRThreadState {
PR_JOINABLE_THREAD,
PR_UNJOINABLE_THREAD
} PRThreadState;
```

Normally, a thread remains valid until it returns from its root function, at which point the thread terminates and attempts to release its resources. This type of thread is said to be *detached* (or unjoinable), and you don't have precise control over when the thread actually terminates. If, on the other hand, you create an *attached* (or joinable) thread, the thread reference remains valid after the thread returns from its root function, and its lifetime can be extended until another thread joins it using `PR_JoinThread`. `PR_JoinThread` blocks the calling thread until a specified thread terminates and releases its resources. Thus, when `PR_JoinThread` returns, you know that the thread's resources have been released.

Setting Thread Priorities

You set thread priority with the enumerated type, `PRThreadPriority`. Thread priority ranges from low to urgent. When you schedule local threads, higher priority threads execute before lower priority threads. As long as there are higher priority threads waiting, a lower priority thread will not get CPU time.

Thread priority is more of an abstract concept than a concrete one where higher priority threads have more CPU time than lower priority threads, but this behavior depends on the availability of system resources. Further, the scheduling of global threads really depends on the host OS. NSPR can't control the scheduling of global threads and instead depends on the operating system to schedule global threads.

The definition for `PRThreadPriority` is:

```
#include <prthread.h>
typedef enum PRThreadPriority
{
PR_PRIORITY_FIRST = 0,
PR_PRIORITY_LOW = 0,
PR_PRIORITY_NORMAL = 1,
PR_PRIORITY_HIGH = 2,
PR_PRIORITY_URGENT = 3,
PR_PRIORITY_LAST = 3
} PRThreadPriority;
```

The thread priority you'll usually want to use is normal, which is the most common priority. Priorities of first and last are placeholders and shouldn't be used. Other priorities assign more or less CPU time relative to the normal priority and should be used rarely.

Thread Creation and Management

NSPR provides many different functions for creating and managing threads. These functions are:

- `PR_CreateThread`: Creates a thread.

- `PR_JoinThread`: Blocks the calling thread until a specified thread terminates and releases its resources.

- `PR_GetCurrentThread`: Gets the current thread.

- `PR_Interrupt`: Sets an interrupt for a thread so the thread stops executing and returns to a control point.

- `PR_ClearInterrupt`: Clears an interrupt request.

- `PR_Sleep`: Tells a thread to wait for a certain amount of time or to surrender the process to other threads of equal priority.

- `PR_GetThreadPriority`: Gets a thread's priority.

- `PR_SetThreadPriority`: Sets a thread's priority.

- `PR_GetThreadScope`: Gets the scope of a thread as either global or local.

- `PR_NewThreadPrivateIndex`: Creates an index that enables you to associate private data with a thread.

- `PR_SetThreadPrivate`: Sets private thread data using the previously created index.

- `PR_GetThreadPrivate`: Gets private thread data using the previously created index.

- `PR_SetConcurrency`: Sets the number of threads NSPR uses to handle its system resource needs.

Out of all these functions, only a few are used regularly outside of NSPR. With this in mind, the sections that follow examine the most commonly used functions.

Creating a Thread

You use `PR_CreateThread` to create a thread. The syntax for `PR_CreateThread` is:

```
#include <prthread.h>
PRThread* PR_CreateThread(
PRThreadType type,
void (*start)(void *arg),
void *arg,
PRThreadPriority priority,
PRThreadScope scope
PRThreadState state,
PRUint32 stackSize);
```

As you can see, PR_CreateThread uses the parameters outlined in the previous section to define the type, scope, priority, and state of the new thread. The function also expects to be passed a pointer to the thread's root function as the *start parameter. This function becomes the root of the thread, and returning from this function is the only way to terminate a thread. The root function can have only one argument, and you use the arg parameter to set a pointer to this argument. Further, NSPR doesn't care about the validity or type of the argument. The final parameter you must set is the thread's stack size. Normally, stack size is set in bytes, but you can also set the value 0, which lets NSPR choose the best stack size for the host OS.

A successful call to PR_CreateThread returns a pointer to a new thread. The thread pointer remains valid until the thread returns from its root function. If the call to PR_CreateThread isn't successful, the function returns NULL. Generally, a call is unsuccessful when system resources aren't available to allocate to the thread.

Listing 10-1 shows an example of how you could use PR_CreateThread. As you examine the listing, note that the root function for all the threads is threadmain. The threadmain function is called with a single argument, either TestFile1, TestFile2, or TestFile3, depending on the thread, and, in turn, the function calls threadwork and passes this argument in. Note also that PR_Init is called to initialize NSPR. Because NSPR can be initialized implicitly, you normally don't have to initialize the runtime.

LISTING 10-1: WORKING WITH THREADS

```
#include "prinit.h"
#include "prstrms.h"
#include "prio.h"
#include <string.h>
#include <stdio.h>
#ifdef XP_UNIX
#include <sys/types.h>
#include <sys/stat.h>
#endif

const unsigned int MaxCnt = 1;
```

Continued

LISTING 10-1: *(continued)*

```
void threadwork(void *mytag);

typedef struct threadarg {
    void *mytag;
} threadarg;

void
threadmain(void *mytag)
{
    threadarg arg;

    arg.mytag = mytag;

    threadwork(&arg);
}

void
threadwork(void *_arg)
{
   //accessing the passed parameters
   threadarg *arg = (threadarg *)_arg;
   unsigned int i;

   char fname1[256];
   char fname2[256];

   strcpy(fname1, (char *)arg->mytag);
   strcpy(fname2, (char *)arg->mytag);

//do more thread work

}

#define STACKSIZE 1024*1024
int
```

```
main(int argc, char **argv)
{
    PR_Init(PR_SYSTEM_THREAD, PR_PRIORITY_NORMAL, 256);
    threadmain("TestFile");

    //Creating the thread
    PRThread *thr1 = PR_CreateThread(PR_SYSTEM_THREAD,
                threadmain,
                (void *)"TestFile1",
                PR_PRIORITY_NORMAL,
                PR_GLOBAL_THREAD,
                PR_JOINABLE_THREAD,
                STACKSIZE);

    //Joining the thread
    PR_JoinThread(thr1);
    return 0;
}
```

Joining a Thread

To synchronize the termination of a thread, you'll use PR_JoinThread.
PR_JoinThread blocks the calling thread until a specific thread terminates and
releases its resources. The only parameter for the function is a pointer to the
thread you want to join. NSPR doesn't validate the pointer and instead relies on
you to do so in the source code before calling the function.

The syntax for PR_JoinThread is:

```
#include <prthread.h>
PRStatus PR_JoinThread(PRThread *thread);
```

A successful call to PR_JoinThread returns PR_SUCCESS. An unsuccessful call
to PR_JoinThread returns PR_FAILURE. Generally, a call is unsuccessful if the
target thread cannot be found or if the target thread isn't joinable. Further, if multiple threads try to join a single thread, only one of the attempts succeeds and the
other attempts result in failure.

For an example of how to use PR_JoinThread, refer to Listing 10-1.

Getting the Current Thread

If you need to examine the currently running thread, you can do so using
PR_GetCurrentThread. PR_GetCurrentThread returns a pointer to the calling
thread, which enables a thread to discover its identity.

The syntax for PR_GetCurrentThread is:

```
#include <prthread.h>
PRThread* PR_GetCurrentThread(void);
```

You can also use PR_GetCurrentThread to determine if a thread instance is
running. If a thread instance isn't available, the function returns NULL. You can use
this to determine the availability of a thread, such as:

```
if ( PR_GetCurrentThread() == NULL )
{
  //No thread is available
}
```

A more complete example of working with the current thread is shown in
Listing 10-2. The example implements the nsIBlockingNotification
Observer interface, which uses threaded event queues.

LISTING 10-2: WORKING WITH THE CURRENT THREAD

```
NS_IMETHODIMP
nsDefaultProtocolHelper::Notify(nsIBlockingNotification
*aCaller,
                                nsIURL *aUrl,
                                PRThread *aThread,
                                PRInt32 aCode,
                                nsISupports *aExtraInfo)
{
  nsresult rv;
  NotificationEvent *ev;

  /*
   * Initialize the return code
   */
```

```
    rv = NS_NOTIFY_BLOCKED;

  /*
   * If no thread switch is necessary, then handle the
   * notification immediately
   */
  if (PR_GetCurrentThread() == aThread) {
    rv = HandleNotification(aCaller, aUrl, aCode,
aExtraInfo);
  }
  else {
    /*
     * Post a message to the appropriate thread event queue
     * to handle the notification...
     */
    PLEventQueue *evQ = nsnull;

    /* locate the event queue for the thread... */
    if (mEventQService) {
      mEventQService->GetThreadEventQueue(aThread, &evQ);
    }

    /* Create and dispatch the notification event... */
    if (evQ) {
      ev = new NotificationEvent(this, aCaller, aUrl, aCode,
                                 aExtraInfo);
      if (ev) {
        PRStatus status;

      /* dispatch event into the appropriate event queue */
        status = ev->Fire(evQ);

        if (PR_SUCCESS != status) {
       /* If the event was not dispatched, then clean up */
          NotificationEvent::DestroyPLEvent(ev);
          rv = NS_ERROR_FAILURE;
```

Continued

LISTING 10-2: *(continued)*

```
            }
        }
        else {
            /* allocation of the Notification event failed */
            rv = NS_ERROR_OUT_OF_MEMORY;
        }
    } else {
        /* No event queue was found! */
        NS_ASSERTION(0, "No Event Queue is available!");
        rv = NS_ERROR_FAILURE;
    }
  }
  return rv;
}
```

Getting and Setting Thread Priority

When you create a thread with `PR_CreateThread`, you set its NSPR priority. If
necessary, you can obtain or change this priority setting. To obtain the current priority setting, you can use `PR_GetThreadPriority`. The syntax for
`PR_GetThreadPriority` is:

```
#include <prthread.h>
PRThreadPriority PR_GetThreadPriority(PRThread *thread);
```

To change a thread's priority, you can use `PR_SetThreadPriority`. The syntax for `PR_SetThreadPriority` is:

```
#include <prthread.h>
void PR_SetThreadPriority(
PRThread *thread,
PRThreadPriority priority);
```

As you can see, `PR_SetThreadPriority` expects two parameters, `thread` and
`priority`. The `thread` parameter is an identifier for the thread whose priority
you want to set. The `priority` parameter is the priority you want to set.

Interrupting a Thread

NSPR provides several ways to interrupt a thread. You can use PR_Interrupt to set an interrupt request or you can use PR_Sleep to cause a thread to wait. When you use PR_Interrupt, you tell the thread to stop its current task and return to a control point.

While setting an interrupt is good in theory, in practice causing a thread to wait is usually better than using an interrupt. Interrupts can be delayed for a number of reasons. For example, if there is a blocking I/O function the interrupt may be delayed for up to 5 seconds. Also note that if a thread reaches the control point before it receives an interrupt (and after you've called PR_Interrupt), you may need to clear the interrupt with PR_ClearInterrupt.

When you call PR_Interrupt, you pass the function a pointer to the thread you want to interrupt. The syntax for PR_Interrupt is:

```
#include <prthread.h>
PRStatus PR_Interrupt(PRThread *thread);
```

The function returns PR_SUCCESS if successful or PR_FAILURE if unsuccessful. However, because of possible delays, PR_SUCCESS doesn't mean that the thread is interrupted. You may want to check for the error PR_PENDING_INTERRUPT_ERROR. If this error is set, the thread didn't stop and you should handle the error, such as:

```
if (PR_GetError() == PR_PENDING_INTERRUPT_ERROR) {
 userTargetErrMsg = "ThreadDeath: thread tried to proceed
after being stopped";
} else {
 userTargetErrMsg = NULL;
}
```

CROSS-REFERENCE

You'll find more information on error handling and error codes in Chapter 12.

PR_ClearInterrupt clears an interrupt for the calling thread. The syntax for PR_ClearInterrupt is:

```
#include <prthread.h>
void PR_ClearInterrupt(void);
```

Because it isn't always advantageous to work with interrupts, you may want to use PR_Sleep instead of PR_Interrupt. With PR_Sleep, you cause a thread to wait on a condition for a specified amount of time or simply have the thread surrender the process to other threads of equal priority. The latter method is the easiest way to allow other threads to execute and return a thread to the queue.

You'll find that PR_Sleep is the most common technique used to suspend threads. The function accepts a single parameter, which is the timeout interval in CPU ticks. In lieu of an actual timeout period, you can use the value PR_INTERVAL_NO_TIMEOUT to have the thread surrender the process. The syntax for PR_Sleep is:

```
#include <prthread.h>
PRStatus PR_Sleep(PRIntervalTime ticks);
```

CAUTION

Calling PR_Sleep with a parameter equal to PR_INTERVAL_NO_TIMEOUT is an error.

PR_Sleep can use an existing lock on the thread, and all you have to do is call the function with a timeout value, such as:

```
PR_Sleep( PR_MillisecondsToInterval(ThreadSleepTime) );
```

Or

```
PR_Sleep(50);
```

A more complete example of suspending a thread is shown in Listing 10-3. Note the use of locking and unlocking in the example. Locking is covered later in the chapter.

LISTING 10-3: SUSPENDING A THREAD WITH PR_SLEEP

```
static int
js_SuspendThread(JSThinLock *p)
{
JSFatLock *fl;
JSStatus stat;
```

```
while ((fl = (JSFatLock*)js_AtomicSet((jsword*)&p->fat,1))
== (JSFatLock*)1) /* busy wait */
 PR_Sleep(PR_INTERVAL_NO_WAIT);

if (fl == NULL)
 return 1;

PR_Lock(fl->slock);
js_AtomicSet((jsword*)&p->fat,(jsword)fl);
fl->susp++;

if (fl->susp < 1) {
 PR_Unlock(fl->slock);
 return 1;
}

stat = (JSStatus)PR_WaitCondVar(fl-
>svar,PR_INTERVAL_NO_TIMEOUT);
if (stat == JS_FAILURE) {
 fl->susp--;
 return 0;
}
PR_Unlock(fl->slock);
return 1;
}
```

Synchronizing Threads

When you use threads that are scheduled within processes, synchronization is critical. Synchronization ensures that shared data is locked when it is being used and unlocked when it is not in use. Synchronization also ensures that threads can communicate with one another and can track the status of certain conditions.

In NSPR, locking is handled through mutually exclusive locks, and state changes are communicated through condition variables. When a mutually exclusive lock and one or more condition variables are associated with shared data, they establish a monitor relationship. In this relationship, a thread must have exclusive access to a lock on shared data before it can access, modify, or check the shared data. In this way, locks prevent multiple threads from working with data simultaneously.

Two types of exclusive locks are defined in NSPR: `PRLock` and `PRMonitor`. `PRLock` is the standard type of locking mechanism and is used in conjunction with one or more condition variables to control access to shared data. `PRMonitor` is a special type of lock that is re-entrant and has a single built-in condition variable. The sections that follow examine `PRLock`, condition variables, and `PRMonitor`.

Working with Locks

Locks enable you to control access to data and ensure that only one thread manipulates protected data at a time. As stated previously, locks are used in conjunction with condition variables. These condition variables are used to communicate changes in state to threads. Methods you'll use to work with locks are:

- `PR_NewLock`: Creates an instance of the lock object.

- `PR_Lock`: Locks a lock object.

- `PR_Unlock`: Unlocks a lock object.

- `PR_DestroyLock`: Destroys a lock object.

Creating a New Lock

Because locks are object-based, you must first create an instance of a lock object with `PR_NewLock` before you can set a lock on a thread. The syntax for `PR_NewLock` is:

```
#include <prlock.h>
PRLock* PR_NewLock(void);
```

If the call is successful, the function returns a pointer to a new lock object. Otherwise, the function returns `NULL`. Generally, failure occurs when system resources aren't available. An example using `PR_NewLock` follows:

```
jsd_CreateLock()
{
  JSDStaticLock* lock;
```

```
   if( ! (lock = calloc(1, sizeof(JSDStaticLock))) ||
      ! (lock->lock = PR_NewLock()) )
  {
    if(lock)
    {
     free(lock);
     lock = NULL;
    }
  }
  return lock;
  }
```

Working with the Lock

Once you create a lock object, you can lock and unlock shared data using PR_Lock and PR_Unlock, respectively. PR_Lock expects to be passed a pointer to a lock object. When the function returns, the calling thread has exclusive access to the shared data and is holding the monitor's lock. If another thread tries to obtain a lock on the shared data, the call is blocked until the first thread releases the lock. The locking process doesn't have a timeout and cannot be interrupted.

When you are finished with the shared data, you release the lock by passing PR_Unlock a pointer to the lock object. If unlock is successful, the function returns PR_SUCCESS. Otherwise, the function returns PR_FAILURE, which can occur if the calling thread doesn't own the lock.

The syntax for PR_Lock and PR_Unlock follows:

```
#include <prlock.h>
void PR_Lock(PRLock *lock);
#include <prlock.h>
PRStatus PR_UnLock(PRLock *lock);
```

An example of how you could use these functions follows:

```
PR_Lock(freelist_lock);
if ((rv = freelist[k]) != NULL) {
 freelist[k] = rv->next;
}
PR_Unlock(freelist_lock);
```

Destroying the Lock

When you are finished with the lock object, use PR_DestroyLock to destroy the lock object and release the resources it used. This function has the following syntax:

```
#include <prlock.h>
void PR_DestroyLock(PRLock *lock);
```

Before you call this function, you should ensure that no other thread is using the lock object. When you call PR_DestroyLock, you pass in a pointer to the lock object to destroy, such as:

```
static void
freeFatlock(JSFatLock *fl)
{
 PR_DestroyLock(fl->slock);
 PR_DestroyCondVar(fl->svar);
 free(fl);
}
```

Using Condition Variables

Condition variables are used to communicate state changes to threads. When monitored data changes, you notify condition variables of changes and make threads wait accordingly. You determine how data is monitored when you create a condition variable, and this relationship exists for the life of the condition variable. Anytime you work with condition variables, you do so within a monitor. Generally, a monitor consists of a mutex type for locking, one or more condition variables that check for conditions and state, and the data you are monitoring.

Threads can be designed to wait for a certain condition to exist in the monitored data. To set a wait condition, you use the PR_WaitCondVar function. Waiting threads are set in a "waiting on condition" state. Threads can also notify other threads of state changes. Notification is handled with PR_NotifyCondVar and PR_NotifyAllCondVar. When a thread receives notice of a state change, the thread's state changes from waiting on condition to ready. In the ready state, the thread enters the scheduling queue, and, when scheduled, the thread can perform the following tasks:

1. Enter the monitor by locking access to the shared data with PR_Lock.

2. Work with the shared data.

3. Notify the condition associated with the data with `PR_NotifyCondVar` or `PR_NotifyAllCondVar`.

4. Exit the monitor by unlocking the shared data with `PR_Unlock`.

The structure for creating and manipulating condition variables is `PRCondVar`. When you use a variable of this type, follow this syntax:

```
#include <prcvar.h>
typedef struct PRCondVar PRCondVar;
```

The sections that follow examine how you can work with condition variables.

Creating a New Condition Variable

To create a new condition variable, you use `PR_NewCondVar`. The function has one parameter, which is the identity of the mutex type used for locking; and its syntax is:

```
#include <prcvar.h>
PRCondVar* PR_NewCondVar(PRLock *lock);
```

A successful call to `PR_NewCondVar` returns a pointer to the new condition variable object. An unsuccessful call to `PR_NewCondVar` returns NULL. Generally, a call is unsuccessful if no system resources are available.

An example of using this function follows:

```
home.cv = PR_NewCondVar(home.ml);
shared->cv = PR_NewCondVar(home.ml);
```

Waiting for a Condition

You set a condition to wait for using `PR_WaitCondVar`. The function has two parameters: `cvar` and `timeout`; `cvar` sets the condition variable on which to wait, and `timeout` sets the wait requirements. The syntax for the function is:

```
#include <prcvar.h>
PRStatus PR_WaitCondVar(
PRCondVar *cvar,
PRIntervalTime timeout);
```

Before you call `PR_WaitCondVar`, the calling thread must hold the lock associated with the referenced condition variable. After the call, the lock is released and the thread is blocked with a state of "waiting on condition." The thread maintains this state until another thread notifies the condition variable or a caller-specified timeout elapses. If the condition variable is notified, the thread's state changes to ready, and then, when scheduled, the thread attempts to reacquire the lock that it held when `PR_WaitCondVar` was called.

While the previous scenario outlines how waiting for a condition normally works, the function's second parameter actually controls the wait requirements. If you pass timeout the value `PR_INTERVAL_NO_TIMEOUT`, either the condition variable must be notified or the thread must be interrupted before the thread will resume from the wait. If you pass timeout the value `PR_INTERVAL_NO_WAIT`, the thread releases the lock and then attempts to reacquire the lock and resume. If you use a different value for the timeout parameter, the thread will be rescheduled, and this rescheduling occurs because either the caller-specified timeout has elapsed or there has been explicit notification.

`PR_WaitCondVar` returns a status that indicates success or failure. If the call succeeds, the function returns `PR_SUCCESS`. If the call fails, the function returns `PR_FAILURE`. Although failure can occur for many different reasons, the most common reasons are that either the thread was interrupted or the caller didn't have a lock on the associated condition variable. You can use `PR_GetError` to check the error.

An example of how you could use `PR_WaitCondVar` follows:

```
timeout = PR_INTERVAL_NO_TIMEOUT;

PRStatus RCCondition::Wait()
{
 PRStatus rv;
 PR_ASSERT(NULL != cv);
 if (NULL == cv)
 {
  SetError(PR_INVALID_ARGUMENT_ERROR, 0);
  rv = PR_FAILURE;
 }
 else
  rv = PR_WaitCondVar(cv, timeout.interval);
 return rv;
}
```

Notifying a Condition Variable of a Change

If the condition of the monitored data changes, you notify other threads of the state change using PR_NotifyCondVar or PR_NotifyAllCondVar. PR_NotifyCondVar and PR_NotifyAllCondVar set a pointer to a condition variable to notify of a state change. Their syntax is:

```
#include <prcvar.h>
PRStatus PR_NotifyCondVar(PRCondVar *cvar);
PRStatus PR_NotifyAllCondVar(PRCondVar *cvar);
```

These functions return a status that indicates success or failure. If the call succeeds, the functions return PR_SUCCESS. If the call fails, the functions return PR_FAILURE. Generally, failure is because the caller didn't have a lock on the associated condition variable. You can use PR_GetError to check the error.

While either function can be used to notify threads of a condition change, the function behavior is slightly different. Before you call PR_NotifyCondVar, the calling thread must hold the lock associated with the referenced condition variable. After the call, the runtime promotes a thread with a state of "waiting on condition" to the ready state. If multiple threads are waiting on the condition, only one of the threads is promoted, and you cannot reliably predict which thread it will be. With PR_NotifyAllCondVar, on the other hand, all threads waiting on the specified condition are promoted to the ready state.

Listing 10-4 shows how you could use PR_NotifyCondVar. The example creates a structure called notifyData, and then sets up a Notifier method. As you examine the source code, note how the condition variables are locked and unlocked.

LISTING 10-4: NOTIFYING OF CONDITION CHANGES

```
typedef struct notifyData {
 PRLock *ml;
 PRCondVar *child;
 PRCondVar *parent;
 PRBool pending;
 PRUint32 counter;
 } NotifyData;
```

Continued

LISTING 10-4: *(continued)*

```
static void Notifier(void *arg)
{
 NotifyData *notifyData = (NotifyData*)arg;
 PR_Lock(notifyData->ml);
 while (notifyData->counter > 0)
 {
  while (!notifyData->pending)
   PR_WaitCondVar(notifyData->child,
PR_INTERVAL_NO_TIMEOUT);
   notifyData->counter -= 1;
   notifyData->pending = PR_FALSE;
   PR_NotifyCondVar(notifyData->parent);
  }
  PR_Unlock(notifyData->ml);
}
```

Destroying a Condition Variable

To destroy a condition variable, you use PR_DestroyCondVar. Pass
PR_DestroyCondVar a pointer to the condition variable that you want to destroy.
The syntax is:

```
#include <prcvar.h>
void PR_DestroyCondVar(PRCondVar *cvar);
```

Before calling this function, the caller must ensure that the condition variable is
no longer in use. Otherwise, an error occurs. An example using
PR_DestroyCondVar follows:

```
PR_DestroyCondVar(home.cv);
PR_DestroyCondVar(shared->cv);
```

Using Special Locks with PRMonitor

Special locks created with PRMonitor are another NSPR feature used extensively
in modules. These special locks combine features of the standard locking mechanism and condition variables to create a unique way to protect shared data. While

`PRLock` types can have multiple conditions associated with them, a `PRMonitor` type has a single built-in condition. Another difference between `PRLock` and `PRMonitor` is in the way the locking mechanism uses monitors.

When you create locks with `PRLock`, the locking process is rather sequential. A thread enters a monitor, works with the shared data, and then exits the monitor after notifying other threads of any condition changes. Although multiple condition variables can be associated with the monitor, no other threads can work with the shared data while the monitor is locked, and the locking thread cannot re-enter the monitor without first completing its work and exiting.

When you create locks with `PRMonitor`, the process is more circular than sequential. A single thread can enter a monitor multiple times. The first time the thread enters the monitor, it acquires a lock and the thread's entry count is set to 1. The thread can then re-enter the monitor, and each time it does so, the thread's entry count is increased incrementally. The entry count is decremented each time the thread exits the monitor. The thread holds the lock on the monitor until the entry count reaches zero, at which point the thread releases the lock and other threads can be scheduled to enter the monitor.

Because `PRMonitor` types combine features of standard locks and condition variables, you'll find the functions available are very familiar. These functions include:

- `PR_NewMonitor`: Creates a new lock object of type `PRMonitor`.
- `PR_EnterMonitor`: Enters the lock associated with a specified monitor, increasing the entry count.
- `PR_ExitMonitor`: Exits the monitor and decrements the entry count associated with a specified monitor.
- `PR_Wait`: Waits for notification on a monitor's condition variable.
- `PR_Notify`: Notifies a thread waiting on a monitor's condition variable.
- `PR_NotifyAll`: Notifies all threads waiting on a monitor's condition variable.
- `PR_DestroyMonitor`: Destroys the lock object.

Creating a Special Lock

Because locks are object-based, you must first create an instance of a special lock object with `PR_NewMonitor` before you can enter the lock associated with a monitor. The syntax for `PR_NewMonitor` is:

```
#include <prmon.h>
PRMonitor* PR_NewMonitor(void);
```

If the call is successful, the function returns a pointer to a `PRMonitor` object. Otherwise, the function returns `NULL`. Generally, failure occurs when system resources aren't available. An example using `PR_NewMonitor` follows:

```
void SU_InitMonitor(void)
{
  su_monitor = PR_NewMonitor();
  XP_ASSERT( su_monitor != NULL );
}
```

Entering and Exiting the Monitor

For a new monitor, the entry count is set to zero, which makes it available to waiting threads. A thread can enter the lock associated with the monitor by passing `PR_EnterMonitor` a pointer to the `PRMonitor` object you want to work with. `PR_EnterMonitor` has the following syntax:

```
#include <prmon.h>
void PR_EnterMonitor(PRMonitor *mon);
```

A call to `PR_EnterMonitor` has one of two results. If the lock on the monitor is available, the call thread returns with the monitor's lock. Otherwise, the calling thread is blocked until the lock is released. Calls to enter the monitor's lock cannot be interrupted and do not have a timeout period.

Once a thread enters the monitor, it can re-enter the monitor as many times as necessary. Each time it does, the entry count is incremented. To decrease the entry count, the thread must call `PR_ExitMonitor`. When you decrease the entry count to zero, the lock on the monitor is released. `PR_ExitMonitor` expects to be passed a pointer to a `PRMonitor` object and has the following syntax:

```
#include <prmon.h>
PRStatus PR_ExitMonitor(PRMonitor *mon);
```

If the calling thread doesn't hold the lock on the referenced monitor object, the call fails and returns `PR_FAILURE`. If the call is successful, `PR_SUCCESS` is returned.

Generally, you'll find that `PR_EnterMonitor` and `PR_ExitMonitor` follow each other in the source code, such as you see in Listing 10-5.

LISTING 10-5: ENTERING AND EXITING A MONITOR

```
void su_NetExitProc(URL_Struct* url, int result, MWContext *
context)
{
 su_startCallback * c;
 if (result == MK_UNABLE_TO_CONVERT)
 {
  PR_EnterMonitor(su_monitor);
  DnLoadInProgress = FALSE;

  if (context)
  {
   FE_Alert(context, XP_GetString(SU_NOT_ENOUGH_SPACE));
  }
  PR_ExitMonitor(su_monitor);
 }

 else if (result != MK_CHANGING_CONTEXT)
 {
  PR_EnterMonitor(su_monitor);
  if ((c = QGetItem()) != NULL)
  {
   FE_SetTimeout( su_FE_timer_callback, c, 1 );
  }
  else
  {
   DnLoadInProgress = FALSE;
  }
 PR_ExitMonitor(su_monitor);
 }
}
```

Releasing the Monitor's Lock

To release the lock before the entry count reaches zero, you can use PR_Wait.
PR_Wait releases the lock on the thread temporarily and enables other threads to
access the monitor. When control is returned to the waiting thread, the entry

count is restored to its previous value, and the thread can continue using the monitor. PR_Wait expects to be passed a pointer to a PRMonitor object and a timeout value, giving it a syntax of:

```
#include <prmon.h>
PRStatus PR_Wait( PRMonitor *mon, PRIntervalTime ticks);
```

The calling thread must hold the lock associated with the monitor. After the call, the lock is released and the calling thread is blocked with a state of "waiting on condition." The thread maintains this state until another thread notifies it of a condition change or the specified timeout elapses. If the condition variable is notified, the thread's state changes to ready and it regains control of the monitor with the same entry count it had before the wait.

While the previous scenario outlines how waiting for a condition normally works, the function's second parameter actually controls the wait requirements. If you pass timeout the value PR_INTERVAL_NO_TIMEOUT, the thread must be notified or interrupted before it will resume from the wait. For an example, see Listing 10-6.

PR_Wait returns a status that indicates success or failure. If the call succeeds, the function returns PR_SUCCESS. If the call fails, the function returns PR_FAILURE. Although failure can occur for many different reasons, the most common reasons are that the thread was interrupted or the caller didn't have a lock on the associated condition variable. You can use PR_GetError to check the error.

LISTING 10-6: WORKING WITH MONITORS AND PR_WAIT

```
PRIVATE void
si_lock_signon_list(void)
{
  if(!signon_lock_monitor) {
   signon_lock_monitor =
   PR_NewNamedMonitor("signon-lock");
  }

  PR_EnterMonitor(signon_lock_monitor);
  while(TRUE) {
   /* no current owner */
   PRThread * t = PR_CurrentThread();
```

```
  if(signon_lock_owner == NULL || signon_lock_owner == t) {
    signon_lock_owner = t;
    signon_lock_count++;
    PR_ExitMonitor(signon_lock_monitor);
    return;
  }
  PR_Wait(signon_lock_monitor, PR_INTERVAL_NO_TIMEOUT);
  }
}
```

Notifying Other Threads of a Condition Change

If the condition of the monitored data changes, you can notify other threads of the state change by passing PR_Notify or PR_NotifyAll a pointer to a PRMonitor object whose state has changed. Following this, the syntax for PR_Notify is:

```
#include <prmon.h>
PRStatus PR_Notify(PRMonitor *mon);
```

And the syntax for PR_NotifyAll is:

```
#include <prmon.h>
PRStatus PR_NotifyAll(PRMonitor *mon);
```

These functions return a status that indicates success or failure. If a call succeeds, PR_SUCCESS is returned. Otherwise, PR_FAILURE is returned. Generally, failure occurs because the caller didn't have a lock on the referenced monitor. Use PR_GetError to check the error.

While either function can be used to notify threads of a condition change, the behavior the functions is slightly different. With PR_Notify, the runtime promotes a thread with a state of "waiting on condition" to the ready state. If multiple threads are waiting on the condition, only one of the threads is promoted, and you cannot reliably predict which thread it will be. With PR_NotifyAllCondVar, on the other hand, all threads waiting on the specified condition are promoted to the ready state.

Listing 10-7 shows an example using PR_Notify. Here, when the lock count reaches zero, the lock owner is set to NULL and a waiting thread is notified that the monitor's state has changed.

LISTING 10-7: USING PR_NOTIFY

```
PRIVATE void
si_unlock_signon_list(void)
{
 PR_EnterMonitor(signon_lock_monitor);
 signon_lock_count--;

 if(signon_lock_count == 0) {

  signon_lock_owner = NULL;
  PR_Notify(signon_lock_monitor);
 }

 PR_ExitMonitor(signon_lock_monitor);
}
```

Destroying the Special Lock

When you are finished with the `PRMonitor` object, use `PR_DestroyMonitor` to destroy the object and release the resources it used. This function has the following syntax:

```
#include <prmon.h>
void PR_DestroyMonitor(PRMonitor *mon);
```

Before you call this function, you should ensure that no other thread is using the `PRMonitor` object. When you call `PR_DestroyMonitor`, you pass in a pointer to the `PRMonitor` object to destroy, such as:

```
void SU_DestroyMonitor(void)
{
 if ( su_monitor != NULL )
 {
  PR_DestroyMonitor(su_monitor);
  su_monitor = NULL;
 }
}
```

Summary

Thread handling and synchronization are two of the most important core concepts for Mozilla source code development. As you've learned in this chapter, user and system threads, as well as threads with global and local scope, are available. Threads also have state and priority. Thread state controls what happens to a thread when it returns from the root function. Thread priority controls thread execution. Local threads of a higher priority execute before threads of a lower priority. To ensure that threads are handled properly, thread execution must also be synchronized. Synchronization ensures that shared data is locked when it is being used and unlocked when it is not in use. Synchronization also ensures that threads can communicate with one another and can track the status of certain conditions.

Managing File I/O in Mozilla

F ile input and output (I/O) is an essential part of any application, and Mozilla is no exception. NSPR's file I/O types and functions provide the core file handling facilities for Mozilla modules. Whenever you work with files or directories, you use these facilities. Because these facilities are platform-independent, you don't have to worry about developing platform-specific implementations and can instead concentrate on the tasks you need to accomplish, such as:

■ Creating files and directories

■ Accessing file and directory information

■ Reading, writing, and searching files

■ Removing files and directories

■ Renaming files

Before examining functions used in file I/O, this chapter looks at common types used by these functions. Most file I/O functions make use of one or more file I/O types, and you can learn a lot by examining their structures.

Understanding File I/O Types

Three files I/O types are commonly used with file I/O functions. These are directory types, file descriptor types, and file information types.

Directory Types

NSPR represents open directories in the file system with the directory type `PRDir`. The definition for a directory type is:

```
#include <prio.h>
typedef struct PRDir PRDir;
```

Directory types are pointers to open directories and as such can be used to work with directories. You obtain a pointer to a directory type using `PR_OpenDir` and then you access the directory using `PR_ReadDir`. When you are finished with the directory, you close the directory and release the pointer using `PR_CloseDir`.

File Descriptor Types

Most file I/O functions make use of file descriptor types. File descriptor types are pointers to I/O objects, such as open files, and are defined as follows:

```
#include <prio.h>
struct PRFileDesc {
PRIOMethods *methods;
PRFilePrivate *secret;
PRFileDesc *lower, *higher;
void (*dtor)(PRFileDesc *fd);
PRDescIdentity identity;
```

```
};
typedef struct PRFileDesc PRFileDesc;
```

NOTE

File descriptor types can act as descriptors for open files, sockets, and I/O streams. While this chapter is on files, most functions that work with a file descriptor can be used with sockets as well. You'll also find a specific set of functions for working with sockets in the NSPR header file `prio.h`.

File descriptor types are fairly complex and have many different fields. These fields are used as follows:

- `methods`: A pointer to the method to invoke, as defined in the I/O methods table, which is a structure of type `PRIOMethods`

- `secret`: A pointer to the private implementation data, which is defined as a structure of type `PRFilePrivate`

- `lower`: A pointer to the lower protocol layer

- `higher`: A pointer to the higher protocol layer

- `dtor`: A destructor function for a protocol layer

- `identify`: The identity for the file descriptor's protocol layer

As you can see, some file descriptor fields are defined with their own structures. The first structure, `PRIOMethods`, creates an I/O methods table that is used to invoke I/O functions, such as read, write, and seek. For example, the seek method in the I/O table corresponds to the `PR_Seek` function.

You need to work with a function's type declaration only when you implement a protocol layer on top of NSPR, such as Secure Sockets Layer (SSL). When you implement a protocol layer, you should provide functions that correspond to each method in the table. If a protocol layer doesn't implement a function, it should call a corresponding function of a lower or higher layer. For example, the open method could return the corresponding function in a lower layer `fd->lower->method->open(fd->lower)`.

`PRFileDesc` also makes use of `PRFilePrivate` and `PRDescIdentity` structures. `PRFilePrivate` is a protocol layer implementor that is used to collect all the private data of an OS layer. Because each protocol layer is distinct and separate from other layers, the private data isn't accessible in other layers. PRDescIdentity is the identity for the file descriptor's protocol layer and it can be used to determine which layer to use.

File Information Types

File information types are used with functions that examine information about files. Two file information types are defined: PRFileInfo and PRFileInfo64. PRFileInfo is designed to be used with files whose size is 4MB or less (that is, the file size can be expressed as a 32-bit integer). PRFileInfo64 is designed to be used with files larger than 4MB (that is, the file size can be expressed as a 64-bit integer).

PRFileInfo and PRFileInfo64 use the same fields and have similar definitions. PRFileInfo is defined as:

```
#include <prio.h>
struct PRFileInfo {
PRFileType type;
PRUint32 size;
PRTime creationTime;
PRTime modifyTime;
};

typedef struct PRFileInfo PRFileInfo;
```

And PRFileInfo64 is defined as:

```
#include <prio.h>
struct PRFileInfo64 {
PRFileType type;
PRUint64 size;
PRTime creationTime;
PRTime modifyTime;
};

typedef struct PRFileInfo64 PRFileInfo64;
```

Here, `type` sets the file type, `size` is the size of the file in bytes, `creationTime` is the time the file was created, and `modifyTime` is the time the file was last modified.

As with file descriptor types, some fields are defined with their own structures — namely, `PRTime` and `PRFileType`. NSPR represents time as 64-bit signed integers relative to 00:00:00, January 1, 1970 Greenwich Mean Time. You'll find the definition for `PRTime` and its associated functions in `prtime.h`.

`PRFileType` is an enumerated type with the following definition:

```
#include <prio.h>
typedef enum PRFileType{
PR_FILE_FILE = 1,
PR_FILE_DIRECTORY = 2,
PR_FILE_OTHER = 3
} PRFileType;
```

As you might expect, `PR_FILE_FILE` describes a file, `PR_FILE_DIRECTORY` describes a directory, and `PR_FILE_OTHER` describes other types of file system objects.

Working with Directories

Now that you know a bit about file I/O types, you're ready to work with directories. NSPR provides all the key directory management functions you'll need to use inside of Mozilla-based applications. These functions enable you to:

- Open directories
- Close directories
- Read directories
- Create directories
- Remove directories

The sections to follow examine functions that correspond to these tasks.

TIP
In file I/O operations, NSPR uses Unix-style pathnames. These pathnames support only the ASCII character set and are null-terminated character strings. Directories in the path are separated with a forward slash (/), and you should use this convention if you specify path names. Before making calls to the operating system, NSPR converts the forward slash to the directory separator of the host operating system.

Opening Directories

You open a directory by passing `PR_OpenDir` the pathname to the directory you want to open. If the directory exists and can be opened, the function returns a pointer to a directory stream, which is a dynamically allocated `PRDir` object.

The directory stream, in turn, can be passed on to `PR_ReadDir` to access the directory's files and subdirectories. Then when you are finished working with the directory, you use `PR_CloseDir` to close the directory stream. Closing the directory stream frees memory used by the `PRDir` object.

The syntax for `PR_OpenDir` is:

```
#include <prio.h>
PRDir* PR_OpenDir(const char *name);
```

If the referenced directory doesn't exist or cannot be opened, the function returns `NULL`. In this case, you shouldn't attempt to work with the directory.

You could use PR_OpenDir as follows:

```
PRDir* dir = PR_OpenDir(dirPath);
if (dir != NULL) {
  //read the directory
}
```

Reading Directories

Once you open a directory, you use `PR_ReadDir` to read the directory's contents. You pass `PR_ReadDir` a pointer to the directory stream (the `PRDir` object) and a flag that specifies the entries to skip. The function is defined as:

```
#include <prio.h>
PRDirEntry* PR_ReadDir(PRDir *dir, PRDirFlags flags);
```

Flags used by `PR_ReadDir` are:

- `PR_SKIP_NONE`: Do not skip any directory entries.

- `PR_SKIP_DOT`: Skip the current directory, which is represented as a parent directory entry (.)

- `PR_SKIP_DOT_DOT`: Skip the parent directory, which is represented as a current directory entry (..).

- `PR_SKIP_BOTH`: Skip both the current and parent directory entries.

- `PR_SKIP_HIDDEN`: Skip hidden file entries. On Win32 and Mac, hidden files have the "hidden" attribute set. On Unix, hidden files have names that begin with a dot (".").

A successful call to `PR_ReadDir` returns a pointer to the next entry in the directory. If an error occurs or the end of the directory is reached, `NULL` is returned. For error handling purposes, `PR_GetError` returns `PR_NO_MORE_FILES_ERROR` when the end of directory is reached.

NSPR manages memory allocation for directory entries. Because of this, you don't have to worry about clearing out old entries. However, you do need to think about the lifetime of directory entries. A directory entry is only valid until the next call to `PR_ReadDir` or until you close the directory with `PR_CloseDir`.

Directory entry structures are defined as:

```
struct PRDirEntry {
const char *name;
};
typedef struct PRDirEntry PRDirEntry;
```

As you can see, `name` is the only field defined for directory entries. This field represents the name of the entry, relative to the directory name.

One of the easiest ways to use `PR_ReadDir` is to place the function call in a `while` loop and continue to read while the directory contains entries, such as:

```
while ((dirent = PR_ReadDir(dir, PR_SKIP_BOTH)) != NULL) {
  //read directory entries
}
```

Closing Directories and Freeing Resources

When you are finished working with a directory, you should close it with
PR_CloseDir. Closing a directory destroys the associated PRDir object, freeing
the memory it used. Pass PR_CloseDir a pointer to the PRDir object you want to
close, following this syntax:

```
#include <prio.h>
PRStatus PR_CloseDir(PRDir *dir);
```

The function returns PR_SUCCESS if successful or PR_FAILURE if an error occurred. Use PR_GetError to check the error code.

Listing 11-1 provides an example of opening, reading, and closing a directory.
Note the test for NULL to ensure the directory is valid and the while loop to repeatedly access entries in the directory. These techniques were highlighted previously.

LISTING 11-1: WORKING WITH DIRECTORIES

```
PRDir* dir = PR_OpenDir(dirPath);
if (dir != NULL) {
 PRDirEntry* dirent;
 while ((dirent = PR_ReadDir(dir, PR_SKIP_BOTH)) != NULL) {
  PRFileInfo info;
  char* path = PR_smprintf("%s%c%s", dirPath,
              PR_DIRECTORY_SEPARATOR, PR_DirName(dirent));

  if (path != NULL) {
   PRBool freePath = PR_TRUE;
   if ((PR_GetFileInfo(path, &info) == PR_SUCCESS)
     && (info.type == PR_FILE_FILE)) {
    int len = PL_strlen(path);

    /* Is it a zip or jar file? */
    if ((len > 4) &&
      ((PL_strcasecmp(path+len-4, ".zip") == 0) ||
      (PL_strcasecmp(path+len-4, ".jar") == 0))) {
     fClassPathAdditions->Add((void*)path);
```

```
      if (jvm) {
       /* Add this path to the classpath: */
       jvm->AddToClassPath(path);
      }
      freePath = PR_FALSE;
    }
  }

  // Don't leak the path!
  if (freePath)
    PR_smprintf_free(path);
  }
 }
 PR_CloseDir(dir);
}
```

Creating and Removing Directories

While the most common directory tasks you'll perform involve opening, reading, and closing directory paths, NSPR also provides facilities for creating and removing directories. Create directories with PR_MkDir and remove directories with PR_RmDir.

PR_MkDir creates a directory with a specified pathname and access mode, giving the function syntax of:

```
#include <prio.h>
PRStatus PR_MkDir(const char *name, PRIntn mode);
```

While the path name should include the directory path as well as the directory name, NSPR can create directories only along paths that already exist. For example, if home/usr/wrs exists, you can specify a path name as home/usr/wrs/test for the new directory. On the other hand, if home/usr/wrs doesn't exist, you cannot specify a path name of home/usr/wrs/test.

Access modes for directories follow Unix conventions and, as such, are valid only on Unix systems. If you are familiar with the Unix chmod command, you'll feel right at home setting access mode values. Because of differences between Windows/Macintosh and Unix systems, you'll usually want to set this to a generic value, such as 0777, which allows full access on Unix systems. In this way, you can be sure the application can access the directory as necessary.

NOTE

Access modes really work only on Unix systems. Setting an access mode on another system has no effect.

As with most other file I/O functions, PR_MkDir returns PR_SUCCESS if successful or PR_FAILURE if an error occurred. Use PR_GetError to check the error code.

Listing 11-2 shows how you could create a directory.

LISTING 11-2: CREATING A DIRECTORY

```
static char*
AssureDir(char* path)
{
 char *autoupdt_dir = PR_smprintf("%sSilentDL", path);
 if (PR_SUCCESS != PR_Access(autoupdt_dir,
PR_ACCESS_WRITE_OK))
  {
   if ((PR_MkDir(autoupdt_dir, 0777)) < 0) {
     /* Creation of directory failed. Don't do SilentDownload.
*/
    return NULL;
   }
 }
 return autoupdt_dir;
}
```

PR_RmDir removes a directory with a specified pathname, giving the function a syntax of:

```
#include <prio.h>
PRStatus PR_RmDir(const char *name);
```

The directory you want to remove must be empty. If it isn't, the operation fails with PR_FAILURE and PR_GetError returns the error code PR_DIRECTORY_ NOT_EMPTY_ERROR. If successful, the call returns PR_SUCCESS.

Listing 11-3 provides an example of how you could remove files and directories. In the example, the `isNative` flag tests to see whether you're working with the native OS file system.

LISTING 11-3: REMOVING FILES AND DIRECTORIES

```
if(!file->isNative){
  if ((js_isDirectory(file) ? PR_RmDir(file->path) :
PR_Delete(file->path))==PR_SUCCESS) {
    js_ResetAttributes(file);
    *rval = JSVAL_TRUE;
  } else {
    JS_ReportErrorNumber(cx, js_GetErrorMessage, NULL,
    JSFILEMSG_REMOVE_FAILED, file->path);
    return JS_FALSE;
  }
}else{
  if ((js_isDirectory(file) ? rmdir(file->path) :
remove(file->path))==PR_SUCCESS) {
    js_ResetAttributes(file);
    *rval = JSVAL_TRUE;
  } else {
    JS_ReportErrorNumber(cx, js_GetErrorMessage, NULL,
    JSFILEMSG_REMOVE_FAILED, file->path);
    return JS_FALSE;
  }
}
```

Managing Files

File management is very similar to directory management. When you manage files, you manipulate files as a whole and not their contents. In most circumstances, file management works like this:

1. Check the file information and access permissions.

2. Open or create the file you want to work with.

3. Work with the file.

4. Close the file.

You can also rename and delete files. The sections that follow examine key file management tasks. Because there are a lot of steps involved with working with file contents, this step is examined in a separate section.

NOTE

As stated earlier, file I/O operations use Unix-style pathnames, which support the ASCII character set only and are null-terminated character strings. Further, path names must use a forward slash (/) as a separator. Before making calls to the operating system, NSPR converts the forward slash to the directory separator of the host operating system.

Checking File Information

If you want to examine information about a closed file, use PR_GetFileInfo for files of 4MB or less and PR_GetFileInfo64 for files larger than 4MB. Pass either function both the pathname to the file you want to work with and a pointer to a file information object (PRFileInfo or PRFileInfo64 type) to hold the results. Information about the file is then stored in the file information object, including file type, size in bytes, creation time, and modification time.

The syntax for PR_GetFileInfo is:

```
#include <prio.h>
PRStatus PR_GetFileInfo(const char *fn, PRFileInfo *info);
```

The syntax for PR_GetFileInfo64 is:

```
#include <prio.h>
PRStatus PR_GetFileInfo64( const char *fn, PRFileInfo64
*info);
```

If you already have an open file, you can use the counterparts to these functions: PR_GetOpenFileInfo or PR_GetOpenFileInfo64. In the function call, pass a pointer to a file descriptor for the open file you want to work with and a pointer to a file information object to hold the results. The syntax for PR_GetOpenFileInfo is:

```
#include <prio.h>
PRStatus PR_GetOpenFileInfo(PRFileDesc *fd, PRFileInfo
*info);
```

And the syntax for PR_GetOpenFileInfo is:

```
#include <prio.h>
PRStatus PR_GetOpenFileInfo64(PRFileDesc *fd, PRFileInfo64
*info);
```

These functions return PR_SUCCESS if successful or PR_FAILURE if an error occurs. You can use PR_GetError to check the error code.

The following example shows how you could create an instance of PRFileInfo and then obtain file information for an open file or closed file:

```
PRFileInfo info;

if ((file->isOpen)?
  PR_GetOpenFileInfo(file->handle, &info):
  PR_GetFileInfo(file->path, &info)!=PR_SUCCESS){
  return JS_FALSE;
}else
  return (info.type==PR_FILE_DIRECTORY);
```

Checking to See if a File Is Accessible

Before you try to work with a file, you may want to see if the file exists and is accessible. To do this, pass PR_Access the pathname to a file and a value that specifies the type of access you want to check.

The syntax for PR_Access is:

```
#include <prio.h>
PRStatus PR_Access( const char *name, PRAccessHow how);
```

As shown, access type values are set with the enumerated type PRAccessHow. The syntax for this enumerated type is:

```
typedef enum PRAccessHow {
    PR_ACCESS_EXISTS = 1,
```

225

```
        PR_ACCESS_WRITE_OK = 2,
        PR_ACCESS_READ_OK = 3
} PRAccessHow;
```

Using the predefined enumerators, you can check for the existence of a file, write permission, and read permission. If the access permission is valid, the function returns PR_SUCCESS. Otherwise, the function returns PR_FAILURE.

Listing 11-4 shows sample functions that test for read and write permissions. Note that the source assumes that a special access function for non-native files called *access* has been defined to handle files that aren't native to the OS.

LISTING 11-4: TESTING FOR READ AND WRITE PERMISSIONS

```
static JSBool
js_canRead(JSFile *file)
{
 if(file->isOpen&&!(file->mode&PR_RDONLY)) return JS_FALSE;

 if(!file->isNative){
    return (PR_Access(file->path,
          PR_ACCESS_READ_OK)==PR_SUCCESS);
  }else{
    return (access(file->path,
PR_ACCESS_READ_OK)==PR_SUCCESS);
  }
}

static JSBool
js_canWrite(JSFile *file)
{
 if(file->isOpen&&!(file->mode&PR_WRONLY)) return JS_FALSE;

 if(!file->isNative){
   return (PR_Access(file->path,
          PR_ACCESS_WRITE_OK)==PR_SUCCESS);
  }else{
   return (access(file->path,
PR_ACCESS_WRITE_OK)==PR_SUCCESS);
```

```
    }
}
```

Opening and Creating Files

NSPR provides a single function for opening and creating files. This function is
PR_Open. PR_Open creates a file descriptor as a PRFileDesc object for the file
with the specified pathname and sets its status flag. If a new file is created as a result of the call to PR_Open, a permission mode is also set for the file. The syntax
for PR_Open is:

```
#include <prio.h>
PRFileDesc* PR_Open(const char *name,
PRIntn flags, PRIntn mode);
```

As with directories, pathnames and permission modes should follow Unix conventions. With this in mind, pathnames should include the directory path as well
as the directory name, using the forward slash as a directory separator; and permission modes should be set using an integer value for the mode, such as 0777,
which allows full access on Unix systems.

Permission modes determine who can access a file. Status flags determine the
mode of the file, such as read only, read/write, and so on. The available status flags are:

- PR_APPEND: Opens an existing file in append mode. Here, the file pointer is set to the
  end of the file prior to each write.

- PR_CREATE_FILE: Creates a file if it doesn't exist. Otherwise, the flag has no effect.

- PR_RDONLY: Opens a file in read-only mode.

- PR_RDWR: Open a file for reading and writing.

- PR_TRUNCATE: Truncates an existing file and sets its length to zero.

- PR_WRONLY: Opens a file in write-only mode.

TIP

If you plan to work with the open file, you will probably want to open the file in read/write
mode. This allows you to check for available bytes and move the file pointer as well as read
and write.

While an unsuccessful call to PR_Open returns a NULL pointer, a successful call to PR_Open returns a pointer to a file stream, which is a dynamically allocated PRFileDesc object. Once opened, the file can be used as appropriate for its status flag.

An example using PR_Open is shown as Listing 11-5. As you study the example, note the way PR_GetError is used to check for and handle errors.

LISTING 11-5: OPENING FILES

```
static REGERR nr_OpenFile(char *path, FILEHANDLE *fh)
{
    PR_ASSERT( path != NULL );
    PR_ASSERT( fh != NULL );

    /* Open the file for read/write */
    (*fh) = PR_Open(path, PR_RDWR|PR_CREATE_FILE, 00700);
    if ( !VALID_FILEHANDLE(*fh) )
    {
        switch (PR_GetError())
        {
        case PR_FILE_NOT_FOUND_ERROR: /* file not found */
            return REGERR_NOFILE;

        case PR_FILE_IS_BUSY_ERROR: /* file in use */
        case PR_FILE_IS_LOCKED_ERROR: /* file is locked */
        case PR_ILLEGAL_ACCESS_ERROR:
            (*fh) = PR_Open(path, PR_RDONLY, 00700);
            if ( VALID_FILEHANDLE(*fh) )
                return REGERR_READONLY;
            else
                return REGERR_FAIL;
        default:
            return REGERR_FAIL;
        }
    }
    return REGERR_OK;
}
```

Closing a File

When you are finished with a file, use PR_Close to close the file stream and release its associated memory. Pass PR_Close a pointer to the file stream you want
to close. File streams are represented with PRFileDescr objects.

The syntax for PR_Close is:

```
#include <prio.h>
PRStatus PR_Close(PRFileDesc *fd);
```

If the call to PR_Close is successful, the function returns PR_SUCCESS.
Otherwise, the function returns PR_FAILURE.

You can use PR_Close as follows:

```
if ( fOut != NULL )
  PR_Close( fOut );
```

Deleting and Renaming Files

You'll use PR_Delete and PR_Rename to delete and rename files, respectively.
Both functions return the same values on success and failure: either PR_SUCCESS
or PR_FAILURE.

PR_Delete expects to be passed the pathname of the file you want to delete
and has the following syntax:

```
#include <prio.h>
PRStatus PR_Delete(const char *name);
```

You can use PR_Delete as follows:

```
//Remove file from the disk
if (PR_SUCCESS == PR_Delete(filepath)
{
  bStatus = PR_TRUE;
}
else
{
  //Failed to delete the file off the disk!
  bStatus = PR_FALSE;
}
```

PR_Rename expects to be passed the original path and filename as the from parameter and the new path and filename as the to parameter. Although you must
specify path information in the parameters, PR_Rename is not designed to move
files from one location to another. PR_Rename will not overwrite existing files either. If you try to name a file and the new name already exists, the operation fails
and PR_GetError returns the error code PR_FILE_EXISTS_ERROR.

The syntax for PR_Rename is:

```
#include <prio.h>
PRStatus PR_Rename( const char *from, const char *to);
```

You can use PR_Rename as follows:

```
nsresult nsFileSpec::Rename(const char* inNewName)
{
if (strchr(inNewName, '/'))
  return NS_FILE_FAILURE;

char* oldPath = PL_strdup(mPath);
SetLeafName(inNewName);

if (PR_Rename(oldPath, mPath) != NS_OK)
{
  // Could not rename, set back to the original.
  mPath = oldPath;
  return NS_FILE_FAILURE;
}

delete [] oldPath;
return NS_OK;
}
```

Manipulating File Contents

Opening a file gives you a pointer to a file stream, which is a PR_FileDesc object.
You can use this pointer to randomly access a file, to read its contents, and to write
new data. In most circumstances, the steps you follow to read from a file are

different from the steps you follow to write to a file. For example, you may read from a file as follows:

1. Open the file you want to work with in the correct mode, such as read only or read write.

2. If necessary, move the file pointer to a start location.

3. Determine the number of bytes that can be read from this position.

4. Read from the file as necessary.

5. Close the file when you are finished.

And you may follow these steps to write to a file:

1. Open the file you want to work with in the correct mode, such as append or read write.

2. If necessary, move the file pointer to a start location.

3. Write to the file as necessary.

4. Synchronize the file buffer.

5. Close the file when you are finished.

The sections that follow examine the functions you use to perform the read and write operations.

Determining the Number of Bytes Available for Reading

NSPR provides two functions for determining the number of bytes available for reading: `PR_Available` and `PR_Available64`. `PR_Available` is designed to be used with files 4MB or less and `PR_Available64` is designed to be used with files larger than 4MB.

The syntax for `PR_Available` is:

```
#include <prio.h>
PRInt32 PR_Available(PRFileDesc *fd);
```

The syntax for `PR_Available64` is:

```
#include <prio.h>
PRInt64 PR_Available64(PRFileDesc *fd);
```

To use either of these functions, you pass in a pointer to a file stream (a PRFileDesc object), and the function returns the number of bytes that are available for reading beyond the current file pointer position. If an error occurs, such as what can happen when the end of file is reached, these functions return –1 and you can use PR_GetError to examine the error code.

You could use PR_Available as follows:

```
if ((mFileDesc = PR_Open((const char*)nsFileSpec(inFile),
nsprMode, accessMode)) == 0)
   return NS_FILE_RESULT(PR_GetError());


mLength = PR_Available(mFileDesc);
```

Setting the File Pointer Position

When you work with fixed-length records or fields, you'll often want to move the file pointer to the previous or next record. To do this, you move the file pointer to a position designated by an offset from its current position. For example, to move forward 80 characters, you would set the offset to 80, but to move backward 80 characters, you would set the offset to –80. You can also move the pointer to a position from the start or end of a file.

The functions you'll use to manipulate the file pointer are PR_Seek and PR_Seek64. PR_Seek is designed to be used with files 4MB or less and PR_Seek64 is designed to be used with files larger than 4MB. If you are unsure of the file size, first use PR_GetFileInfo64 to examine the byte size of the file and then work with the file using the appropriate function (either PR_Seek or PR_Seek64).

PR_Seek and PR_Seek64 expect to be passed three parameters: fd, offset, and whence. The fd parameter is a pointer to the file you want to work with. You set the pointer offset with the offset parameter and the pointer start location with the whence parameter. Following this, you see that these functions have this syntax:

```
#include <prio.h>
PRInt32 PR_Seek( PRFileDesc *fd,
                 PRInt32 offset, PRSeekWhence whence);
```

And:

```
#include <prio.h>
PRInt64 PR_Seek64( PRFileDesc *fd,
                    PRInt64 offset, PRSeekWhence whence);
```

As indicated earlier, the offset can be a positive or negative integer. However, the whence parameter really controls the acceptable range of values. For example, if you position the pointer to the beginning of the file, you really shouldn't use a negative offset. Instead, use an offset of zero or a positive value. Similarly, if you position the pointer at the end of the file, you shouldn't use a positive offset. Here, you'll want to use an offset of zero or a negative value.

The acceptable values for the whence parameter are:

- PR_SEEK_CUR: Sets the file pointer relative to its current position.

- PR_SEEK_SET: Sets the file pointer relative to the beginning of the file.

- PR_SEEK_END: Sets the file pointer to the end of the file.

Upon success, these functions return the resulting pointer location, which is measured in bytes from the beginning of the file. On failure, -1 is returned and you can use PR_GetError to examine the error. Generally, the seek fails when you try to move the pointer to an invalid pointer location, such as beyond the end of the file.

Listing 11-6 shows an example that implements a seek function in a module. Note how the pointer is positioned for each possible value and how the file size is obtained when you add the current pointer position to the number of available bytes.

LISTING 11-6: WORKING WITH FILE POINTERS AND PR_SEEK

```
NS_IMETHODIMP FileImpl::Seek(PRSeekWhence whence, PRInt32
offset)
{
    if (mFileDesc==PR_STDIN || mFileDesc==PR_STDOUT ||
mFileDesc==PR_STDERR || !mFileDesc)
        return NS_FILE_RESULT(PR_BAD_DESCRIPTOR_ERROR);
    mFailed = PR_FALSE; // reset on a seek.
```

Continued

LISTING 11-6: *(continued)*

```
    mEOF = PR_FALSE; // reset on a seek.

    //get current pointer position
    PRInt32 position = PR_Seek(mFileDesc, 0, PR_SEEK_CUR);

    //check available bytes
    PRInt32 available = PR_Available(mFileDesc);

    //check file size
    PRInt32 fileSize = position + available;
    PRInt32 newPosition = 0;
    switch (whence)
    {
        case PR_SEEK_CUR: newPosition = position + offset;
                          break;
        case PR_SEEK_SET: newPosition = offset; break;
        case PR_SEEK_END: newPosition = fileSize + offset;
                          break;
    }
    if (newPosition < 0)
    {
        newPosition = 0;
        mFailed = PR_TRUE;
    }
    if (newPosition >= fileSize) // nb: not "else if".
    {
        newPosition = fileSize;
        mEOF = PR_TRUE;
    }
    if (PR_Seek(mFileDesc, newPosition, PR_SEEK_SET) < 0)
        mFailed = PR_TRUE;
    return NS_OK;
}
```

Reading from a File

After opening a file and setting the file pointer, you can read from the file using PR_Read. PR_Read expects to be passed three parameters: fd, buf, and amount. The fd parameter is a pointer to a file stream (a PRFileDesc object). The buf parameter is a pointer to an output buffer for the data you are reading. The amount parameter is the amount of data to read (which should be equal to the buffer size).

The syntax for PR_Read is:

```
#include <prio.h>
PRInt32 PR_Read(PRFileDesc *fd, void *buf, PRInt32 amount);
```

PR_Read invokes a thread that blocks other threads until the operation succeeds or fails. If successful, the function returns the number of bytes read. Otherwise, the function returns 0 if the end of file is reached or –1 if a read error occurred.

The following example shows how you can read from a file and handle errors:

```
PRInt32 bytesRead = PR_Read(mFileDesc, aBuf, aCount);
if (bytesRead < 0)
{
  *aReadCount = 0;
  mFailed = PR_TRUE;
  return NS_FILE_RESULT(PR_GetError());
}
*aReadCount = bytesRead;
```

Writing to a File and Synchronizing Buffers

Writing to a file is much like reading from it. To write to a file, you'll use PR_Write. PR_Write expects to be passed three parameters: fd, buf, and amount. The fd parameter is a pointer to a file stream (a PRFileDesc object). The buf parameter is a pointer to an input buffer containing the data you want to write. The amount parameter is the amount of data to write from the buffer.

The syntax for PR_Write is:

```
#include <prio.h>
PRInt32 PR_Write( PRFileDesc *fd, const void *buf, PRInt32
amount);
```

NOTE

NSPR also provides a function for writing to a file using multiple buffers. This function is `PR_Writev`. While the function is useful in some instances, `PR_Writev` is rarely used in the source code.

As with `PR_Read`, `PR_Write` invokes a thread that blocks other threads until all the data is written or the operation fails. If successful, the function returns the number of bytes written, which should be equal to `amount`. Otherwise, the function returns -1.

Often when you write to a file, information is buffered in a file buffer rather than written directly to the file. Because of this, you may want to synchronize the buffer before you try to modify its contents. Synchronizing forces the file buffer to write its contents to the file. You sync the buffer with the file by passing `PR_Sync` a pointer to the file stream, which is a `PRFileDesc` object. The syntax for `PR_Sync` is:

```
#include <prio.h>
PRStatus PR_Sync(PRFileDesc *fd);
```

Listing 11-7 shows examples of how you can use `PR_Write` and `PR_Sync`. Note the way errors are checked for and then handled.

LISTING 11-7: WRITING AND SYNCING

```
nsresult nsNetFile::FileWrite(nsFile *aFile, const char
*aBuf,
                              PRInt32 *aLen,
                              PRInt32 *aBytesWritten) {
    PRErrorCode error; // for testing, not propagated.
    NS_PRECONDITION( (aFile != nsnull), "Null pointer.");

    if (*aLen < 1)
        return NS_OK;

    *aBytesWritten = PR_Write(aFile->fd, aBuf, *aLen);

    if (*aBytesWritten == -1) {
        error = PR_GetError();
```

```
        return NS_ERROR_FAILURE;
    }
    return NS_OK;
}

nsresult nsNetFile::FileSync(nsFile *aFile) {
    NS_PRECONDITION( (aFile != nsnull), "Null pointer.");

    if (PR_Sync(aFile->fd) == PR_FAILURE)
        return NS_ERROR_FAILURE;

    return NS_OK;
}
```

Summary

NSPR's file I/O types and functions make it easy to work with files in a platform-independent manner. You can use these types and functions whenever you need to work with files or directories—and you don't need to worry about tailoring code for various operating systems. This way you are able to concentrate on tasks you need to accomplish rather than have to reinvent the wheel each time you need to perform file I/O.

Memory Management and Error Handling

In this chapter, you'll learn about the Netscape Portable Runtime (NSPR) functions and macros for memory management and error handling. You'll use these functions and macros extensively as you develop Mozilla modules. Proper memory management and error handling are two of the most important ingredients for successful programming. Applications that don't manage memory properly have memory leaks, and can cause serious problems on the end user's system. Applications that don't detect and handle errors properly can freeze, fail to respond as expected, or, worse, crash the system.

Managing Memory in Mozilla Modules

NSPR provides heap-based memory management functions and macros, which you can use with C and C++ source code. The primary reason for using these structures is that they are *thread safe,* which means they can be used with multi-threaded processes. The key memory management functions you'll use are `PR_Calloc`, `PR_Free`, `PR_Malloc`, and `PR_Realloc`. These functions have similar signatures to the corresponding `libc` functions `calloc`, `free`, `malloc`, and `realloc`, respectively. The key difference is that NSPR uses the type `PRUInt32` rather than `size_t`. Most NSPR memory management functions have corresponding macros, provided for convenience. You'll find additional convenience macros in NSPR as well.

Allocating Memory

`PR_Malloc` is used to allocate memory. Normally, `PR_Malloc` returns a pointer to the allocated memory of size `_size` from the heap. However, if there isn't enough memory for the request, a null pointer is returned instead. Because of this, you should always verify that the return value is not `NULL` before you try to work with the memory. To free memory allocated by `PR_Malloc`, you must use `PR_Free`.

The syntax for `PR_Malloc` is:

```
#include <prmem.h>
void *PR_Malloc(PRUint32 size);
PR_EXTERN(void *) PR_Malloc(PRUint32 size);
```

You can use `PR_Malloc` as follows:

```
char* buf = (char*)PR_Malloc(ZIP_BUFLEN);

if ( buf == NULL )
    return ZIP_ERR_MEMORY;
```

Two convenience macros are based on `PR_Malloc`: `PR_MALLOC` and `PR_NEW`. `PR_MALLOC` allocates an untyped item of size `_bytes` from the heap and returns a pointer to the item. `PR_NEW` allocates an item of type `_struct` from the heap and returns a pointer to the structure. The size of the memory allocated is equal to the size of the structure.

Both macros return a null pointer if there isn't enough memory for the request. Additionally, to free memory allocated by these macros, you should use PR_DELETE or PR_FREEIF.

PR_MALLOC is defined as:

```
#define PR_MALLOC(_bytes) (PR_Malloc((_bytes)))
```

and has a syntax of:

```
#include <prmem.h>
void * PR_MALLOC(_bytes)
```

PR_NEW is defined as:

```
#define PR_NEW(_struct) ((_struct *)
PR_MALLOC(sizeof(_struct)))
```

and has a syntax of:

```
#include <prmem.h>
(_struct *) PR_NEW(_struct)
```

Examples using PR_MALLOC and PR_NEW follow:

```
private_data->r8torgbn = PR_MALLOC(256);

SDL_TaskList* taskNode =
(SDL_TaskList*)PR_MALLOC(sizeof(SDL_TaskList));

GetURLEvent* e = PR_NEW(GetURLEvent);
DBT * rv = PR_NEW(DBT);
```

Allocating Memory for an Array of Objects

PR_Calloc allocates sufficient memory for an array of nelem objects with a size of elsize. The total memory used by the function is equal to nelem * elsize and all bytes in the allocated memory are cleared. The syntax for PR_Calloc is:

```
#include <prmem.h>
void *PR_Calloc(PRUint32 nelem, PRUint32 elsize);
```

`PR_Calloc` returns a pointer to the allocated memory. If there isn't enough memory for the request, a null pointer is returned. Before you try to work with the memory, you should always verify that the return value is not NULL. To free memory allocated by `PR_Calloc`, you must use `PR_Free`.

An example using `PR_Calloc` follows:

```
fs->width = ic->image->header.width;
fs->direction = 1;

fs->err1 = (long*) PR_Calloc(fs->width+2, sizeof(long));
fs->err2 = (long*) PR_Calloc(fs->width+2, sizeof(long));
fs->greypixels = (uint8 *)PR_Calloc(fs->width+7, 1);
fs->bwpixels = (uint8 *)PR_Calloc(fs->width+7, 1);
```

The corresponding macro for `PR_Calloc` is `PR_CALLOC`. `PR_CALLOC` is defined as:

```
#define PR_CALLOC(_size) (PR_Calloc(1, (_size)))
```

and has a syntax of:

```
#include <prmem.h>
void * PR_CALLOC(_size)
```

Using `PR_CALLOC`, you can easily allocate memory for a one-object array with a size of _size. As with the corresponding function, all bytes in the allocated memory are cleared. To free memory allocated by `PR_CALLOC`, you should use `PR_DELETE` or `PR_FREEIF`.

An example using `PR_CALLOC` follows:

```
totalNumberOfInterfaces += header->num_interfaces;

if (k == 0) {
   IDE_array = PR_CALLOC(totalNumberOfInterfaces *
sizeof(XPTInterfaceDirectoryEntry));
   fix_array = PR_CALLOC(totalNumberOfInterfaces *
sizeof(fixElement));
}
```

Another macro based on `PR_Calloc` is `PR_NEWZAP`. `PR_NEWZAP` allocates an item of type `_struct` from the heap and clears all the bytes in the allocated memory. The size of the memory allocated is equal to the size of the structure. As with other functions and macros, if there is insufficient memory available, the macro returns a null pointer.

`PR_NEWZAP` is defined as:

```
#define PR_NEWZAP(_struct) ((_struct*)PR_Calloc(1,
sizeof(_struct)))
```

and has a syntax of:

```
#include <prmem.h>
(_struct *) PR_NEWZAP(_struct)
```

You can use `PR_NEWZAP` in several ways, such as:

```
if ( (obj = PR_NEWZAP(NET_SimpleStreamData)) == NULL ) {
return NULL;
}
```

or

```
CRAWL_Tag tag = PR_NEWZAP(CRAWL_TagStruc);
if (tag == NULL) return NULL;
```

Freeing Memory

`PR_Free` returns the memory pointed to by `ptr` to the heap. This frees the memory and makes it available for allocation. `PR_Free` should be used only to free memory allocated by the functions `PR_Calloc`, `PR_Malloc`, and `PR_Realloc`. Before you call `PR_Free`, you should ensure that the pointer is valid. Calling `PR_Free` with an invalid pointer can crash the system.

The syntax for `PR_Free` is:

```
#include <prmem.h>
void PR_Free(void *ptr);
```

You can use PR_Free as follows:

```
nsJVMManager::~nsJVMManager()
{
  int count = fClassPathAdditions->GetSize();
  for (int i = 0; i < count; i++) {
    PR_Free((*fClassPathAdditions)[i]);
  }

  delete fClassPathAdditions;
  if (fClassPathAdditionsString)
    PR_Free(fClassPathAdditionsString);
}
```

Two macros are based on PR_Free: PR_DELETE and PR_FREEIF. PR_DELETE returns the memory pointed to by _ptr to the heap and then sets _ptr to null. PR_FREEIF conditionally returns memory to the heap. If the memory pointed to by _ptr exists, the memory is returned to the heap. Otherwise, the memory isn't freed.

The definition for PR_DELETE is:

```
#define PR_DELETE(_ptr) { PR_Free(_ptr); (_ptr) = NULL; }
```

and it has a syntax of:

```
#include <prmem.h>
void PR_DELETE(_ptr)
```

The definition for PR_FREEIF is:

```
#define PR_FREEIF(_ptr)        if (_ptr) PR_DELETE(_ptr)
```

and it has a syntax of:

```
#include <prmem.h>
void PR_FREEIF(_ptr)
```

Listing 12-1 shows an extended example using macros to assign memory and then free it. Note the difference in usage for PR_DELETE and PR_FREEIF.

LISTING 12-1: ALLOCATING AND FREEING MEMORY

```
XPT_PUBLIC_API(XPTInterfaceDescriptor *)
XPT_NewInterfaceDescriptor(uint16 parent_interface, uint16
                                num_methods, uint16
num_constants)
{

XPTInterfaceDescriptor *id =
PR_NEWZAP(XPTInterfaceDescriptor);
if (!id)
    return NULL;

if (num_methods) {
    id->method_descriptors = PR_CALLOC(num_methods *
                        sizeof(XPTMethodDescriptor));
    if (!id->method_descriptors)
        goto free_id;
    id->num_methods = num_methods;
}

if (num_constants) {
    id->const_descriptors = PR_CALLOC(num_constants *
                        sizeof(XPTConstDescriptor));
    if (!id->const_descriptors)
        goto free_meth;
    id->num_constants = num_constants;
}

if (parent_interface) {
        id->parent_interface = parent_interface;
} else {
    id->parent_interface = 0;
}

return id;
```

Continued

LISTING 12-1: *(continued)*

```
free_meth:
    PR_FREEIF(id->method_descriptors);
free_id:
    PR_DELETE(id);
    return NULL;
}
```

Resizing Memory Allocations

PR_Realloc changes the size of previously allocated memory pointed to by ptr to that specified by size. The value of size can be smaller or larger than the original. For a larger memory size, the PR_Realloc may need to move the memory to a new address. If this happens, the contents of the old memory block are copied to the new location and the information is not lost.

PR_Realloc returns a pointer to the allocated memory. If the memory pointed to by ptr is null, the function allocates memory of the size specified. If the size is zero, the memory pointed to by ptr is freed. Additionally, if more memory can't be allocated as necessary, a null pointer is returned and the original memory block is unchanged.

The syntax for PR_Realloc is:

```
#include <prmem.h>
void *PR_Realloc(void *ptr, PRUint32 size);
```

The following shows how you could use PR_Realloc:

```
if (inLength > mData->mLength && inLength > kMinStringSize)
    mData = (Data*)PR_Realloc(mData, inLength + sizeof(Data));
mData->mLength = inLength;
```

Another example is:

```
m_pStart = PR_Realloc(m_pStart, m_AllocSize+kPageSize);
```

The convenience macro for PR_Realloc is PR_REALLOC. PR_REALLOC changes the size of previously allocated memory pointed to by _ptr to that specified by _size. The macro is defined as:

```
#define PR_REALLOC(_ptr, _size) (PR_Realloc((_ptr),
(_size)))
```

and has a syntax of:

```
#include <prmem.h>
void * PR_REALLOC(_ptr, _size)
```

The following shows how you could use PR_REALLOC:

```
newIDE = PR_REALLOC(IDE_array, totalNumberOfInterfaces *
sizeof(XPTInterfaceDirectoryEntry));

newFix = PR_REALLOC(fix_array, totalNumberOfInterfaces *
sizeof(fixElement));

if (!newIDE) {
  perror("FAILED: PR_REALLOC of IDE_array");
  return 1;
}
if (!newFix) {
  perror("FAILED: PR_REALLOC of newFix");
  return 1;
}
```

Error Handling

Error handling is another core service provided by NSPR. You can use this service to detect and set errors. Error functions are defined in prerror.h. Although there are many different error functions, this section focuses on the key functions you'll use in your development efforts.

Checking for Errors

NSPR preserves error codes on a per-thread basis for its own runtime environment as well as the operating system. If you want to extend the error handling to other areas of the application, you'll need to actively manage the error codes and ensure that there are no conflicts.

CROSS-REFERENCE

Appendix B provides a guide to Mozilla's modules and troubleshooting Mozilla problems. In this guide, you'll find a complete listing of common error codes and their associated constants.

Getting Platform-Independent Errors

To retrieve the most recent error code generated by NSPR, you can use PR_GetError. The function returns an error code as a 32-bit integer. NSPR defines error codes as 32-bit integers, starting at –6000 and moving toward zero. These error codes are platform-independent and are set by errors that occur in the runtime environment. NSPR creates a lookup table that matches error codes to constants, which makes it easier to handle errors.

The syntax for PR_Error is:

```
#include <prerror.h>
PRErrorCode PR_GetError(void)
```

You can use the function to handle a PR_PENDING_INTERRUPT_ERROR as follows:

```
if (PR_GetError() == PR_PENDING_INTERRUPT_ERROR) {
  //interrupt error
}
```

Another example using PR_GetError is:

```
if (bytesRead < 0)
{
  *aReadCount = 0;
  mFailed = PR_TRUE;
  return NS_FILE_RESULT(PR_GetError());
}
```

Getting OS-Specific Errors

You examine OS-specific errors with PR_GetOSError. The function returns an error code that is a 32-bit signed integer. Because these error codes are OS-specific, they are really useful only during development.

The syntax for PR_GetOSError is:

```
#include <prerror.h>
PRInt32 PR_GetOSError(void)
```

The following shows how you could use this function:

```
TRACEMSG(("HTTP: Unable to connect to host for `%s'
  (errno = %d).", ce->URL_s->address, PR_GetOSError()));
```

Getting Error Text

To examine the text associated with the current thread's error, you'll use PR_GetErrorTextLength and PR_GetErrorText. PR_GetErrorTextLength gets the length of the error text, and, if error text is available, the function returns a 32-bit integer value sufficient to contain the error text. Otherwise, the function returns zero.

The syntax for PR_GetErrorTextLength is:

```
#include <prerror.h>
PRInt32 PR_GetErrorTextLength(void)
```

PR_GetErrorText copies the current error text to an array, which is specified when the function is called. The function returns the number of bytes copied to the array. If the function returns zero, no text was copied.

The syntax for PR_GetErrorText is:

```
#include <prerror.h>
PRInt32 PR_GetErrorText(char *text);
```

PR_GetErrorTextLength and PR_GetErrorText are normally used together, such as:

```
error = (char*)PR_MALLOC(PR_GetErrorTextLength());
(void) PR_GetErrorText(error);
```

Setting Error Codes and Text

If you want to preserve an error condition for the current thread, you can use PR_SetError and PR_SetErrorText. PR_SetError sets the error code.

`PR_SetErrorText` sets the text for the error. NSPR translates the error and stores it but doesn't validate it. The error remains set until it is overwritten by another error condition or a subsequent call to `PR_SetError` is made.

Using PR_SetError

`PR_SetError` sets a platform-independent error code, `errorCode`, and an OS-specific error code, `oserr`. If there is no OS-specific error code, use zero. The syntax for `PR_SetError` is:

```
#include <prerror.h>
void PR_SetError(PRErrorCode errorCode, PRInt32 oserr)
```

An example using `PR_SetError` follows:

```
primordialThread = PR_NEWZAP(PRThread);
if( NULL == primordialThread )
{
 PR_SetError( PR_OUT_OF_MEMORY_ERROR, 0 );
 return;
}
```

You'll find a list of the most common error codes in Appendix B. Use this list to determine which error code you may want to set.

Using PR_SetErrorText

`PR_SetErrorText` sets an integer value representing the length of the text, `textLength`, and a pointer to the error text, `text`. The syntax for `PR_SetErrorText` is:

```
#include <prerror.h>
void PR_SetErrorText(PRIntn textLength, const char *text)
```

Summary

Use the functions and macros discussed in this chapter to help you implement thread-safe memory management and adequate error handling. Proper memory management and error handling are essential. Applications must manage memory properly to prevent memory leaks and other memory related problems. Applications must detect and handle errors properly to minimize adverse affects on the operating system. Otherwise, the system may run out of memory, freeze, or fail to respond as expected.

PART

IV

Developing and Building Mozilla

IV
Developing and Building Mozilla

Before you compile and build the source, you'll need to learn about Mozilla's build systems. You'll also need to learn development techniques and necessities for your platform. Part IV covers development environments and build systems for Windows, Unix, and Macintosh systems.

Understanding Mozilla's Build System

After exploring the Mozilla front-end and back-end interfaces, you are probably more than ready to begin developing or coding your own custom solutions. Before you do this, however, there's one last thing you should know, and that's how Mozilla's build systems work. To accommodate the needs of a changing environment, Mozilla uses several different build systems. These build systems include Autoconf, GNU Make, and a CodeWarrior/MacPerl combination.

The Autoconf build system is used to create the necessary configuration files for building Mozilla in its entirety. GNU Make and CodeWarrior are used to compile and recompile specific modules within the Mozilla source code. As a Mozilla developer, you must have a basic understanding of each of these build systems, and the sections that follow should help you in this effort.

Working with Autoconf

Building the source code for a complex application such as Mozilla can be tricky. The original Mozilla source code relied heavily on platform-specific `#ifdef` structures in the source code to determine features supported by various platforms. To help with the build process and make it easier to build on multiple platforms and architectures, the team at mozilla.org updated Mozilla to use a build system that eliminates the need for most platform-specific #ifdef structures. This build system is called *Autoconf,* and it is the primary build system used in Mozilla.

Introducing Autoconf

Autoconf is a utility for creating scripts that automatically configure source code. Instead of relying on platform-specific definitions, Autoconf configuration scripts test for the presence of system features. Because of this, Autoconf scripts can easily handle architecture variations.

Generally, Autoconf scripts are created from template files that list system features needed by the application and test for the presence of these features. Once the template files and the scripts needed to recognize and respond to system features have been written, you can generate Autoconf configure scripts by running a simple configure command.

Autoconf enables the scripts to be shared with other applications that can use these features. If you need to update the scripts at a later date, you need to do so only in the template files. Once you update the template files, your configure scripts can be regenerated automatically to take advantage of the updates.

Autoconf Template Files

Mozilla's main template file is called `configure.in`. You'll find this file at the root of the source code directory tree. To access the directory tree root in the Mozilla Cross Reference, access any of the reference pages and click on the `mozilla` link at the top of the source listing. This will take you to `cvs-mirror.mozilla.org/webtools/lxr/source/`.

The template file defines the environment settings, libraries, and makefiles used by Mozilla. Here are some examples:

- Optimize the build by default:

```
OPTIMIZE="${OPTIMIZE=-O}"
COMPILER_WARNINGS=-Wall
CFLAGS="${CFLAGS}"
CXXFLAGS="${CXXFLAGS}"
```

- Set the version number of the libraries included with Mozilla:

```
MOZJPEG=62
MOZPNG=95
```

- Set the minimum version of toolkit libraries used by Mozilla:

```
GTK_VERSION=1.1.13
```

- Set the Mail/News makefiles:

```
MAILNEWS_MAKEFILES="
network/protocol/certld/Makefile
network/protocol/imap4/Makefile
network/protocol/mailbox/Makefile
network/protocol/nntp/Makefile
network/protocol/pop3/Makefile
network/protocol/smtp/Makefile
mailnews/Makefile
mailnews/base/Makefile
mailnews/base/public/Makefile
mailnews/base/src/Makefile
mailnews/base/build/Makefile
mailnews/base/tests/Makefile
mailnews/imap/Makefile
mailnews/imap/public/Makefile
mailnews/local/Makefile
mailnews/local/public/Makefile
mailnews/local/src/Makefile
mailnews/local/tests/Makefile
mailnews/imap/src/Makefile
```

```
mailnews/news/Makefile
mailnews/news/public/Makefile
mailnews/news/src/Makefile
mailnews/news/tests/Makefile
mailnews/mime/Makefile
mailnews/mime/public/Makefile
mailnews/mime/src/Makefile
mailnews/compose/Makefile
mailnews/compose/public/Makefile
mailnews/compose/src/Makefile
mailnews/compose/tests/Makefile
mailnews/public/Makefile
"
```

NOTE

As Mozilla modules move toward standalone functionality, the reliance on a single configure script could go away. Instead of one main script, you may have one script per module. This would enable each module to be completely independent.

Where to Go for More Information on Autoconf

Autoconf is a complex utility with many features — too many to cover in this book. If you'd like to learn more about Autoconf, here are some good resources:

- The GNU configure and Build System (`www.cygnus.com/~ian/configure/`)

- AutoConf, Creating Automatic Configuration Scripts at Delorie (`www.delorie.com/gnu/docs/autoconf/`)

- AutoConf, Creating Automatic Configuration Scripts at Cornell (`www.lns.cornell.edu/public/COMP/info/autoconf/`)

Working with GNU Make

Mozilla uses GNU Make to compile source modules on Unix and Windows systems. The key component of this build system is a utility called *make.* Make can automatically determine which source files in a large program need to be recompiled and can issue commands to recompile them.

Learning About make

To use make, you must create a Makefile. A Makefile describes the relationships among files in your application and provides commands for updating these files. These relationships and commands tell make how to compile and link the application.

Makefiles are similar to Autoconf templates in that they provide a central location to handle updates. For example, if you update the source files in a module, you don't need to recompile these source files separately. Instead, you re-run the make utility, and the utility uses the Makefile to determine which files have changed.

Make determines changes by checking the modification dates on the source files and comparing them with the entries in the Makefile database. If a source file has changed, make looks in the Makefile and executes the command associated with the source file.

Understanding Makefiles

The most basic structures in Makefiles are rules. A rule defines a command or set of commands to execute on a target based on certain dependencies. A typical rule has the following structure:

```
target: dependencies
        commands
```

Targets are usually the names of executables or object files. However, targets can also be the names of actions to execute, such as the `clean` action that is often used to instruct make to clean up after itself by removing unneeded files.

A single target usually has multiple dependencies. Dependencies are input files used to create targets. As stated, when these input files change, the commands associated with them are usually executed on the target, which is how source files are recompiled based on changes. Dependencies are followed by commands that should be executed, such as the command to execute the C compiler.

Listing 13-1 is a sample Makefile. The Makefile shows the relationships and commands necessary to create an executable called *widget*. As you can see, widget depends on several object files (`main.o`, `input.o`, `command.o`, and `display.o`), and these files in turn depend on several C source and header files. For example, `main.o` depends on `main.c` and `defs.h`.

LISTING 13-1: A SAMPLE MAKEFILE

```
widget : main.o input.o command.o display.o
 cc -o widget main.o input.o command.o display.o

main.o : main.c defs.h
        cc -c main.c

input.o : input.c defs.h command.h
        cc -c input.c

command.o : command.c defs.h command.h
        cc -c command.c

display.o : display.c defs.h display.h
        cc -c display.c

clean :
        rm widget main.o input.o command.o display.o
```

Given the Makefile shown in Listing 13-1, there are several things you can do. You can create the widget executable by typing `make` at the command line or you can type `make clean` at the command line to remove the widget executable and object files.

GNU Make in Mozilla

In the Mozilla source, you'll find a lot of Makefiles. Each module has its own Makefile, and each folder within a module usually has its own Makefile as well.

Figure 13-1 shows the Makefiles for the RDF module in Mozilla. As you can see, there is a general Makefile called Makefile and two instances of the Makefile that are generated by the system: `MakeFile.in` and `MakeFile.win`.

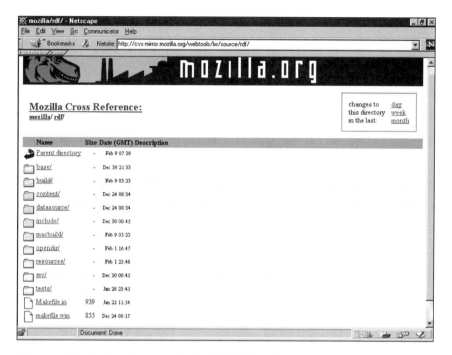

Figure 13-1: Makefiles used in Mozilla's RDF module

If you examine the high-level Makefiles such as the ones listed in the figure, you normally won't find rules. Instead, you'll find information that tells you how the Makefile is to be used. For example, each line in the code that follows sets a variable used by the build system:

```
DEPTH = ../..
DIRS = include src
INCLUDE = $(INCLUDE) -I$(DEPTH)/modules/libimg/public
MODULE        = rdf
LIBRARY_NAME  = $(LITE_PREFIX)rdf
REQUIRES      = nspr dbm java js htmldlgs util img layer
pref ldap network parse
```

These variables tell the build system many things about the source code found in the module:

■ DEPTH: Determines which files are being referenced by the Makefile. In the example, the Makefile applies to directories below this one.

- ■ `DIRS`: Sets the specific directories to which the Makefile applies. In the example, the Makefile applies to the `include` and `src` directories.

- ■ `INCLUDE`: Sets additional directories to include. In the example, the Makefile includes `../../modules/libimg/public`.

- ■ `MODULE`: Sets the module name. Here, the module name is `rdf`.

- ■ `LIBRARY_NAME`: Sets the library name for the module.

- ■ `REQUIRES`: Sets the names of other libraries required by the module.

As you examine the Makefiles in Mozilla, look for these variables. They'll help you keep up with what's happening when you recompile.

Where to Go for More Information on GNU Make

A complete discussion of make is beyond the scope of this book. If you want more information, visit GNU's Web site (`www.gnu.org`) or read the GNU Make documentation (`www.gnu.org/manual/make-3.77/make.html`).

Working with CodeWarrior Projects

CodeWarrior is a modular software development environment. mozilla.org distributes CodeWarrior project files with the module source files. Although these project files are generally host-neutral and not platform specific, the files distributed with Mozilla are designed to be used by Macintosh developers.

Mac Build Directories and CodeWarrior Project Files

If available, you'll find the CodeWarrior project files in module subdirectories called *macbuild*. Figure 13-2 shows the contents of the `macbuild` folder used in the XPCOM module. The file listing shown is fairly typical.

As you can see from the figure, `macbuild` folders usually contain prefix files that point to includes, `toc` files that list files used in the project, C header files, and mcp files that point to the raw binary files used in the module.

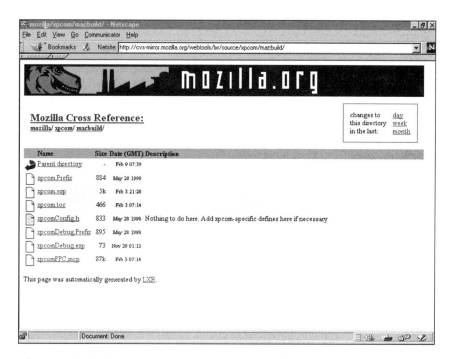

Figure 13-2: The `macbuild` folder contains CodeWarrior project files for Mac developers.

The Mac Build System

On the Macintosh, the build system uses MacPerl to work with Mozilla via AppleScript and AppleEvents. The core of the build system revolves around Perl scripts that control the build process. The main scripts in the build process are PullNGLayout.pl, NGLayoutBuildList.pm, and BuildNGLayoutDebug.pl.

PullNGLayout.pl checks out the source tree required to build core Mozilla projects. NGLayoutBuildList.pm contains a list of directories to check out, lists manifest files to be processed, and lists projects to build. BuildNGLayoutDebug.pl configures various build options and starts a build of the project.

CROSS-REFERENCE

You'll learn more about these scripts in Chapter 15.

Where to Go for More Information on CodeWarrior

CodeWarrior is an extensive development environment. If you want more information, visit MetroWerk's Web site (`www.metrowerks.com`) or read the CodeWarrior documentation (`www.metrowerks.com/tools/documentation/overview.html`).

Summary

Mozilla uses the Autoconf, GNU Make, and CodeWarrior build systems. Autoconf is used to create the configuration files for building Mozilla in its entirety. GNU Make and CodeWarrior are used to compile individual modules within the source code. You'll use these build systems whenever you work with Mozilla.

IN THIS CHAPTER

— Using the GNU Tools

— Using the Netscape Build Tools

— Using Perl 5 for Win32

— Setting up a Build Environment

— Running the Build

14

Developing Mozilla on Windows Systems

ozilla has a specific build process for Windows systems. This process involves setting up a developer environment, obtaining the source code, setting up a build environment, and then finally running the build. To learn more about the build process, read this chapter, follow the techniques I discuss, and then jump to the troubleshooting sections of Appendix B if you have problems.

Setting up the Developer Environment

You need to set up a developer environment for Mozilla. The tools you need are:

- Microsoft Visual C++ Version 5.0 or later

- GNU Tools for Microsoft Windows

- Netscape's Windows Build Tools package

- Perl5 for win32

All the tools except Visual C++ are shareware or freeware. Once you install Visual C++ on your system, you will need to set up the additional developer tools. Start with the GNU Tools and then install Netscape's toolkit. Afterward, install Perl5.

Obtaining and Installing GNU Tools

To build Mozilla, you need the Cygnus Windows GNU toolkit. This toolkit sets up a Unix-like environment on your system and enables you to work with standard GNU tools. One of the tools you'll use the most is make, which is used to compile source files.

You can obtain the most current versions of these tools as follows:

1. Visit `http://sourceware.cygnus.com/cygwin/download.html` and select a download site that's close to your area of the world.

2. Access the latest directory and download the file `full.exe`. This file is a self-extracting ZIP file and is about 14MB. To install the toolkit, you'll need about 30MB of free disk space.

TIP

Such a large file can be difficult to download, especially if your connection is unreliable. If you have problems downloading the 14MB file, access the full-split directory where you'll find files that have been split into smaller segments. After you download all the split files, copy all of the segment files into a file called `full.exe`. For example, if there are six segment files, you will type the following at the command prompt:

```
copy /b xaa + xab + xac + xad + xae + xaf full.exe
```

As you can see, you need to name each file you are copying into `full.exe`. Once you re-create `full.exe`, you can delete the old split files and proceed with the installation.

Install the Cygnus Windows GNU toolkit by following these steps:

1. Run `full.exe` to begin the installation process.

2. On the Welcome screen, click Next.

3. Use of the toolkit is subject to the GNU Public License. After you read the license, click Yes to accept its terms.

4. Click Next again.

5. Next, you will be prompted for an installation location (see Figure 14-1). The default location is *system-drive:*`\cygnus\cygwin-b20`. If you change the default, you will need to note this for the Netscape tools and Perl5 installations.

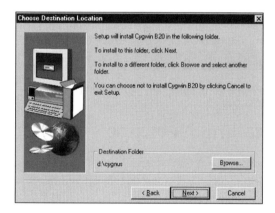

Figure 14-1: Select an installation location.

6. Afterward, select a name for the program files folder and the GNU toolkit (see Figure 14-2). By default, the installation program creates a folder called `Cygnus Solutions` that contains an entry for Cygwin B20.

7. Proceed with the remaining steps. When the installation program finishes, you should be able to start Cygwin B20, which will open a command window called the *bash shell window*.

NOTE
If you want to use the bash shell environment for other development efforts beyond Mozilla, you need to set up the GNU toolkit environment. You do this in the bash window as follows: (1) Mount the drive you want to use as the root, such as C:\. (2) Type **mkdir -p /tmp** to create a directory for temporary files. (3) Type **mkdir -p /bin** to create a bin directory. (4) Finally, copy sh.exe into the bin directory.

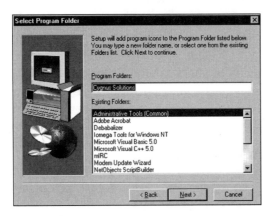

Figure 14-2: Select a name for the program files folder.

Obtaining and Installing Netscape's Build Tools

Netscape's build tools contain modified versions of the standard GNU tools. You need these modified versions in order to build Mozilla on Windows systems.

You can obtain the most current version of the Netscape build tools as follows:

1. Visit http://www.mozilla.org/mirrors.html and select a mirror site. The mirror sites are organized geographically, and with this in mind you should normally select the mirror site closest to your area of the world.

2. At the mirror site, access the mozilla/source directory. In this directory, you'll find a file called wintools.zip. Download this file.

Extracting Files from wintools.zip

Using your favorite unzipping utility, extract the files from wintools.zip to a folder called wintools on your hard drive. Ensure that you preserve the directory and naming structure. The Netscape Windows build tools are stored in binary and source file format.

In the directory where you've extracted the build tools, you'll find several directories. The key folder you'll want to work with is called *windows*. In the windows\bin folder, you'll find the modified GNU build tools for Alpha and Intel x86 chip architectures. In the windows\source folder, you'll find the source files for compiling the build tools individually.

The Netscape build tools are:

- **gmake.exe:** a modified version of GNU Make that is designed to use shmsdos.exe as its shell.

- **shmsdos.exe:** a shell environment developed by Netscape programmers that includes the necessary file manipulation operations needed by gmake. These commands include cp for copying files, rm for removing files, and mkdir for creating directories.

NOTE

Because the file manipulation commands are built into the shell environment, gmake and shmsdos always use these internal commands. This means that if you have cp installed elsewhere on your system, you don't have to worry about its being invoked and causing a conflict.

- **uname.exe:** a utility that returns the operating system name in the format needed by gmake. For example, on Windows NT systems, uname returns WINNT, which is the OS string expected by gmake on these systems.

- **nsinstall.exe:** a file installer used by shmsdos.

Installing the Build Tools on Alpha and x86

On a system that uses Alpha or Intel x86 chip architecture, the build tools are already compiled for you. You can complete the installation as follows:

1. The Alpha folder contains the build tools for Alpha systems. The x86 folder contains build tools for Intel x86 systems.

2. Copy the appropriate version of the Netscape build tools to the bin folder of the Cygnus Windows toolkit. By default, this folder is located in cygnus\cygwin-b20\H-i586-cygwin32\bin. If necessary, overwrite the existing files in the bin folder with the files for the Netscape build tools.

3. In the bin folder of the Cygnus Windows toolkit, you'll find a utility called date.exe. Rename this utility as unix_date.exe.

Installing the Build Tools on Other Chip Architectures

The windows/source folder from the installation contains source files that you'll need if your system uses other chip architectures. If you use a different chip architecture, such as AMD K6, you may need to compile the Netscape build tools from the source. The reason for doing this is to optimize the build tools for your chip architecture and environment.

You will need to build make, shmsdos, nsinstall, and uname. Before you do this, ensure that Microsoft Visual C++ and nmake are properly installed on your system. Nmake is a Microsoft build utility that is a part of the standard Visual C++ install.

To build make, follow these steps:

1. Change to the directory containing the make source files. If you installed the build tools in the wintools folder, this location is wintools\windows\source\make.

2. Execute the following command: **nmake /f Nmakefile**.

3. It will take a few minutes to compile make. When the process is finished, you'll find two new subdirectories: WinDebug, which contains a non-optimized version of make.exe, and WinRel, which contains an optimized version of make.exe. Normally, you'll want to use the optimized version.

4. Rename make.exe to gmake.exe and then copy it to the bin folder of the Cygnus Windows toolkit. By default, the bin folder is located in cygnus\cygwin-b20\H-i586-cygwin32\bin.

To build shmsdos and nsinstall, follow these steps:

1. Change to the directory containing the source files. If you installed the build tools in the wintools folder, this location is wintools\windows\source\shmsdos.

2. Build shmsdos by executing the following command: **nmake /f shmsdos.mak**.

3. Build nsinstall by executing the following command: **nmake /f nsinstall.mak**.

4. When the build process is finished, you'll find a new subdirectory called Release. This directory will contain the executables for shmsdos and nsinstall.

5. Copy shmsdos.exe and nsinstall.exe to the bin folder of the Cygnus Windows toolkit. By default, the bin folder is located in cygnus\cygwin-b20\H-i586-cygwin32\bin.

To build uname, follow these steps:

1. Change to the directory containing the uname source files. If you installed the build tools in the `wintools` folder, this location is `wintools\windows\source\uname`.

2. Build uname by executing the following command: **nmake /f uname.mak**.

3. When the build process is finished, you'll find a new subdirectory called `Release`. This directory will contain the executable for uname.

4. Copy uname.exe to the bin folder of the Cygnus Windows toolkit. By default, the bin folder is located in `cygnus\cygwin-b20\H-i586-cygwin32\bin`. Overwrite the existing file.

Obtaining and Installing Perl5 for Win32

To build Mozilla on Windows systems, you need Perl5 for Win32. Perl is a scripting language that is often used for system administration and Web programming. Mozilla's build tools use Perl to handle common tasks and provide core functions during the build process.

mozilla.org recommends that you use ActivePerl from Activestate (`http://www.activestate.com/ActivePerl`). Once you download and unarchive ActivePerl, you can begin the installation process by running the executable file in the x86 or Alpha directory from the installation folder.

NOTE

If you use the Perl Resource Kit for Win32, you shouldn't install ActivePerl. Instead, you'll want to install the latest service pack for the resource kit, which includes updates to ActivePerl. You can obtain the service pack online at `www.activestate.com/PRK/`.

If you are using a chip architecture other than Alpha or x86, you'll need to build the source files for ActivePerl. Download the source from Activestate, then, using your favorite unzipping utility, extract the source archive to a folder on your hard drive called `ActivePerl`. Ensure that you preserve the directory and naming structure. Once you extract the source, you'll find a subfolder called `win32`. This folder contains the makefile you'll need to compile the source. After you compile the source, you can complete the installation process following the instructions from ActivePerl's `readme` files.

To install ActivePerl, follow these steps:

1. Run the ActivePerl executable to begin the installation process.

2. On the Welcome screen, click Next.

3. Use of the ActivePerl is subject to the ActiveState Community License. After you read the license, click Yes to accept its terms.

4. Read the installation notes and then click Next again.

5. Next, you will be prompted for an installation location. The default location is *system-drive:*\perl.

6. Select the components you want to install. As shown in Figure 14-3, the only component you really need is Perl. Other components aren't needed with Mozilla.

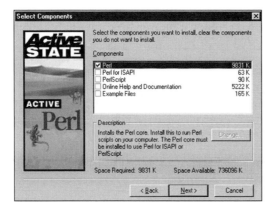

Figure 14-3: To save space, deselect the unneeded components before you proceed with the installation.

7. Set the installation options. I recommend deselecting all of these options or electing to add only Perl to your path (see Figure 14-4).

8. Proceed through the remaining steps. When the installation program finishes, ActivePerl will be configured on your system.

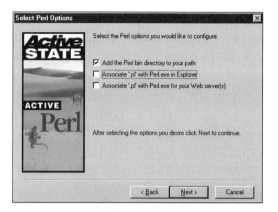

Figure 14-4: Select the installation options that make sense for your system and development needs.

9. Create a directory called `perl5` in the `cygnus\cygwin-b20\H-i586-cygwin32` directory. As you may recall, the latter directory is part of the Cygnus Windows toolkit installation.

10. Copy the contents of ActivePerl's bin directory to `cygnus\cygwin-b20\H-i586-cygwin32\perl5`. Mozilla's build tools look for Perl in this location.

Obtaining the Source Code

The CD-ROM contains several months' worth of source files with which you can practice. These files are in the `mozilla\source` directory and are organized by date. To obtain the latest files, however, you'll need to do so via FTP/HTTP or through CVS.

If you've already installed the source files from the CD-ROM, you can update them via CVS. The advantage to this is that you have to download only files that have changed since your installation, and this can save a few hours of downloading. To update files via CVS, follow these steps:

1. At the command prompt, enter the command: **set CVSROOT=:pserver:anonymous@cvs-mirror.mozilla.org:/cvsroot** and then **type set HOME=\TEMP**.

2. Next, enter **cvs login** and when prompted enter the password **anonymous**.

3. Finally, enter the command: **cvs -z3 checkout SeaMonkeyAll**.

The CVS server and Mozilla will begin transferring the source files.

If you decide to obtain the source code via FTP or HTTP, you should do so using the mirror sites listed at `http://www.mozilla.org/mirrors.html`. As shown in Figure 14-5, the mirror sites are organized geographically, and with this in mind you should normally select the mirror site closest to your area of the world. At the mirror site, access the `mozilla/source` directory and download the most recent mozilla source file.

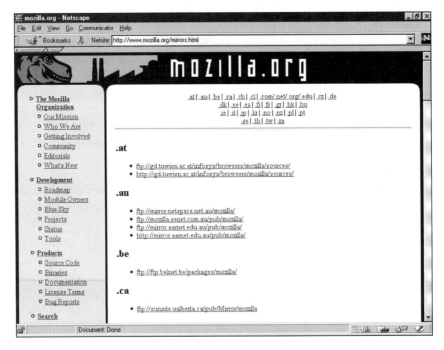

Figure 14-5: Using the mirror sites to download the source is quicker than using CVS.

Setting up the Build Environment

On the CD-ROM, you'll find a directory called `bin\win32\build`. These batch files are designed to help you set up the build environment. You simply run the batch file from the command prompt each time you want to work with the Mozilla source code.

The `bin\win32\build` folder on the CD-ROM includes the following batch files:

- **Win32VC50LITE.bat**: Sets a client-only build for standard Win32 and Visual C++ 5.0.

- **Win32VC50MED.bat:** Sets a client/composer build for standard Win32 and Visual C++ 5.0.

- **Win32VC50DARK.bat:** Sets a full build with client, composer, and Mail/News for standard Win32 and Visual C++ 5.0.

- **Win32VC60LITE.bat:** Sets a client-only build for standard Win32 and Visual C++ 6.0.

- **Win32VC60MED.bat:** Sets a client/composer build for standard Win32 and Visual C++ 6.0.

- **Win32VC60DARK.bat:** Sets a full build with client, composer, and Mail/News for standard Win32 and Visual C++ 6.0.

- **TargetWin95.bat:** Sets the build environment variables for a Windows 95 target system.

- **TargetWin98.bat:** Sets the build environment variables for a Windows 98 target system.

These batch files are meant to be used as starting points, and you'll probably want to edit their contents. The environment variables in these batch files are used as follows:

- `BUILD_OPT`: Optimizes the build. If you want an optimized build, set this variable to 1.

- `CM_BLDTYPE`: Sets the build type. If you want a release build, set this variable to rel. Otherwise, set this to dbg for a debugging build.

- `MODULAR_NETLIB`: Turns on the module settings for netlib. This variable should be set to 1.

- `MOZ_BITS`: Mozilla is set for 32-bit systems, and this variable should be set to 32.

- `MOZ_DEBUG`: Sets the debug mode. If you want to build Mozilla in debug mode, set this variable to 1.

- `MOZ_LITE`: An optional build parameter that enables you to build only the client. To do this, set this parameter to 1 and remove the `MOZ_MEDIUM` or `MOZ_DARK` parameters.

- `MOZ_MEDIUM`: An optional build parameter that enables you to build the client and composer components. To do this, set this parameter to 1 and remove the `MOZ_LITE` or `MOZ_DARK` parameters.

- `MOZ_DARK`: An optional build parameter that enables you to build the client, composer, and Mail/News components. To do this, set this parameter to 1 and remove the `MOZ_LITE` or `MOZ_MEDIUM` parameters.

- `MOZ_NT`: Sets the NT version number. If you are running NT 3.51, you need to set this variable to 351. Otherwise, this variable isn't needed.

- `MOZ_OUT`: Optional variable that sets the location of output files.

- `MOZ_SRC`: The top of your source tree, such as `d:\mozilla_source`. This is the directory into which you checked out or unzipped the source. (Don't end the directory name with a '\'.)

- `MOZ_TOOLS`: The parent directory of the GNU tools bin directory. The build looks for `MOZ_TOOLS\bin\gmake.exe`.

- `NGLAYOUT_PLUGINS`: Sets NGLayout plug-in mode. This variable is set to 1 by default and shouldn't be changed in most instances.

- `OS_TARGET`: Sets the target operating system. This variable is useful if you want to compile the source for an operating system other than the one you are using. Use WINNT for Windows NT, WIN95 for Windows 95, and WIN98 for Windows 98.

- `STANDALONE_IMAGE_LIB`: Sets the mode for the image library. This variable is set to 1 by default and shouldn't be changed in most instances.

- `_MSC_VER`: Sets the version of MS C++ you are using. Use 1100 for VC++ 5.0 and 1200 for VC++ 6.0.

Running the Build

Once you've set up everything else, running the build is the easy part. You simply change to the directory where the source resides and then tell `nmake` to compile Mozilla using the command **nmake /f client.mak**. For example, if you installed the source in `d:\mozilla_main`, you'll find a subdirectory called `mozilla`. This subdirectory is where the source resides. So, you'd change to this subdirectory and enter the command:

```
nmake /f client.mak
```

Mozilla is very a large application, and it will take a while to compile the application. Be patient. The typical compile time is about 30 minutes.

Keep in mind that compile time is directly related to the speed of your processor, drives, and memory, as well as the size of your memory and the available free space in memory and on disk. To speed up the compile process, you should reduce the workload on the system by closing unneeded applications.

Here are some example compile times:

- 300 minutes on a 486DX4/100 system with 16MB RAM

- 25 minutes on a DEC-ALPHA with 512MB RAM

- 30 minutes on a Pentium Pro 200 with 128MB RAM

- 25 minutes on a PowerMac G3/300 with 128MB RAM

CROSS-REFERENCE
If you have problems building the source, see the troubleshooting guide in Appendix B.

Summary

If you plan to compile Mozilla on your system, setting up a build environment is a necessity. The build environment for Windows includes Microsoft Visual C++, GNU utilities, Netscape build tools, and Perl 5 for Win32. Once you've installed these tools, you can configure the build environment and build the source. Don't forget that Appendix B provides troubleshooting tips and resources.

IN THIS CHAPTER

— Setting Up a Developer Environment

— Obtaining the Mac Source Code

— Setting Up the Mac Build Environment

— Building Mozilla on the Mac

Developing Mozilla on Macintosh Systems

The Macintosh version of Mozilla is designed to be used with MacOS 8.5 and MetroWerks CodeWarrior Pro 4.1 or later. When you install CodeWarrior, you must choose the full MacOS install, which requires about 250MB of free space. You will need an additional 15 to 20 MB of free space to install the rest of the developer tools.

Once the CodeWarrior development environment is installed, you can begin developing for Mozilla. The Mac build process has several steps that involve setting up a developer environment, obtaining the source code, setting up a build environment, and then, finally, building the application.

For the latest Mac build instructions, see `http://www.mozilla.org/build/mac.html`. If you have problems building Mozilla, jump to the troubleshooting sections of Appendix B.

NOTE

You should be building on a MacPPC. If you're not, you'll need the specific build source for your environment, such as Rhapsody.

Setting up the Developer Environment

Beyond the need for CodeWarrior Pro and MasOS 8.5, you need to set up a fairly extensive developer environment to build Mozilla on Macintosh systems. The tools you need are:

- Universal Headers 3.2+
- GA classes from the CodeWarrior Pro Reference CD
- ToolServer from the CodeWarrior Pro Reference CD
- Waste 1.3+
- CWASTE 1.6.2+
- Menu Sharing Toolkit
- Internet Config 1.4+ SDK
- AEGizmos 1.4.2+
- MacPerl5 5.20r4 MPW Tool
- `Mac::AppletEvents::Simple`
- `Mac::Apps::Launch`
- GNU Patch 2.1
- XPIDL Plug-in

All the tools, except Code Warrior Pro and its related tools, are shareware or freeware. While the number of tools you need may seem dizzying, don't worry. I'll go through each of them one by one. Still, keep in mind that with the need for so many developer tools, it is hard to go into real depth on the installation and use of each tool. Thus, the sections to follow provide a quick overview of each and how to install each for use with Mozilla.

Working with Universal Headers

Universal Headers 3.2 adds support files for C/C++ headers and libraries. To obtain the most recent version of this utility, visit `ftp://ftp.apple.com/developer/Development_Kits/CIncludes-Libraries.3.2.sit.hqx`.

Uncompress and install Universal Headers 3.2 in the CodeWarrior folder, in `':MacOS Support:Headers:Universal Headers:'`, `':MacOS Support:Libraries:MacOS Common:'`, and `':MacOS Support:Libraries:MacOS PPC:'` as appropriate.

Working with GA Classes and ToolServer

The CodeWarrior Pro Reference CD has several tools that are needed for Mozilla. First of all, you need the CD's obsolete GA classes. Uncompress and install these classes in the CodeWarrior folder, in `':MacOS Support:PowerPlant:_Will Be Obsolete:'`.

After you install the GA classes, you need to install ToolServer. Ideally, ToolServer and MPW will share the same Tools folder; this way you don't have multiple versions of tools and you'll have only a single instance of ToolServer on your machine. After you delete any existing ToolServer installations, follow these steps to reinstall and configure ToolServer:

1. Uncompress ToolServer from the CodeWarrior Pro Reference CD.

2. Access ToolServer's Tools folder on your system. You'll find a file called `RMetrowerks`. Move `RMetrowerks` to the Tools folder of MPW, which should be located at `Metrowerks:Codewarrior MPW:MPW`.

3. Remove ToolServer's Tools folder.

4. Create an alias of the Tools folder in CodeWarrior MPW and move this to your ToolServer folder.

5. Rename the alias Tools.

Working with WASTE, CWASTE, and AEGizmos

WASTE, CWASTE, and AEGizmos are all a part of the Mac developer environment for similar reasons. WASTE 1.3 is a text-editing library for MacOS. CWASTE 1.6.2 is a C Port of WASTE. And AEGizmos 1.4.2 is an editor extension toolkit. You'll find these utilities online at:

- `ftp://ftp.boingo.com//dan/WASTE/`

- `ftp://www.bact.wisc.edu//Bact%20Web/Public/`

- `http://www.mooseyard.com/Jens/Software/`

To install these utilities, uncompress their archive files and then drag the resulting folders to the MacOS Support folder in your CodeWarrior folder.

Working with the Menu Sharing Toolkit and Internet Config SDK

The Menu Sharing Toolkit adds shared menu support to PowerPlant applications. You'll find this toolkit online at `ftp://ftp.scripting.com/userland /menuSharingToolkit4.1.sit.hqx`. To install the toolkit, uncompress the HQX file and then drag the resulting folder to the MacOS Support folder in your CodeWarrior folder.

Internet Config 1.4 SDK enables you to set Internet preferences in one place and have them read by any other application configured to use this library. The SDK also supports "Get URL" AppleEvents and routes them to the appropriate helper application. You'll find Internet Config online at `ftp://ftp.share. com/pub/internet-configuration/ICProgKit1.4.sit` or `http:// hyperarchive.lcs.mit.edu/HyperArchive/Archive/comm/inet/ internet-config-14.hqx`. To install the SDK, uncompress the archive file and then drag the resulting folder to the MacOS Support folder in your CodeWarrior folder.

Working with MacPerl5 and Related Files

To build Mozilla on Windows systems, you need Perl5 for the Mac. Perl is a scripting language that is often used for system administration and Web programming. Mozilla's build tools use Perl to handle common tasks and provide core functions during the build process. To build Mozilla on Mac systems, you need Perl5's Application and MPW Tool modules.

You can obtain the Perl5 Application module online at `http://www.perl.com/CPAN/ports/mac/Mac_Perl_520r4_appl.bin`. Install the Application module by running the installer program and then dragging the resulting folder into your CodeWarrior folder. Next, you need to set a preference to enable Perl scripts to start with a double-click. In CodeWarrior, you set this preference by selecting Edit ⇨ Preferences, clicking on the Script button, and then selecting the radio button Run Scripts opened from Finder.

After you set up the application module, you should install the MPW Tool module. You can obtain the Perl 5 MPW Tool module online at `http://www.perl.com/CPAN/ports/mac/Mac_Perl_520r4_tool.bin`. Run the installer program. In the MacPerl folder, there will be an MPW tool called Perl. Install this tool in the MPW Tools folder.

Next, you need to install the GNU patch 2.1 for MPW tools, which can be obtained online at `ftp://sunsite.cnlab-switch.ch/software/platform/macos/src/mpw_c/Patch_21.sit.bin`. Install the patch in the MPW Tools folder.

For MacPerl, you also need to install the AppletEvents and Apps library updates for Mozilla. You'll find these online at `http://www.perl.com/CPAN/modules/by-category/04_Operating_System_Interfaces/Mac/Mac-AppleEvents-Simple-0.60.tgz` and `http://www.perl.com/CPAN/modules/bycategory/04_Operating_System_Interfaces/Mac/Mac-Apps-Launch-1.60.tar.gz`. Uncompress `Mac::AppleEvents::Simple` and install it in your MacPerl folder in `:lib:Mac:AppleEvents`. Uncompress `Mac::Apps::Launch` and install it in your MacPerl folder in `:lib:Mac:Apps`.

Working with the XPIDL Plug-in

The XPIDL plug-in is an add-on toolkit for CodeWarrior. You can obtain the toolkit online at `http://www.mozilla.org/build/xpidl_plugin_1.0d5.sit`. After uncompressing the archive, you'll find that the toolkit consists of three tools: XPIDL, XPIDL Settings, and XPT Linker. You'll need to install these tools in specific locations within the CodeWarrior Plugins folders. XPIDL is installed in the Compilers folder. XPIDL Settings is installed in Preference Panels. XPT Linker is installed in Linkers.

You'll use these tools when you build projects that contain IDL. In CodeWarrior, create a new empty project for the module you are working with, and then add the .IDL files to the new project. You can now generate the headers and type libraries needed to build the project. To generate headers, follow these steps:

1. Open the Target Settings panel and change the Target Name field to headers, and then set the Linker preference to None.

2. Select the xpidl Settings panel and set the Mode field to Header Files.

3. Click Save.

To generate type libraries, follow these steps:

1. Open the Target Settings panel and change the Target Name field to typelibs and then set the Linker preference to xpt Linker.

2. Select the xpidl Settings panel and set the Mode field to Type Libraries.

3. In the xpidl Settings panel, set the Linker output field to an appropriate name for the module, such as xpcom.xpt.

4. Click Save. XPT Linker will combine all of the .XPT files generated for each .IDL file into a single type library.

Obtaining the Mac Source Code

The CD-ROM contains several months worth of source files that you can use to practice with. These files are in the mozilla\source directory and are organized by date. To obtain the latest files, however, you'll need to do so via the Mac CVS client.

Checking out the Mac Build

I discuss obtaining and getting started with the MacCVS client in Chapter 3. After you obtain and install the client, you need to create a new CVS session file and set your CVS preferences using Edit ➪ Sessions Settings.

CROSS-REFERENCE

See Chapter 3 for a discussion of getting started with the MacCVS client.

Next, you can start retrieving Mozilla modules from mozilla.org. The module you want at this point is mozilla/build/mac. If this is your default module in MacCVS, you can simply select Action ⇨ Check Out Default Module. Otherwise, check out the module using Action ⇨ Module checkout.

Because you are checking out a lot of data, it may take a while to complete the action. Be patient, as you are downloading several megabytes of data.

Making Updates and Completing the Source Pull

When CVS is done checking out the build directory, you can access your local tree directory and drill down to the `:mozilla:build:mac:` folder. This folder should contain several build scripts.

You should also see the RunTSScript MPW compiler. You'll need to place a copy of the compiler in your `CodeWarrior Pro 4` folder, in `Metrowerks CodeWarrior:CodeWarrior Plugins:Compilers:`.

Next, you need to obtain the `NGLayout` files. These files complete the directory tree for Mac Mozilla. You obtain the `NGLayout` files by dragging `PullNGlayout.pl` onto MacPerl or running it in MacPerl to begin the process. The first time you run `PullNGlayout.pl`, the scripts prompts you for the location of your CVS session file. The session file is used to check out the rest of Mozilla's source tree.

Setting up the Mac Build Environment

Once you obtain the source code, you can set up the build environment. On the Mac, the build system uses MacPerl to work with Mozilla via AppleScript and AppleEvents. The core of the build system revolves around several different Perl scripts, which in turn call other Perl scripts.

Working with the Build Scripts

If you want to examine the build scripts, you can do so via the CVS directory tree. Figure 15-1 shows some of the scripts in the `mozilla/build/mac` (`http://lxr.mozilla.org/mozilla/source/build/mac/`) folder of the Mozilla Cross Reference.

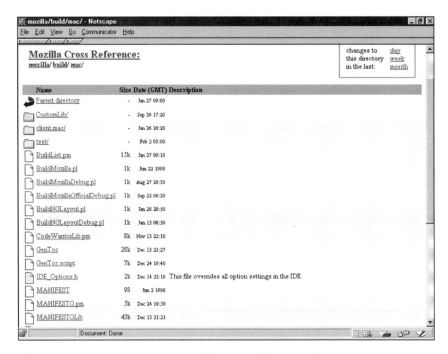

Figure 15-1: You can use the Mozilla Cross Reference to browse scripts or access them in the CVS directory tree.

The key scripts you'll need to work with are `PullNGLayout.pl`, `NGLayoutBuildList.pm`, and `BuildNGLayoutDebug.pl`. As you learned in the previous section, `PullNGLayout.pl` checks out the source tree required to build NGLayout. The other scripts are used to build the CodeWarrior project file and the Mozilla application.

Examining NGLayoutBuildList.pm

`NGLayoutBuildList.pm` has three main functions: `Checkout`, `BuildDist`, and `BuildProjects`. `Checkout` contains a list of directories to check out.

BuildDist lists files to be processed for inclusion in :mozilla:dist:. BuildProjects lists the projects to build.

The actions the script takes depend on the build options set in BuildNGLayoutDebug.pl. As with PullNGLayout.pl, NGLayoutBuildList.pm prompts you for the location of the CVS session file the first time the script is run.

Configuring Build Options in BuildNGLayoutDebug.pl

BuildNGLayoutDebug.pl starts a build of the project files and the Mozilla application. In this file, you may want to update various configuration and build options.

You have several options for editing the script. You can use BBEdit and BBEdit Perl extensions as your build environment, which enable you to edit build scripts inside BBEdit and use the extensions to run the scripts inside MacPerl. Other possibilities include running build scripts from MPW or on Alpha, using the native Perl mode.

Configuration variables you may want to set include $DEBUG, $CLOBBER_LIBS, and $FULL_CIRCLE. The $DEBUG variable is used to create a debugging build of Mozilla. The $CLOBBER_LIBS is used to overwrite existing libs and .xSYM files before you build the project. The $FULL_CIRCLE variable enables you to add optional modules/features to the build.

By default, $DEBUG and $CLOBBER_LIBS are set to 1, which means they are on. If you want to build a normal release of Mozilla, set $DEBUG to 0. If you don't want to clobber existing libs and .xSYM files before building the project, set $CLOBBER_LIBS to 0. If you want to add extra modules/features to the build, set $FULL_CIRCLE to 1.

Another feature of BuildNGLayoutDebug.pl is that the script determines which modules are downloaded from the CVS source repository. By default, no modules are downloaded. You can change this if you want to update your modules. The variables you'll use to do this are:

$pull{all}: Set to 1 to download all source modules.
$pull{lizard}: Set to 1 to download the client modules.
$pull{xpcom}: Set to 1 to download the XPCOM source modules.
$pull{imglib}: Set to 1 to download the imglib source modules.
$pull{netlib}: Set to 1 to download the netlib source modules.
$pull{nglayout}: Set to 1 to download NGLayout modules.

BuildNGLayoutDebug.pl also determines which modules are built when the script is run. By default, all modules are built and you can change this setting if you want to. The variables you'll use to change the build settings are:

$build{all}: Set to build all modules and projects, which is the default. If you want to do individual builds for modules, set this to 0 and set one of the other parameters to 1.

$build{stubs}: Set to build stub-related projects such as MemAllocator, NSStdLib, NSRuntime, and Client.

$build{common}: Set to build common projects, such as those used for Java, JavaScript, and LiveConnect.

$build{nglayout}: Set to build NGLayout-related projects such as HTMLParser, DOM, GFX, Plugin, View, Widget, Webshell, and RDF.

$build{editor}: Set to build editor-related projects such as txmgr, EditorGUIManager, and editor.

$build{viewer}: Set to build viewer-related projects such as viewer and xpfeviewer.

$build{xpapp}: Set to build XPAPP-related projects such as AppShell, AppCores, and apprunner.

Building Mozilla on the Mac

Building Mozilla sets up the CodeWarrior projects and creates a Mac application directory within your source tree. Before you build Mozilla, you should ensure that the Macintosh build column in Tinderbox is green. If the tree isn't green, the build won't run, so be sure to check Tinderbox as outlined in Chapter 5 before proceeding.

Two different techniques are used to build Mozilla. To build Mozilla for the first time, simply run BuildNGLayoutDebug.pl from MacPerl. This script builds the project and creates a Macintosh application directory in :mozilla:dist: viewer_debug: within your source tree. The next time you need to build Mozilla, you'll need to follow a different process.

On subsequent Mozilla builds, you will usually want to delete all files in :mozilla:dist: and then check out the Mac build again (:mozilla:build :mac:). The reason you need to check out the Mac build again is that the build scripts are stored in the tree, and if someone has changed these scripts, you need to get the latest version. When you are finished, run BuildNGLayoutDebug.pl from MacPerl.

Summary

If you plan to compile Mozilla on your system, setting up a build environment is a necessity. The build environment for Macintosh systems includes CodeWarrior Pro, Mac Perl, and many different add-on tools. Once you've installed these tools, you can configure the build environment and build the source. Don't forget that Appendix B provides troubleshooting tips and resources.

Developing Mozilla on Unix Systems

Mozilla has a specific build process for Unix systems. This process involves setting up a developer environment, obtaining the source code, and then running the build. To learn more about the build process, read this chapter, follow the techniques I discuss, and then jump to the troubleshooting sections of Appendix B if you have problems.

NOTE

For the latest Unix build instructions, see `http://www.mozilla.org/build/unix-details.htm`.

Setting up the Unix Developer Environment

You need to set up a developer environment for Mozilla. The tools you need are:

- GNU Make 3.74 or higher

- Perl 5

- CVS 1.9 or higher

- C/C++ compiler, such as egcs Version 1.0.3 or gcc Version 2.7.2

- GTK+ and Glib 1.2 or higher

- libIDL 6.3 (or higher)

- NSPR Library

NOTE

GNU Make and Perl5 are available on most Unix systems these days. Because of this, I won't go into detail on how to install these tools. If you need GNU make or Perl5, visit one of the GNU mirror sites listed at `http://www.gnu.org/order/ftp.html`.

CROSS-REFERENCE

Working with and installing CVS is covered in Chapter 4.

If you want to edit and manage configuration files, such as `configure.in`, you'll also need to install:

- Autoconf 2.12 or higher

- GNU m4 1.4+

All of these tools are freeware or shareware, and while the number of tools you need may seem dizzying, don't worry. I'll go through each of these one by one.

Still, keep in mind that with the need for so many developer tools, it is hard to go into real depth on the installation and use of each tool. Thus, the goal of the sections that follow is to provide a quick overview of the tools and how to install them with Mozilla.

Setting up the C/C++ Compiler

The compiler is an important part of the developer environment. Although you can use your favorite C/C++ compiler, such as gcc Version 2.7.2, mozilla.org recommends using egcs Version 1.0.3. The egcs compiler (`http://egcs.cygnus.com`) is an enhanced version of the standard GNU C compiler, gcc. Usually you'll find that egcs compiles faster than gcc and with fewer complaints. You can find egcs online at `ftp://egcs.cygnus.com/pub/egcs/releases/index.html`.

Because egcs is the recommended C/C++ compiler, let's look at how to set up this compiler on your system. After you copy and extract the compiler archive, you must:

- Configure the compiler
- Build the compiler
- Install the compiler

Configuring egcs

Start the configuration process by creating an object directory where you'll build the compiler. The object directory should be separate from the directory where the compiler source files are located. I recommend using `/tmp/obj` as the object directory and `/temp/egcs` as the source directory, which ensures that the directories are separate from each other.

Once you set up the object directory, ensure that either the native compiler cc or gcc is in your path. If it isn't, you need to set the path or set the CC environment variable. Next, if you've used the suggested directory structure, change to the object directory and type:

```
egcs/configure
```

Otherwise, type the relative path to the source directory's configure file, such as:

```
../source/egcs/configure
```

293

This command will configure egcs to use the default target and options. The command also sets the top level of the installation to /usr/local. When you install egcs later, this is where the compiler libraries and executables are installed. You can change the installation location by adding the following options when you run configure:

- --prefix=dirname: Sets the top-level installation directory. The default is /usr/local, meaning that egcs is installed in /usr/local/bin.
- --with-local-prefix=dirname: Sets the installation directory for local include files. The default is /usr/local/include.
- --with-gxx-include-dir=dirname: Sets the installation directory for g++ header files. The default is /usr/local/include/g++.

NOTE
For more configuration options, consult the documentation included with the egcs source files.

Building and Installing egcs

After you configure egcs, you can build it. To do this, issue the command **make bootstrap** in the object directory. The build process is handled is several stages. First, host tools are built, and then target tools are built. Afterward, the compiler is built using a three-stage bootstrap process. Finally, the runtime libraries are built from the third-stage compiler.

TIP
If you don't have a lot of disk space, try using make boostrap-lean. This version of Make cleans up the object files during the build process, thus reducing the amount of space needed for the build.

When the build process is finished, you can install egcs. In the object directory, type **make install**. This installs the compiler libraries and executables in the installation directory.

Setting up GNU m4 and Autoconf

GNU m4 is a macro processor for Unix systems that has functions for handling file includes, executing shell commands, and performing mathematical computations. GNU m4 can also handle the automated build processes needed by Autoconf. As you know from previous chapters, Autoconf is the primary build system for Mozilla. What you don't know is that Autoconf is actually an extension of m4 — it is an extensible set of m4 macros used to configure and build source code. You can obtain GNU m4 and Autoconf from the GNU mirror sites listed at `http://www.gnu.org/order/ftp.html`.

Getting Ready to Use GNU m4

In order to use Autoconf, you must first install GNU m4. Installing m4 is a fairly straightforward process that involves configuring and building the m4 libraries.

To install m4, follow these steps:

1. Unarchive the m4 source files and store them on your hard drive.

2. Change to the directory containing the source files and type **`./configure`**. This command configures m4 to use the default target and options. The command also sets the top level of the installation to `/usr/local`. When you install m4 later, this is where the m4 libraries and related files are installed. You can change the installation location using the `--prefix` option when you run configure, such as `--prefix=/usr/bin/local`.

3. Your system will start configuring the source. When it finishes, type **`make`** to build m4.

4. Next, install m4 by typing **`make install`**.

5. After you test the installation, you can remove unneeded binaries and object files by typing **`make clean`**. To remove distribution files created by configure, type **`make distclean`**.

NOTE

For more configuration options, consult the documentation included with the m4 source files.

Getting Ready to use Autoconf

Once you install m4 on your system, you can install Autoconf. As you'll see, the Autoconf installation process is almost identical to the m4 installation process, and that's because they are configured the same. With this in mind, if there are any special options you need to get m4 to install and run correctly on your system, you should use these same options with Autoconf.

You can install Autoconf as follows:

1. Unarchive the Autoconf source files and store them on your hard drive.

2. Change to the directory containing the source files and type `./configure`. This command configures Autoconf to use the default target and options. The command also sets the top level of the installation to `/usr/local`. When you install Autoconf later, this is where the Autoconf libraries and related files are installed. You can change the installation location using the `--prefix` option when you run configure, such as `--prefix=/usr/bin/local`.

3. Your system will start configuring the source. When it finishes, type **make** to build Autoconf.

4. Next, install Autoconf by typing **make install**.

5. After you test the installation, you can remove unneeded binaries and object files by typing **make clean**. To remove distribution files created by configure, type **make distclean**.

NOTE
For more configuration options, consult the documentation included with the Autoconf source files.

Setting up GTK+, GLib, and libIDL

With Mozilla, you should use GTK+, GLib 1.2.0 (or later) and libIDL 6.3 (or later). GTK+ is a GUI toolkit and Glib is a C library that includes functions for memory allocation, lists, trees, and other support routines; libIDL adds functions needed to create IDL headers and type libraries.

You can obtain GTK+ and GLib from one of the GNU mirror sites listed at `http://www.gnu.org/order/ftp.html`. These utilities are also distributed on the mozilla.org mirror sites in the `mozilla/libraries/source` directory. You can obtain libIDL from `http://www.rpi.edu/~veliaa/libIDL/libIDL-0.6.3.tar.gz`.

On Red Hat Linux systems, you should remove any existing developer packages before you install these tools. To do this, enter these commands:

```
rpm -e glib-devel
rpm -e gtk+-devel
rpm -e libidl-devel
```

You can install these tools exactly as you installed m4 and Autoconf. Simply repeat the steps outlined previously for GTK+, for Glib, and then for libIDL. Note that on Solaris systems, you must have X11R6, which is in Solaris 2.6, and you must also configure GTK+ and GLib using the option `--enable-xim=no`.

On x86 Linux systems, another way to install GTK+ and GLib is to get their RPM files. These files are available at any Mozilla mirror site. Access the folder `mozilla/libraries/RPMS/i386`.

The RPM files you want are for gtk+, gtk+devel, glib, glib-devel, libidl, libidl-devel. If you store these files in a single directory, you can install them with the following command:

```
rpm -i *.rpm
```

Otherwise, install the RPM files individually.

Installing the NSPR Library

NSPR is the portable runtime environment used by Mozilla. There are several different ways to install NSPR. You can get the RPM files or download the source from `client.mk`. You can also check out the source from CVS.

Setting up NSPR Using the RPM Files

On x86 Linux systems, you can install NSPR using the RPM package files. These files are in `source\mozilla` on the CD-ROM. Or you can visit the Mozilla mirror sites and access the folder `mozilla/libraries/RPMS/i386`.

In these folders, you'll find different versions of the NSPR RPM files: `nspr-pthreads` and `nspr-pthreads-devel`. Usually, you want to install the most recent versions of these files (the ones with the highest rev number). If you store these RPM files in the same directory, you can install them with the following command:

```
rpm -i *.rpm
```

Otherwise, install the RPM files individually.

Setting up NSPR Via CVS

While RPM files are great if you're on a Linux x86 system, most other Unix systems can't use these files. Instead, you'll have to check out the source via CVS. Before you get started, make sure you set the CVSROOT environment variable as follows:

```
setenv CVSROOT :pserver:anonymous@cvs-mirror.mozilla.org:/cvsroot
```

This setting for CVSROOT tells CVS to log you in to mozilla.org's CVS mirror using an anonymous login. Once the variable is set, you can access the server and login using the password anonymous. To check out NSPR, use the following command:

```
cvs co NSPR
```

Next, ensure that your LD_LIBRARY_PATH environment variable includes the path to the NSPR shared objects. If your NSPR distribution is in /usr/local/nspr, the shared objects are on /usr/local/nspr/lib and you can update LD_LIBRARY_PATH using either of the following commands:

```
setenv LD_LIBRARY_PATH
${LD_LIBRARY_PATH}:/usr/local/nspr/lib
export
LD_LIBRARY_PATH=${LD_LIBRARY_PATH}:/usr/local/nspr/lib
```

NOTE

HP-UX and AIX systems don't use the `LD_LIBRARY_PATH` variable. Instead, use `SHLIB_PATH` on HP-UX and `LIBPATH` on AIX.

Once the path is set up, you can build NSPR. NSPR's default build settings are usually sufficient. Still, you may want to change the threading options. Table 16-1 can help you determine the right options for your system.

TABLE 16-1: THREAD OPTIONS FOR NSPR

UNIX VERSION	THREAD OPTIONS
AIX: 4.2.1	By default, this system is configured to use pthreads. Local threads only and pthreads-user versions are also available. To build a local threads only version, set `CLASSIC_NSPR=1`. To build a pthreads-user version, set `PTHREADS_USER=1`.
BSD/386: 3.0, 2.1	By default, this system is configured to use local threads only.
Digital Unix: V4.0B	By default, this system is configured to use pthreads. To build a local threads-only version, set `CLASSIC_NSPR=1`.
FreeBSD: 2.2	By default, this system is configured to use local threads only.
HP-UX: B.10.10	By default, this system is configured to use DCE threads (Posix thread draft 4). To build a local threads-only version, set `CLASSIC_NSPR=1`.
HP-UX: B.11.00	By default, this system is configured to use pthreads. Local threads only and pthreads-user versions are also available. To build a local threads-only version, set `CLASSIC_NSPR=1`. To build a pthreads-user version, set `PTHREADS_USER=1`.
Irix: 6.2	By default, this system is configured to use combined (MxN) threading. A global thread is mapped to an Irix sproc, and local threads are implemented using user-level context switching. A pthreads version is also available. To build the pthreads version, set `USE_PTHREADS=1`.

Continued

TABLE 16-1: *(continued)*

UNIX VERSION	THREAD OPTIONS
Linux: 2.0	By default, this system is configured to use local threads only. A pthreads version, based on LinuxThreads, is also available. To build the pthreads version, set USE_PTHREADS=1.
MkLinux/PPC: 2.0	By default, this system is configured to use local threads only.
NCR: 3.0	By default, this system is configured to use local threads only.
NEC: 4.2	By default, this system is configured to use local threads only.
SCO_SV: 3.2	By default, this system is configured to use local threads only.
SINIX: 5.42	By default, this system is configured to use local threads only.
Solaris: 2.5.1 sparc, 2.5.1 x86	By default, this system is configured to use global threads only, in which every NSPR thread is mapped to a native Solaris UI thread. Local threads only and pthreads versions are also available. To build a local threads only version, set LOCAL_THREADS_ONLY=1. To build a pthreads version, set USE_PTHREADS=1. Additionally, if you are building NSPR with gcc and g++, set NS_USE_GCC=1.
SunOS 4: 4.1.3_U1	By default, this system is configured to use local threads only.
UNIXWARE: 2.1	By default, this system is configured to use local threads only.

Once you determine the threading you want for NSPR, you can add this option to the make command when you build the source.

NOTE
When you work with the source code, there are several terms you should be familiar with. The top of your source tree is the directory into which you checked out or extracted the source. The Mozilla source directory is where the Mozilla source files are located. If the top of your source tree is /moz_files, the Mozilla source files are located in /moz_files/mozilla. Within the Mozilla source directory, you'll find a directory called nsprpub. This directory contains the NSPR source files that you just checked out.

To build NSPR, follow these steps:

1. Access the NSPR source directory, which is usually located at `mozilla/nsprpub` within your source tree.

2. Enter the `gmake` command followed by any threading or build options you want to use.

Setting up NSPR by Downloading the Source

Another way to install NSPR is to download the source from `client.mk`. However, this assumes you've already checked out the Mozilla client using CVS as outlined in the section "Obtaining the Mozilla Source Code." Once you check out the client, you can use the following command to download the NSPR source and build it:

```
gmake -f mozilla/client.mk nspr
```

Obtaining the Mozilla Source Code

The CD-ROM contains several months' worth of source files that you can use to practice with. These files are in the `mozilla\source` directory and are organized by date. To obtain the latest files, however, you'll need to do so via FTP/HTTP or through CVS.

Getting the Code with CVS

If you've already installed the source files from the CD-ROM, you can update them via CVS. The advantage to this is that you have to download only files that have changed since your installation, and this can save a few hours of downloading. To download the source files with CVS, follow these steps:

1. Ensure that your `LD_LIBRARY_PATH` environment variable includes the path to the NSPR shared objects. If necessary, set the `CVSROOT` environment variable as follows:

```
setenv CVSROOT :pserver:anonymous@cvs-mirror.
mozilla.org:/cvsroot
```

NOTE

HP-UX and AIX systems don't use the `LD_LIBRARY_PATH` variable. Instead, use `SHLIB_PATH` on HP-UX and `LIBPATH` on AIX.

2. Next, login to CVS and check out the source code using the following command:

   ```
   cvs co mozilla/client.mk
   ```

3. If prompted for a password, enter anonymous.

4. Check out the source from the client make file as follows:

   ```
   gmake -f mozilla/client.mk checkout
   ```

5. This process builds only the viewer and apprunner. You still need to build Mozilla. If you want to update the build later, check out the source again by repeating the build process.

Getting the Code with FTP/HTTP

If you decide to obtain the source code via FTP or HTTP, you should do so using the mirror sites listed at `www.mozilla.org/mirrors.html`. The mirror sites are organized geographically and with this in mind, you should normally select the mirror site closest to your area of the world. At the mirror site, access the `mozilla/source` directory. Afterward, download and unarchive the most recent Mozilla source file.

Building Mozilla on Unix Systems

Once you've set up everything else, building Mozilla is fairly easy. Yet as you might expect, there are several ways to build Mozilla. You can manually drive the build or you can automate the build process by accepting the default build options.

Options for a Manual Build

The key reason to manually drive the build process is to set build options. Table 16-2 shows build options that you may want to use. The first column shows the configure options. The second column shows the corresponding make variables. The last column shows a usage for the option functions.

TABLE 16-2: KEY BUILD OPTIONS

CONFIGURE OPTION	ASSOCIATED MAKE VARIABLE	FUNCTION
--disable-asserts	UNIX_SKIP_ASSERTS=1	Disable error asserts during debugging
--disable-async-dns	NO_UNIX_ASYNC_DNS=1	Disable separate DNS thread
--disable-shared	NO_SHARED_LIB=1	Disable building of internal shared libs
--disable-static	NO_STATIC_LIB=1	Disable building of internal static libs
--enable-crypto	MOZ_SECURITY=1	Enable use of SSL
--enable-debug	MOZ_DEBUG=1	Enable debug symbols
--enable-editor	MOZ_EDITOR=1	Enable editor
--enable-gprof	GPROF="-pg"	Enable gprof symbols
--enable-homedir=\$val	MOZ_USER_DIR=$val	Set the home directory to \$val. The location of the mozilla user directory (default is ~/.mozilla).
--enable-idltool	MOZ_IDL_TOOL=1	Build IDL tool
--enable-java	MOZ_JAVA=1	Enable use of java applets; setting this will also unset FULL_STATIC_BUILD and NO_SHARED_LIB
--enable-ldap	NO_UNIX_LDAP=1	Enable LDAP
--enable-ldap	MOZ_LDAP=1	Enable LDAP directory access
--enable-mailnews	MOZ_MAIL_NEWS=1	Enable Mail & News

Continued

TABLE 16-2: *(continued)*

CONFIGURE OPTION	ASSOCIATED MAKE VARIABLE	FUNCTION
--enable-netcast	MOZ_NETCAST	Enable use of netcast
--enable-oji	MOZ_OJI=1	Enable use of Open JVM Interface; setting this will also unset FULL_STATIC_BUILD and NO_SHARED_LIB
--enable-profile	MOZILLA_GPROF=1	Enable profiling (Solaris only)
--enable-smart-mail	MOZ_SMART_MAIL=1	Enable HTML/RDF-based client-side mail
--enable-tests	ENABLE_TESTS=1	Enable test stubs
--enable-xterm-	Updates MOZ_UPDATE_XTERM=1	Update XTERM titles with current command
--enable-wrap-malloc	WRAP_MALLOC_CFLAGS= flags, MKSHLIB=opts	Wrap malloc calls (GNU linker only)
--with-fullcircle=\$dir	FULLCIRCLE_DIR=\$withval	Set the location of FullCircle headers and libraries
--with-jpeg=\$dir	JPEG_DIR=\$withval	Use system libjpeg in \$dir if more recent
--with-nspr=\$dir	NSPR_DIR=\$withval	Set the location of nspr headers and libraries
--with-png=\$dir	PNG_DIR=\$withval	Use system libpng in \$dir if more recent
--with-static-gtk	sysstaticgtk=\$withval	Link FTK statically if possible
--with-static-motif	sysstaticmotif=\$withval	Link motif statically if possible
--with-wrap-malloc=\$dir	WRAP_MALLOC_LIB=\$withval	The location of the malloc wrapper library
--with-zlib=\$dir	ZLIB_DIR=\$withval	Use system zlib in \$dir

When you build Mozilla, you pass build options directly to the configuration file, `configure.in`. `Configure.in` defines the environment settings, libraries, and make files used by Mozilla. The file also detects build options you set at the command line. This file is located in the root of the source code directory tree and can be found online in the folder `cvs-mirror.mozilla.org/webtools/lxr/source/`.

Environment variables can be used in addition to or in lieu of passing command-line options to the configuration file. You set environment variables in the `client.mk` file, which is also found in the root of the source code directory tree.

Building Mozilla Manually

Once you've determined the options you want to use, you can build Mozilla. Keep in mind that compile time is directly related to the speed of your processor, drives, and memory as well as the size of your memory and the available free space in memory and on disk. To speed up the compile process, you should reduce the workload on the system by closing unneeded applications. Here are some example compile times:

- 300 minutes on a 486DX4/100 system with 16MB RAM
- 25 minutes on a DEC-ALPHA with 512MB RAM
- 30 minutes on a Pentium Pro 200 with 128MB RAM
- 25 minutes on a PowerMac G3/300 with 128MB RAM

You have several build options. You can build Mozilla by passing in command-line options or by setting environment variables in `client.mk`. Or you can use the Unix Build Configurator to generate a script containing your build options and then use this script to build Mozilla. If you want to pass in command-line options, follow these steps to build Mozilla:

1. Access the Mozilla source directory, which is the directory where the Mozilla source files are located.

2. Generate the configure script by entering the command:

```
autoconf -l build/autoconf
```

3. Configure the build and put objects in the source tree. Here are several examples:

```
./configure --with-nspr=/usr/local/nspr --with-pthreads
./configure --with-nspr=/usr/local/nspr --enable-editor
./configure --with-nspr=/usr/local/nspr --enable-debug
```

NOTE

If you specified USE_PTHREADS when building NSPR, you must use the --with-pthreads option.

4. Build the necessary linking by entering the command:

gmake depend

5. Complete the build process typing the command:

gmake

6. The obj*/dist/bin contains the objects you need to run viewer and apprunner.

7. Set the MOZILLA_HOME environment variable to the absolute path to the binaries.

CROSS-REFERENCE

If you have problems building the source, see the troubleshooting guide in Appendix B.

If you want to use the Unix Build Configurator, follow these steps to build Mozilla:

1. Generate a configuration script by filling out the online form at http://cvs-mirror.mozilla.org/webtools/build/config.cgi and clicking the Preview Build Script button.

2. Save the script.

3. Build Mozilla by typing the following commands:

```
cvs co mozilla/client.mk
cd mozilla
gmake -f client.mk
```

When you work with the Mozilla source code, you need to keep in mind the following:

- If you change the configuration file, `configure.in`, you will need to re-run Autoconf to generate a new configure script. Also, anytime you check in a configuration file, CVS runs Autoconf automatically for you.

- Once you run configure, you have to run configure again only if you add or remove Makefiles. Unfortunately, you may accidentally check in new Makefiles. If this happens, you'll need to re-run configure. However, if you change a Makefile (rather then add or delete one), run `./config.status`, which updates the necessary files.

Running an Automated Build

Compared with a manual build, the automated build process is a snap. All you need to do is the following:

1. Access the Mozilla source directory, which is the directory where the Mozilla source files are located.

2. Enter the following command:

   ```
   gmake -f mozilla/client.mk build
   ```

3. Your system will build Mozilla for you. Be patient—it'll take a while.

Keep in mind that as you work with the Mozilla source code, you may need to re-run the build. If you want to update the source tree, repeat the CVS check out process outlined in the section "Obtaining the Mozilla Source."

Summary

If you plan to compile Mozilla on your system, setting up a build environment is a necessity. The build environment for Unix systems includes GNU Make, Perl 5, CVS, a C/C++ compiler, and essential libraries, such as Glib and libIDL. Once you've installed these tools, you can configure the build environment and build the source. Don't forget that Appendix B provides troubleshooting tips and resources.

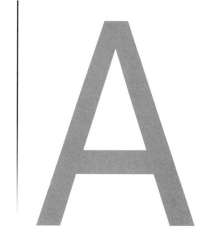

CVS Commands and Syntax

This appendix provides a summary of Concurrent Versions System (CVS) commands and syntax. CVS is a version control system that tracks file changes, enabling you to obtain current versions of files without having to download all of the Mozilla source code. Every time you work with the Mozilla source, you'll use CVS to check out modules and to check in your source changes.

NOTE
Because mozilla.org recommends that you use CVS Version 1.10 or later, this appendix doesn't list the commands that are applicable only to older versions of CVS.

CVS Command Syntax

Regardless of whether you use Windows, Unix, or Mac, the command syntax for CVS is generally the same. In a command-line version of CVS, you enter commands at the shell or command prompt. In a graphical version of CVS, you usually have to enter the options and arguments as inputs.

The basic command syntax for CVS is:

```
cvs [global_options] command [cmd_options] [cmd_args]
```

where *global_options* represents global options you want to specify for all CVS commands (if applicable), *command* represents the CVS command you want to issue, *cmd_options* represents the options for the command you are issuing, and *cmd_args* represents the arguments for the command. The command is the only mandatory parameter.

Global CVS Options

Global options are parameters you want to apply to all CVS commands (if applicable). Generally, once you set a global option, the option applies to all commands issued in the current sessions as well as future sessions. Because of this, you may actually need to unset a global option.

Key global options and their arguments are shown in Table A-1.

TABLE A-1: GLOBAL OPTIONS FOR CVS

QUICK LOOKUP	DESCRIPTION	OPTION FLAG	ARGUMENTS	USAGE
Authentication	Authenticates all communication between the client and the server. Generally, applicable only if you use a direct connection with GSSAPI.	-a	n/a	`cvs -a co SeaMonkeyAll`
CVS root directory	Sets the CVS root directory. Overrides the setting for the $CVSROOT environment variable.	-d	Rootdir	`cvs -d /src/cvsroot co SeaMonkeyAll`
CVS version	Checks the CVS version.	-v	n/a	`cvs -v`
Editor	Sets the editor use for log messages. Overrides the setting for the $CVSEDITOR and $EDITOR environment variables.	-e	Editor	`cvs -e notepad.exe co SeaMonkeyAll`
Encryption	Encrypts all communication between the client and the server. Generally, applicable only if you are using a direct connection with GSSAPI or Kerberos.	-x	n/a	`cvs -x co SeaMonkeyAll`
Gzip transfers	Sets the Gzip compression level for file transfers. Level 3 and 9 are the most commonly used.	-z	Level	`cvs -z9 update`
Help	Gets help on the options and usage of the specified command.	-H	n/a	`cvs -H add`
History logging	Overrides the default logging of commands in the history.	-l	n/a	`cvs -l commit`

Continued

311

TABLE A-1: *(continued)*

QUICK LOOKUP	DESCRIPTION	OPTION FLAG	ARGUMENTS	USAGE
Quiet mode	Generates output only for errors.	-Q	n/a	cvs -Q update
Read/Write files	Sets new working files to read and write mode.	-w	n/a	cvs -w update
Read-only files	Set new working files to read-only. The default is read and write.	-r	n/a	cvs -r update
Simulate execution	Don't execute the command. Instead give a report.	-n	n/a	cvs -n update
Source File	If your home directory contains a file called .cvsrc, options in this file are used in your CVS sessions. The home directory is set with the $HOMEDIR environment variable. To override .cvsrc settings, set the source file option so that you don't read the .cvsrc file, and thus don't use options set in the file.	-f	n/a	cvs -f co SeaMonkeyAll
Temporary directory	Sets a directory for temporary files. Overrides the setting for the $TMPDIR environment variable.	-T	Tempdir	cvs -T C:\mytemp co SeaMonkeyAll
Terse mode	Generate terse output for commands.	-q	n/a	cvs -q update
Trace	Trace CVS execution. Often used with -n option.	-t	n/a	cvs -t update
User variable	Set a user variable.	-s	Var=value	cvs -s test=BETA update

Common Command Options and Arguments

Some options are used by more than one command. You'll find that some options apply to all commands issued in the current session as well as future sessions. These commands are called *sticky* and must be unset to override the specified value.

Common options for commands and their arguments are shown in Table A-2.

TABLE A-2: COMMON OPTIONS FOR CVS COMMANDS

QUICK LOOKUP	DESCRIPTION	OPTION FLAG	ARGUMENTS	USAGE
Filter	Specified that file names should be filtered and in this case, .cvswrappers is used to determine how various file extensions are handled.	-W	n/a	cvs update -W
Ignore flags	Set to retrieve files even when there isn't a match for the tag or date.	-f	n/a	cvs update -f
Keyword substitution	Change how keywords and files are processed. This command is sticky and you will need to unset it.	-k	flag	cvs add -kb my.gif
Local directory	Run the command only in the current directory. Do not go through subdirectories.	-l	n/a	cvs update -l
Log message	Set the log message.	-m	message	cvs commit -m "updated ifdefs" test.cpp
Process recursively	Set to process directories recursively, which is the default.	-R	n/a	cvs update -R
Prune directories	Set to remove empty directories.	Cvs update -P		

QUICK LOOKUP	DESCRIPTION	OPTION FLAG	ARGUMENTS	USAGE
Revision	Set revision for retrieval/use. This command is sticky and you will need to unset it. Has two special tags: HEAD and BASE. HEAD refers to the most recent version available in the repository. BASE refers to the revision you last checked out into the current working directory.	-r	tag	cvs co -r BASE SeaMonkeyAll
Run program	Do not run the program.	-n	n/a	cvs commit -n test.cpp
Show retrieved source	Set to show retrieved source files in standard output rather than writing them in current directory.	-p	n/a	cvs update -p
Specify date	Used to obtain source files with dates no later than the specified date. This command is sticky and you will need to unset it. A wide variety of date formats are accepted. Examples include: 1999-06-15 06:00, 15 Jun 1999 06:00, and 15 Jun.	-D	"date"	cvs update -D "15 Jun"

Keyword Strings and Substitution

All sources files have default substitution modes, which are set in the repository and in the current working directory. These modes determine how keyword strings are substituted when files are added to the repository, checked out, checked in or updated. You set the substitution mode with the –k option.

The substitution modes are summarized in Table A-3.

TABLE A-3: SUBSTITUTION MODES

MODE	USAGE
-kkv	Creates keyword strings with the default format, such as $Revision: 1.1 $ for the Revision keyword.
-kkvl	Creates keyword strings such as -kkv but adds the name of user's locking revisions.
-kk	Creates only keyword name and omits values. This would create $Revision$ instead of $Revisions: 1.1 $.
-ko	Generates the keyword string as it appeared before the file was checked in.
-kb	Creates keywords as with -ko but also turns off conversion of line endings. Used mostly with binary files.
-kv	Creates only keyword values and omits the keyword strings. Often this value is used when you are exporting files.

Common CVS Commands

The sections that follow summarize commonly used CVS commands. You'll find a brief synopsis of the command and its options.

add

The add command is used to register files and directories in the repository. The syntax for add is:

```
add [options] [files/directories]
```

where *options* represents the command options and *files/directories* represents the files and/or directories you are registering. You can use the add command as follows:

```
cvs add qzs.c
cvs add —m "Updated the looping" qzs.c
```

The command accepts the options shown in Table A-4.

TABLE A-4: OPTIONS FOR ADD

OPTION	ARGUMENTS	USAGE
-k	mode	Changes how files and keywords are processed. This command is sticky and you will need to unset it if you want to remove the special processing.
-m	message	Sets the log message.

checkout

The checkout command is used to check out source modules. The syntax for checkout is:

```
cvs checkout [options] module1 [module2 module3 ... moduleZ]
```

where *options* represents the command options and *module1* is the first module you want to check out, *module2* is the second, and so on.

You can also use co and get to perform the same action. Because of this, the following commands have the same meaning:

```
cvs checkout SeaMonkeyAll
cvs co SeaMonkeyAll
cvs get SeaMonkeyAll
```

The command accepts the options shown in Table A-5.

TABLE A-5: OPTIONS FOR CHECKOUT

OPTION	ARGUMENTS	USAGE
-A	n/a	Removes any sticky options.
-c	n/a	Sorts the checkout files and copies to standard output.
-d	*dir*	Creates the specified directory for the working files instead of using the module name.
-D	*date*	Obtains source files with dates no later than the specified date.
-f	n/a	Ignore data and keyword flags when there otherwise wouldn't be a match. Thus, if no matching file is found, retrieve the most recent file.
-j	*tag:date*	Merges changes from the revision specified in first -j option into the revision specified with the second -j option. Or merges changes to source files in the working directory with the revision specified in the -j option.
-k	*mode*	Changes how files and keywords are processed. This command is sticky and you will need to unset it if you want to remove the special processing.
-l	n/a	Runs the command only in the current directory only (not recursively).
-n	n/a	Do not run any checkout program (as specified with the -o option in.
-N	n/a	Do not shorten module paths if -d is specified.
-p	n/a	Pipes files retrieved to standard output rather than writing them to the working directory.
-P	n/a	Prunes empty directories.
-R	n/a	Checks out directories recursively, which is the default.
-r	*tag*	Sets revision for checkout. This command is sticky and you will need to unset it.
-s	n/a	Sorts the checkout files by the status string and copies to standard output, then adds the status of all modules to the output.

commit

The `commit` command is used to check your changes into the repository. The syntax for `commit` is:

```
cvs commit [options] [files]
```

where *options* represents the command options and *files* represents the files you want to check in. If you don't specify files, all changes are checked in, which can be very bad.

You can also use `ci` to perform the same action. Before you check in new files, you should add them to the repository's master list with the `add` command.

Here's how you could use the `commit` command:

```
cvs commit -r 0.1 qzs.c
cvs commit -f qzs.c
```

The command accepts the options shown in Table A-6.

TABLE A-6: OPTIONS FOR COMMIT

OPTION	ARGUMENTS	USAGE
-F	file	Reads the log message from the specified file.
-l	n/a	Runs the command only in the current directory (not recursively). Does not go through subdirectories.
-m	message	Sets the log message.
-n	n/a	Does not run any module program.
-R	n/a	Commits directories recursively, which is the default.
-r	rev	Sets revision for the check in. Revision must be a branch or a revision on the main trunk that is higher than current revision numbers.

diff

The `diff` command is used to show the difference between versions of named files. The syntax for `diff` is:

```
cvs diff [options] [files]
```

where *options* represents the command options and *files* represents the files you want to examine. If you don't specify files, all files in the current working directory are compared with the revisions on which they are based.

Here's how you could use the `diff` command:

```
cvs diff -u -r 1.1 -r 1.3 qzs.c
cvs diff -u -r 1.1 -r 1.3 qzs.c qzt.c qzu.c > m-diffs
cvs diff —u —D "1999-06-15 06:00" —D "1999-06-18 12:30"
qzs.c
```

The command accepts the options shown in Table A-7.

TABLE A-7: OPTIONS FOR DIFF

OPTION	ARGUMENTS	USAGE
-D	*date1*	Sets the first comparison date.
-D	*date2*	Sets the second comparison date.
-k	*mode*	Processes keywords and their values using the specified mode.
-l	n/a	Runs the command only in the current directory. Does not go through subdirectories.
-R	n/a	Examines directories recursively, which is the default.
-r	*rev1*	Sets the first revision for the comparison.
-r	*rev2*	Sets the second revision for the comparison.

You can also set options to format the output. The most commonly used formatting options are shown in Table A-8.

TABLE A-8: FORMATTING OPTIONS FOR DIFF

OPTION	OUTPUT FORMATTING
-B	Ignores blank lines.
-c	Sets context lines.
-H	Hides common lines (show differences only).

OPTION	OUTPUT FORMATTING
-I	Ignores case.
-s	Reports identical files.
-t	Expands tabs.
-u	Uses unified lines.
-w	Ignores additional spaces.
-y	Shows side by side.

export

The export command is used to create a version of a source module that doesn't contain CVS information. In this way, you can export a module from CVS and use it outside of CVS. The syntax for export is:

```
cvs export [options] [rev/date] module1 [module2 module3 ...
moduleZ]
```

where *options* represents the command options, *rev/date* is the revision or date for exporting, and *module1* is the first module you want to export, *module2* is the second, and so on.

Here's how you could use the export command:

```
cvs export –kv –D "15 Jun" DirectorySDKSourceC
diff export –kv -r 1.1 DirectorySDKSourceC
```

The command accepts the options shown in Table A-9.

TABLE A-9: OPTIONS FOR EXPORT

OPTION	ARGUMENTS	USAGE
-d	*dir*	Exports into the specified directory instead of using the module name.
-D	*date*	Used to source files with dates no later than the specified date.

Continued

TABLE A-9: *(continued)*

OPTION	ARGUMENTS	USAGE
-f	n/a	Ignores data and keyword flags when there otherwise wouldn't be a match. Thus, if no matching file is found, retrieve the most recent file.
-k	*mode*	Changes how files and keywords are processed. This command is sticky, and you will need to unset it if you want to remove the special processing.
-l	n/a	Runs the command only in the current directory only (not recursively).
-n	n/a	Do not run any program (as specified with the -o option in the modules files).
-N	n/a	Do not shorten module paths if –d is specified.
-R	n/a	Checkout directories recursively, which is the default.
-r	tag	Sets revision to export.

history

CVS tracks a command history for each use of key commands. Use the `history` command to display this information. The syntax for `history` is:

```
cvs history [report] [flags] [options] [files]
```

where *report* is the report type, *flags* sets report flags, *options* sets additional options, and *files* is the list of files to examine. If you don't specify files to examine, history examines all files changes using the specified flags and options.

Here's how you could use the `history` command:

```
cvs history -T —a -D "Jan 1"
cvs history -T —a -D "Jan 1" qzs.c qzt.c qzu.c
```

Table A-10 summarizes the reports, flags, and options you can use with `history`.

TABLE A-10: PARAMETERS FOR EXPORT

OPTION	ARGUMENTS	USAGE
REPORTS		
-c	n/a	Creates report for all modified files.
-m	*module*	Creates report for specified module. (repeatable).
-o	n/a	Creates report for all checked out modules.
-T	n/a	Creates report for all tags.
-x	*rtype*	Creates report for a specific record type.
FLAGS		
-a	n/a	Shows report on all users rather than only your own user name.
-e	n/a	Shows report for all record types.
-l	n/a	Shows report for the last modification.
-w	n/a	Shows report where working directory matches.
OPTIONS		
-b	*str*	Go back to record with str in module/file/repos field.
-D	*date*	Reports from the date specified forward.
-f	*file*	Uses specified file (repeatable).
-n	*modulename*	Looks for in module (repeatable).
-p	*repos*	Looks in the named repository (repeatable).
-r	*rev/tag*	Looks for history since revision or tag.
-t	*tag*	Looks for history since tag.
-u	*user*	Looks for user name (repeatable).
-z	*timezone*	Output report for time zone (time offset), such as –0200.

log

The log command prints out log information for source files. The syntax for log is:

```
cvs log [options] [files]
```

where *options* represents the command options and *files* represents the files you want to examine. If you don't specify files or options, log prints all information that is available.

Here's how you could use the log command:

```
cvs log > currlog
cvs log -d "Jan 1"
cvs log -d "Jan 1" > "Feb 20"
```

The command accepts the options shown in Table A-11.

TABLE A-11: OPTIONS FOR LOG

OPTION	ARGUMENTS	USAGE
-b	n/a	Shows information for revisions on the default branch.
-d	*dates*	Shows information about revisions with a check-in date and time in the specified range or from the single specified date forward. Can use < or > symbols.
-h	n/a	Shows header information only.
-l	n/a	Runs only in current working directory and not recursively.
-N	n/a	Do not show tags for files.
-R	n/a	Shows only the name of the RCS file.
-r	*rev*	Shows information for the specified revisions. Don't use a space between the -r and the colon-separated revisions.
-s	*states*	Lists only revisions with the specified states (or Print information about revisions whose state attributes match one of the states given in the comma-separated list of states).

OPTION	ARGUMENTS	USAGE
-t	n/a	Shows headers and descriptive text.
-w	Logins	Shows information for the user names specified in a comma-separated list. Don't use a space between the -w and the logins.

login and logout

To prompt for a password and override the default settings, use the `login` command. To log out of the CVS server and remove login settings, use the `logout` command. The syntax is simply:

```
cvs login
```

or

```
cvs logout
```

update

The `update` command is used to update source files and modules in your local directory tree. Use this command to apply changes from the source repository since your last checkout or update. The syntax for the command is:

```
cvs update [options] [files]
```

where *options* represents the command options and *files* represents the files you want to update.

Here's how you could use the `update` command:

```
cvs update -A
cvs update -j 1.5 -j 1.6
```

The command accepts the options shown in Table A-12.

TABLE A-12: OPTIONS FOR UPDATE

OPTION	ARGUMENTS	USAGE
-A	n/a	Removes any sticky options.
-D	date	Checks out revisions as of the specified date. This option is sticky and you will need to unset it.
-d	n/a	Creates directories for the update.
-f	n/a	Forces a head revisions match if tag or date specified is not found.
-I	ignF	Specified files to ignore for the update. This option is sticky and you unset it by using -I!
-j	rev	Merges changes for the specified revision. This option is repeatable.
-k	mode	Uses the keyword expansion mode specified.
-l	n/a	Runs the command only in the current directory. Do not go through subdirectories.
-P	n/a	Prunes empty directories.
-p	n/a	Pipes files retrieved to standard output rather than writing them to the working directory.
-R	n/a	Updates directories recursively, which is the default.
-r	tag	Sets revision for update. This command is sticky and you will need to unset it.
-w	wrapper	Specifies a file name wrapper for the update.

B

Netscape Module Summary and Troubleshooting Guide

At mozilla.org, you'll find many different open source projects, and this appendix is your guide to them. The appendix starts with a module-by-module resource that you can use to aid your development efforts. You'll find a brief analysis of each major module and its key features — all designed to help you find what you need to work with Netscape open source projects. The final component of the appendix is a guide for troubleshooting build and development problems. Be sure to check the mozilla.org Web site for updates.

Mozilla Projects and Modules

The sections that follow provide a brief summary of source code modules available at mozilla.org. Once you find the module you want to work with, you shouldn't have any problems obtaining the information you need. However, you'll be able to use the references more efficiently if you understand how this section is organized. The first module entry, titled "Module: Sample," explains the structure for entries. You should review this entry before moving forward.

NOTE

The module list, projects, and checkout procedures will change over time. The key reason for this is that outdated projects will be halted and stable projects may eventually be merged into the main Mozilla build.

Module: Sample

Module: Sample provides an example of working with reference entries. (As you can see, the heading provides the module name and a brief summary of the module.)

- **LXR Location:** A Mozilla Cross Reference URL for quick access to the module's source code. Enter the URL in your browser, such as:

  ```
  lxr.mozilla.org/mozilla/source/sample/
  ```

- **Source Location:** The relative location of the source in your local development tree after retrieval, such as:

  ```
  mozilla/modules/sample
  ```

- **Primary Language:** The primary programming language used in the module. If the module uses multiple programming languages, these are separated by commas, such as:

  ```
  C, C++
  ```

- **Project:** The open source project the module is associated with. Basically, this tells you if the module is a part of a larger project or is its own project. Here the Sample module is part of its own project:

  ```
  Netscape Sample Project
  ```

■ **CVS Checkout:** The module/code base to use when checking out the module. Entries separated by commas on a single line provide alternative checkout names. The following module could be checked out with `SeaMonkeyAll` or `mozilla/sample`:

```
SeaMonkeyAll, mozilla/sample
```

When you see entries on different lines, you'll know that you need to obtain more than one source module. In this example, you'll need to check out `mozilla/sample` and `mozilla/process`:

```
mozilla/sample
mozilla/process
```

Module: Aurora/RDF BE

Aurora/RDF BE provides the Resource Description Framework classes needed to manage Internet resources using a graphical UI.

■ **LXR Location**

```
lxr.mozilla.org/mozilla/source/rdf/
```

■ **Source Location**

```
mozilla/rdf
```

■ **Primary Language**

```
C, C++, XUL, IDL, CSS
```

■ **Project**

```
Mozilla
```

■ **CVS Checkout**

```
SeaMonkeyAll, mozilla/rdf
```

Module: Berkeley DB

Berkeley DB provides the database structure used with some Mozilla clients; licensed from the University of California.

■ **LXR Location**

```
lxr.mozilla.org/mozilla/source/dbm
```

329

■ **Source Location**

```
mozilla/dbm
```

■ **Primary Language**

```
C
```

■ **Project**

```
Mozilla
```

■ **CVS Checkout**

```
SeaMonkeyAll, mozilla/dbm
```

Module: Browser Hooks

Browser Hooks provides user-scriptable hooks into the front-end interface.

■ **LXR Location**

```
lxr.mozilla.org/mozilla/source/modules/libhook/
```

■ **Source Location**

```
mozilla/modules/libhook
```

■ **Primary Language**

```
C
```

■ **Project**

```
Mozilla XP-COM
```

■ **CVS Checkout**

```
mozilla/libhook
```

Module: Build Config

Build Config provides source needed to build and configure Mozilla.

■ **LXR Location**

```
lxr.mozilla.org/mozilla/source/build/
lxr.mozilla.org/mozilla/source/config/
```

```
lxr.mozilla.org/mozilla/source/l10n/
```

■ **Source Location**

```
mozilla/build
mozilla/config
mozilla/l10n
```

■ **Primary Language**

```
C
```

■ **Project**

```
Mozilla
```

■ **CVS Checkout**

```
SeaMonkeyAll
```

Module: Calendar

Calendar provides the Netscape calendar client; it is used in conjunction with Netscape Directory SDK.

■ **LXR Location**

```
lxr.mozilla.org/mozilla/source/calendar/
```

■ **Source Location**

```
mozilla/modules/calendar
```

■ **Primary Language**

```
C++
```

■ **Project**

```
Netscape Calendar Client
```

■ **CVS Checkout**

```
CalendarClient
```

Module: CCK

CCK provides tools to help distributors customize the client for download, installation, and distribution.

- **LXR Location**

  `lxr.mozilla.org/mozilla/source/cck/`

- **Source Location**

  `mozilla/cck`

- **Primary Language**

  `C++`

- **Project**

  `Client Customization Kit`

- **CVS Checkout**

  `mozilla/cck`

Module: Clipping and Compositing

Clipping and Compositing provides a view manager for the NGLayout engine.

- **LXR Location**

  `lxr.mozilla.org/mozilla/source/view/`

- **Source Location**

  `mozilla/view`

- **Primary Language**

  `C++`

- **Project**

  `Mozilla NGLayout`

- **CVS Checkout**

  `SeaMonkeyAll, mozilla/view`

Module: Composer

Composer provides Mozilla editor source.

- **LXR Location**

  lxr.mozilla.org/mozilla/source/editor/

- **Source Location**

  mozilla/editor

- **Primary Language**

  C++, XML

- **Project**

  Mozilla Editor

- **CVS Checkout**

  SeaMonkeyAll, SeaMonkeyEditor

Module: Dialup

Dialup implements Internet account client and server for creating Internet accounts online.

- **LXR Location**

  lxr.mozilla.org/mozilla/source/cmd/dialup/

- **Source Location**

  mozilla/cmd/dialup

- **Primary Language**

  JavaScript, Java, HTML

- **Project**

  Online Internet Account Creation

- **CVS Checkout**

  mozilla/cmd/dialup

Module: Directory SDK for C

Directory SDK for C provides the Netscape Directory SDK for LDAP servers with implementations for C.

- **LXR Location**

  `lxr.mozilla.org/mozilla/source/directory/c-sdk/`

- **Source Location**

  `mozilla/directory/c-sdk`

- **Primary Language**

  `C`

- **Project**

  `Netscape Directory SDK`

- **CVS Checkout**

  `DirectorySDKSourceC`
  `DirectorySDKSourceBuild`

Module: Directory SDK for Java

Directory SDK for Java provides the Netscape Directory SDK for LDAP servers with implementations for Java.

- **LXR Location**

  `lxr.mozilla.org/mozilla/source/directory/java-sdk/`

- **Source Location**

  `mozilla/directory/java-sdk`

- **Primary Language**

  `Java`

- **Project**

  `Netscape Directory SDK`

■ CVS Checkout

```
DirectorySDKSourceJava
```

Module: Directory SDK for Perl

Directory SDK for Perl provides the Netscape Directory SDK for LDAP servers with implementations for Perl.

■ **LXR Location**

```
lxr.mozilla.org/mozilla/source/directory/perldap/
```

■ **Source Location**

```
mozilla/directory/perldap
```

■ **Primary Language**

```
Perl
```

■ **Project**

```
Netscape Directory SDK
```

■ **CVS Checkout**

```
PerLDAP
```

Module: Document Object Model

Document Object Model implements Mozilla's core DOM as well as IDL interfaces for JavaScript and HTML.

■ **LXR Location**

```
lxr.mozilla.org/mozilla/source/dom/
```

■ **Source Location**

```
mozilla/dom
```

■ **Primary Language**

```
C++
```

■ **Project**

```
Mozilla NGLayout
```

■ CVS Checkout

```
SeaMonkeyAll, mozilla/dom
```

Module: Electrical Fire

Electrical Fire implements a Java Virtual Machine that uses Just In Time compilation.

■ **LXR Location**

```
lxr.mozilla.org/mozilla/source/ef/
```

■ **Source Location**

```
mozilla/ef
```

■ **Primary Language**

```
C++
```

■ **Project**

```
Electrical Fire
```

■ **CVS Checkout**

```
mozilla/ef
mozilla/nsprpub
```

Module: Embeddable Web Browser

Embeddable Web Browser implements a content container that can be used to host various types of data viewers.

■ **LXR Location**

```
lxr.mozilla.org/mozilla/source/webshell/
```

■ **Source Location**

```
mozilla/webshell
```

■ **Primary Language**

```
C++
```

■ **Project**

```
Mozilla NGLayout
```

■ **CVS Checkout**

```
SeaMonkeyAll, mozilla/webshell
```

Module: GTK

GTK implements the Unix GTK toolkit graphics and widgets.

■ **LXR Location**

```
lxr.mozilla.org/mozilla/source/gfx/src/gtk
lxr.mozilla.org/mozilla/source/widget/src/gtk
```

■ **Source Location**

```
mozilla/gfx/src/gtk
mozilla/widget/src/gtk
```

■ **Primary Language**

```
C++
```

■ **Project**

```
Mozilla Classic (no longer being actively developed)
```

■ **CVS Checkout**

```
MozillaSourceUnix
```

Module: I18N Library

I18N Library provides the internationalization and localization source for Mozilla.

■ **LXR Location**

```
lxr.mozilla.org/mozilla/source/lib/libi18n/
```

■ **Source Location**

```
mozilla/lib/libi18n
```

■ **Primary Language**

```
C
```

- **Project**

  ```
  Internationalization and Localization
  ```

- **CVS Checkout**

  ```
  SeaMonkeyAll
  ```

Module: ImageLib

ImageLib provides an image library and utilities for decoding and displaying images.

- **LXR Location**

  ```
  lxr.mozilla.org/mozilla/source/modules/libimg
  ```

- **Source Location**

  ```
  mozilla/modules/libimg
  ```

- **Primary Language**

  ```
  C, C++
  ```

- **Project**

  ```
  Mozilla
  ```

- **CVS Checkout**

  ```
  SeaMonkeyAll
  ```

Module: Java and JS Capability-Based Security

Java and JS Capability-Based Security provides source for managing privileges and capabilities.

- **LXR Location**

  ```
  lxr.mozilla.org/mozilla/source/caps/
  ```

- **Source Location**

  ```
  mozilla/caps
  ```

- **Primary Language**

  ```
  C, C++
  ```

■ **Project**

```
Mozilla
```

■ **CVS Checkout**

```
SeaMonkeyAll, mozilla/caps
```

Module: Java Stubs (OJI)

Java Stubs (OJI) provides Open JVM Integration extensions that enable Java virtual machines to be plugged into Mozilla.

■ **LXR Location**

```
lxr.mozilla.org/mozilla/source/modules/oji/
lxr.mozilla.org/mozilla/source/nav-java/
lxr.mozilla.org/mozilla/source/sun-java/
```

■ **Source Location**

```
mozilla/modules/oji/
mozilla/nav-java/
mozilla/sun-java/
```

■ **Primary Language**

```
C, C++, Java
```

■ **Project**

```
Open Java Integration
```

■ **CVS Checkout**

```
mozilla/modules/oji
mozilla/nav-java
mozilla/sun-java
```

Module: JavaScript

JavaScript implements core JavaScript support and the JavaScript runtime engine as well as LiveConnect, PerlConnect and XPConnect extensions.

- **LXR Location**

  `lxr.mozilla.org/mozilla/source/js/`

- **Source Location**

  `mozilla/js`

- **Primary Language**

  `C, C++, Java, JavaScript, IDL`

- **Project**

  `Mozilla`

- **CVS Checkout**

  `mozilla/js`

Module: JavaScript Debugger

JavaScript Debugger provides a debugging support module for the Netscape JavaScript engine, a Java-based GUI debugger for JavaScript, a JavaScript logging tool, and a console debugger.

- **LXR Location**

  `lxr.mozilla.org/mozilla/source/js/jsd/`
  `lxr.mozilla.org/mozilla/source/js/jsdj/`

- **Source Location**

  `mozilla/js/jsd`
  `mozilla/js/jsdj/`

- **Primary Language**

  `C, JavaScript`

- **Project**

  `Mozilla NGLayout`

- **CVS Checkout**

  `mozilla/js`

Module: JPEG Image Handling

JPEG Image Handling provides the image libraries and utilities for decoding and displaying JPEG images; it is licensed from the Independent JPEG Group as part of their free JPEG software library.

- **LXR Location**

  lxr.mozilla.org/mozilla/source/jpeg/

- **Source Location**

  mozilla/jpeg

- **Primary Language**

  C, Assembler

- **Project**

  Mozilla

- **CVS Checkout**

  SeaMonkeyAll

Module: Macintosh FE

Macintosh FE provides the platform-dependent front-end for Mac as implemented in Classic Mozilla.

- **LXR Location**

  lxr.mozilla.org/mozilla/source/cmd/macfe

- **Source Location**

  mozilla/cmd/macfe

- **Primary Language**

  C++

- **Project**

  Classic Mozilla (no longer maintained)

- **CVS Checkout**

  `MozillaSourceMac`

Module: MIMELib

MIMELib implements a general-purpose MIME parser for Mozilla.

- **LXR Location**

  `lxr.mozilla.org/mozilla/source/lib/libmime/`

- **Source Location**

  `mozilla/lib/libmime`

- **Primary Language**

  `C`

- **Project**

  `Mozilla`

- **CVS Checkout**

  `SeaMonkeyAll`

Module: NetLib

NetLib implements the core networking libraries for Mozilla.

- **LXR Location**

  `lxr.mozilla.org/mozilla/source/network/`

- **Source Location**

  `mozilla/network`

- **Primary Language**

  `C, C++`

- **Project**

  `Mozilla`

■ CVS Checkout

```
SeaMonkeyAll
```

Module: New HTML Layout Engine

New HTML Layout Engine implements the new layout engine with support for HTML, CSS, DOM, XML, XUL, and XSL.

■ **LXR Location**

```
lxr.mozilla.org/mozilla/source/layout/
```

■ **Source Location**

```
mozilla/layout
```

■ **Primary Language**

```
C++
```

■ **Project**

```
Mozilla NGLayout
```

■ **CVS Checkout**

```
SeaMonkeyAll, SeaMonkeyLayout
```

Module: New HTML Parser

New HTML Parser implements the HTML parser for the new layout engine.

■ **LXR Location**

```
lxr.mozilla.org/mozilla/source/htmlparser/
```

■ **Source Location**

```
mozilla/htmlparser
```

■ **Primary Language**

```
C++
```

■ **Project**

```
Mozilla NGLayout
```

■ **CVS Checkout**

```
SeaMonkeyAll
```

Module: NSPR

NSPR implements the Netscape Portable Runtime API.

■ **LXR Location**

```
lxr.mozilla.org/mozilla/source/nsprpub/
```

■ **Source Location**

```
mozilla/nsprpub
```

■ **Primary Language**

```
C, C++
```

■ **Project**

```
NSPR
```

■ **CVS Checkout**

```
SeaMonkeyAll
ns/nspr20
```

Module: PICS

PICS implements Platform for Internet Content Selection used for rating online content.

■ **LXR Location**

```
lxr.mozilla.org/mozilla/source/lib/libpics/
```

■ **Source Location**

```
mozilla/lib/libpics
```

■ **Primary Language**

```
C
```

■ **Project**

```
Mozilla
```

- **CVS Checkout**

```
SeaMonkeyAll
```

Module: Plug-ins

Plug-ins provides a plug-in manager, plug-in file i/o utilities, and other elements needed to implement support for Netscape plug-ins.

- **LXR Location**

```
lxr.mozilla.org/mozilla/source/modules/plugin/
```

- **Source Location**

```
mozilla/plugin
```

- **Primary Language**

```
C++
```

- **Project**

```
Mozilla
```

- **CVS Checkout**

```
SeaMonkeyAll, mozilla/plugin
```

Module: PNG Image Handling

PNG Image Handling implements additional utilities needed to support PNG images via the Image Library.

- **LXR Location**

```
lxr.mozilla.org/mozilla/source/lib/libcnv/
```

- **Source Location**

```
mozilla/lib/libcnv/
```

- **Primary Language**

```
C
```

■ **Project**

  `Mozilla`

■ **CVS Checkout**

  `SeaMonkeyAll`

Module: Preferences

Preferences provides preference and profile management libraries in Mozilla.

■ **LXR Location**

  `lxr.mozilla.org/mozilla/modules/libpref/`

■ **Source Location**

  `mozilla/modules/libpref`

■ **Primary Language**

  `C, C++`

■ **Project**

  `Mozilla`

■ **CVS Checkout**

  `SeaMonkeyAll, mozilla/modules/libpref`

Module: Progress Window

Progress Window implements the progress windows for Mozilla.

■ **LXR Location**

  `lxr.mozilla.org/mozilla/source/modules/progress/`

■ **Source Location**

  `mozilla/modules/progress`

■ **Primary Language**

  `C++`

■ **Project**

    `Mozilla`

■ **CVS Checkout**

    `SeaMonkeyAll, mozilla/modules/progress`

Module: Registry

Registry implements cross-platform registry functions.

■ **LXR Location**

    `lxr.mozilla.org/mozilla/source/modules/libreg/`

■ **Source Location**

    `mozilla/modules/libreg`

■ **Primary Language**

    `C`

■ **Project**

    `Mozilla`

■ **CVS Checkout**

    `SeaMonkeyAll, mozilla/modules/libreg`

Module: Security Stubs

Security Stubs provides stubs necessary to implement security features into Mozilla, such as support for SSL certificates.

■ **LXR Location**

    `lxr.mozilla.org/mozilla/source/modules/security/`

■ **Source Location**

    `mozilla/modules/security`

■ **Primary Language**

    `C`

- **Project**

  ```
  Mozilla
  ```

- **CVS Checkout**

  ```
  SeaMonkeyAll, mozilla/modules/security
  ```

Module: Silent Download

Silent Download implements Mozilla's silent download feature, whereby files can be downloaded to a user's system without interfering with their network performance.

- **LXR Location**

  ```
  lxr.mozilla.org/mozilla/source/silentdl/
  ```

- **Source Location**

  ```
  mozilla/silentdl
  ```

- **Primary Language**

  ```
  C++, IDL
  ```

- **Project**

  ```
  Silent Download
  ```

- **CVS Checkout**

  ```
  SeaMonkeyAll, mozilla/silentdl
  ```

Module: Smart Update

Smart Update implements Mozilla's smart update feature, enabling the browser to updated components automatically.

- **LXR Location**

  ```
  lxr.mozilla.org/mozilla/source/modules/softupdt/
  ```

- **Source Location**

  ```
  mozilla/modules/softupdt
  ```

- **Primary Language**

  C, C++

- **Project**

  Mozilla

- **CVS Checkout**

  SeaMonkeyAll, mozilla/modules/softupdt

Module: Windows FE

Windows FE implements the platform-dependent front-end for Windows.

- **LXR Location**

  lxr.mozilla.org/mozilla/source/cmd/wincom/
  lxr.mozilla.org/mozilla/source/cmd/winfe/

- **Source Location**

  mozilla/cmd/wincom
  mozilla/cmd/winfe

- **Primary Language**

  C, C++

- **Project**

  Classic Mozilla (no longer maintained)

- **CVS Checkout**

  MozillaSourceWin

Module: XML

XML implements an XML parser for Mozilla.

- **LXR Location**

  lxr.mozilla.org/mozilla/source/expat/

- **Source Location**

  mozilla/expat

- **Primary Language**

  C

- **Project**

  `Mozilla`

- **CVS Checkout**

  `SeaMonkeyAll`

Module: XPApps

XPApps implements the cross-platform application shell.

- **LXR Location**

  `lxr.mozilla.org/mozilla/source/xpfe/`

- **Source Location**

  `mozilla/xpfe`

- **Primary Language**

  `C, C++`

- **Project**

  `Mozilla NGLayout`

- **CVS Checkout**

  `SeaMonkeyAll, SeaMonkeyLayout`

Module: XPCOM

XPCOM implements the cross-platform component object model.

- **LXR Location**

  `lxr.mozilla.org/mozilla/source/xpcom/`

- **Source Location**

  `mozilla/xpcom`

- **Primary Language**

```
C++, IDL
```

- **Project**

  ```
  Mozilla
  ```

- **CVS Checkout**

  ```
  SeaMonkeyAll
  ```

Module: XPToolkit

XPToolkit implements the cross-platform front-end interface and widgets.

- **LXR Location**

  ```
  lxr.mozilla.org/mozilla/source/xpfe/
  ```

- **Source Location**

  ```
  mozilla/xpfe
  ```

- **Primary Language**

  ```
  C++, CSS, HTML, XUL, XML
  ```

- **Project**

  ```
  Mozilla
  ```

- **CVS Checkout**

  ```
  SeaMonkeyAll, SeaMonkeyNGLayout
  ```

Module: Zlib

Zlib implements a general-purpose data compression library and is used in HTTP compression.

- **LXR Location**

  ```
  lxr.mozilla.org/mozilla/modules/zlib/
  ```

- **Source Location**

  ```
  mozilla/modules/zlib
  ```

- ■ **Primary Language**

  C

- ■ **Project**

  `Mozilla`

- ■ **CVS Checkout**

  `SeaMonkeyAll`

Troubleshooting Build and Development Problems

Part IV, "Developing and Building Mozilla," provides extensive coverage of the Mozilla build environment. If you are having problems building Mozilla, this should be your first resource. You'll also find that mozilla.org provides a helpful discussion forum where you can get your build problems resolved. Use the newsgroup `netscape.public.mozilla.builds` or the mailing list `mozilla-builds@mozilla.org`.

Most build problems have to do with environment settings. Appendix C lists open source discussions and forums you can use for guidance and advice on particular development areas. The next sections examine common build problems by platform, and then, you'll find a table containing common error codes used in Mozilla.

Common Build Problems on Windows

You'll find that building Mozilla on Windows systems is much less problematic than Unix, but if you do run into problems, follow these steps:

1. Ensure that you have all the standard tools and are using the recommend versions discussed in Chapter 14, and noted online at `http://www.mozilla.org/build/win32.html`.

2. Build on a Win32 system, such as Windows 95, 98, or NT, even if your target is another Windows platform.

3. Be certain to set the necessary environment variables, especially MOZ_SRC, which points to the source directory, and MOZ_TOOLS, which points to the GNU/build tools. MOZ_TOOLS shouldn't include bin, where the GNU executables are stored. Also, ensure that there are no spaces at the end of variable assignments.

4. Make sure you extracted the source using an Unzip utility that supports long filenames. If you didn't, you may get directory-related errors.

5. Use the standard cmd.exe environment to build. Don't use the 4nt command shell.

6. If you are still unable to build, ask for help in the build newsgroup or mailing list.

Common Build Problems on MacPPC

The Mac build environment is managed through CodeWarrior. CodeWarrior can give you a lot of grief if things aren't set up properly. If you are having build problems, follow these steps to solve common problems:

1. Ensure that you have all the standard tools and are using the recommend versions discussed in Chapter 15 and noted online at http://www.mozilla.org /build/mac.html.

2. Build on a MacPPC. If you do not, you'll need the specific build source for your environment, such as Rhapsody.

3. If you have problems with MacPerl, several things could be wrong. First, ensure that you've mapped the .pl extension properly (and used Mac line feeds in doing so). If Mac Perl freezes repeatedly, it may not be able to find CodeWarrior. Try starting CodeWarrrior before running your script.

4. If you see AppleEvents errors, you are probably having a problem with MacPerl. Try allocating more memory to MacPerl (adding 1MB should do it). This should clear up the problem.

5. If PowerPlant.mcp fails to compile or you have other compile problems, you may need more free memory. Try closing other applications before starting the compiler. You'll need up to 32MB free for some large projects.

6. If you can't build the MemAllocatorStubs, your ToolServer environment is not set up correctly. Double-check the setup. Also, you shouldn't run multiple versions of ToolServer. If you are, this could be causing a problem. You may need to remove other versions of ToolServer or make sure you launch the appropriate version before you try to build Mozilla.

7. If JavaScriptPPC.mcp fails to compile, you may be building the wrong target. Make sure you're using the build scripts in `mozilla/build/mac` and the target is either JavaScriptNoJSJ or JavaScriptNoJSJDebug. If you are using the correct tools and targets, try compiling jsinterp.c by itself. To do this, select jsinterp.c in the JavaScriptPPC.mcp project window and press command-K to compile it.

Common Build Problems on Unix

Trying to build Mozilla on Unix can be frustrating, especially if you are using a variation that doesn't have standard support. A great resource to turn to when you are having problems is the Unix Build Configurator, which produces a script that you can save and use to configure your Mozilla build. Before you try anything else, give configurator a try:

```
http://cvs-mirror.mozilla.org/webtools/build/config.cgi
```

If you are still having build problems, try the following:

1. Ensure that you have all the standard tools and are using the recommend versions discussed in Chapter 16 and noted online at `http://www.mozilla.org /build/unix.html`.

2. Ensure that you've downloaded NSPR; this is required for Unix.

3. Ensure that you've set `LD_LIBRARY_PATH` to point to the necessary libraries, such as GTK and NSPR. On AIX, set `LIBPATH` accordingly. On HP-UX, set `SHLIB_PATH` accordingly.

4. Make sure you have only one installation of your preferred Unix toolkit, such as GTK.

5. If you still can't build, ask for help in the build newsgroup or mailing list.

Common Error Codes

After you resolve build problems, you may also have problems with development — namely syntax, structure, and error checking and handling. In Chapter 12, you'll find pointers on how to check for and handle errors. If you don't check for and handle errors, you'll have problems.

To detect and handle errors, refer to Table B-1, which contains a complete listing of common error codes and their associated constants.

TABLE B-1: COMMON ERROR CODES

ERROR CODE CONSTANT	DESCRIPTION
PR_ACCESS_FAULT_ERROR	An invalid memory address was specified.
PR_ADDRESS_IN_USE_ERROR	Network address specified is in use.
PR_ADDRESS_NOT_AVAILABLE_ERROR	Network address is not available.
PR_ADDRESS_NOT_SUPPORTED_ERROR	Network address specified is not supported.
PR_BAD_ADDRESS_ERROR	Network address specified is invalid.
PR_BAD_DESCRIPTOR_ERROR	File descriptor is invalid.
PR_BUFFER_OVERFLOW_ERROR	Buffer overflow because the value retrieved is too large.
PR_CONNECT_REFUSED_ERROR	Peer refused network connection.
PR_CONNECT_RESET_ERROR	Network connection reset by peer.
PR_CONNECT_TIMEOUT_ERROR	Connection timeout.
PR_DEADLOCK_ERROR	Performing the requested operation would have caused a deadlock. The deadlock was avoided.
PR_DEVICE_IS_LOCKED_ERROR	Device needed to perform request is locked.
PR_DIRECTORY_CORRUPTED_ERROR	Directory requested appears to be corrupt.
PR_DIRECTORY_LOOKUP_ERROR	Directory lookup failed.
PR_DIRECTORY_NOT_EMPTY_ERROR	Directory isn't empty and cannot be deleted.
PR_DIRECTORY_OPEN_ERROR	Directory could not be opened.
PR_END_OF_FILE_ERROR	Encountered end of file unexpectedly.
PR_FILE_EXISTS_ERROR	File creation failed; the file already exists.
PR_FILE_IS_BUSY_ERROR	Operation cannot be performed; the file is busy.
PR_FILE_IS_LOCKED_ERROR	File is already locked.
PR_FILE_NOT_FOUND_ERROR	Requested file cannot be found.
PR_FILE_SEEK_ERROR	Encountered unexpected seek error.
PR_FILESYSTEM_MOUNTED_ERROR	Requested operation cannot be completed; the file system is busy or not mounted.

Continued

355

TABLE B-1: *(continued)*

ERROR CODE CONSTANT	DESCRIPTION
PR_FIND_SYMBOL_ERROR	Symbol could not be found.
PR_ILLEGAL_ACCESS_ERROR	An invalid memory address was specified.
PR_IN_PROGRESS_ERROR	Operation has not completed and is still in progress.
PR_INSUFFICIENT_RESOURCES_ERROR	Insufficient system resources to complete request.
PR_INVALID_ARGUMENT_ERROR	Invalid argument passed in function.
PR_INVALID_METHOD_ERROR	Function cannot be used with the specified file descriptor.
PR_INVALID_DEVICE_STATE_ERROR	Operation cannot be completed; the device is in an invalid state.
PR_INVALID_STATE_ERROR	Operation cannot be completed; the object is in an invalid state.
PR_IO_ERROR	Encountered an unspecified I/O error.
PR_IO_PENDING_ERROR	Attempted I/O operation but file descriptor is currently busy.
PR_IO_TIMEOUT_ERROR	I/O operation has timed out.
PR_IS_CONNECTED_ERROR	Network file descriptor is already connected.
PR_IS_DIRECTORY_ERROR	Attempted to perform a file operation on a directory.
PR_LOAD_LIBRARY_ERROR	Dynamic library did not load.
PR_LOOP_ERROR	Error in the symbolic link loop.
PR_NAME_TOO_LONG_ERROR	Filename is too long.
PR_NETWORK_UNREACHABLE_ERROR	Specified network address currently is unreachable.
PR_NO_ACCESS_RIGHTS_ERROR	Calling thread does not have permission to perform operation.
PR_NO_DEVICE_SPACE_ERROR	Device is full; file is not written.
PR_NO_MORE_FILES_ERROR	No more entries in the directory.

ERROR CODE CONSTANT	DESCRIPTION
PR_NOT_CONNECTED_ERROR	Network file descriptor is not connected.
PR_NOT_DIRECTORY_ERROR	Attempted to perform directory operation on a file.
PR_NOT_IMPLEMENTED_ERROR	Function is not implemented.
PR_NOT_SAME_DEVICE_ERROR	Cannot rename file/directory across devices.
PR_NOT_SOCKET_ERROR	Not a network file descriptor.
PR_NOT_TCP_SOCKET_ERROR	Not a TCP-file descriptor.
PR_OPERATION_NOT_SUPPORTED_ERROR	Operation is not supported by the platform.
PR_OUT_OF_MEMORY_ERROR	Not enough memory to perform request.
PR_PENDING_INTERRUPT_ERROR	Thread interrupted and operation is terminated.
PR_PROC_DESC_TABLE_FULL_ERROR	Cannot complete operation; the process table for holding open file descriptors is full.
PR_PROTOCOL_NOT_SUPPORTED_ERROR	Protocol not supported on host.
PR_READ_ONLY_FILESYSTEM_ERROR	Operation attempted to write to a read-only file.
PR_REMOTE_FILE_ERROR	Connection to the remote file is no longer available.
PR_SOCKET_ADDRESS_IS_BOUND_ERROR	Address is already bound.
PR_SYS_DESC_TABLE_FULL_ERROR	System table for holding open file descriptors is full.
PR_TPD_RANGE_ERROR	Thread-private data index is out of range.
PR_UNKNOWN_ERROR	An unknown error has occurred.
PR_UNLOAD_LIBRARY_ERROR	Failed to unload a dynamic library.
PR_WOULD_BLOCK_ERROR	A blocking operation conflict has occurred.

Netscape Open Source Forums and Discussions

ozilla.org provides many different discussion forums to help programmers stay in touch with others in the Mozilla developer community.
Discussion forums are available as newsgroups and mailing lists. This
way you can choose whether you receive messages from news or by e-mail.

You'll find that two types of discussion forums are available: topic-specific and
project-related. You are able to participate in discussions related to subjects that
interest you, such as discussions on how to improve Mozilla's user interface, as
well as projects you are working on, such as I18N.

Rather than divide the forums into two groups: topics and projects, this appendix lists forums alphabetically by subject. This means that if you are looking for a
discussion on Mozilla's user interface, you'd look under U.

If you don't have time to keep up with the newsgroups, you can catch up with the latest and most important discussions through Newsbot (`http://www.mozilla.org/newsbot/`). Newsbot is a page where summary information for newsgroup articles of general interest to the Mozilla community can be posted.

If you see an important newsgroup article, you can forward it to `newsbot@mozilla.org` and write a summary of the article.

NOTE
Although the discussion forum list in this appendix aims to be comprehensive, mozilla.org's discussion forums change frequently. As a result, you'll find that over time, new forums are added as necessary and old forums are sometimes deleted.

Announcements

The announcement forum is used to post notices of new source releases as they become available. The forum isn't for discussions; it is for announcements only.

- **Newsgroup:** `netscape.public.mozilla.announce`
- **Mailing List:** `mozilla-announce@mozilla.org`
- **Mailing List Requests:** `mozilla-announce-request@mozilla.org`

BeOS

The BeOS forum is used to help support developers who are porting Mozilla to the Be operating system. If you are interested in this effort, start following the discussion.

- **Newsgroup:** `netscape.public.mozilla.beos`
- **Mailing List:** `mozilla-beos@mozilla.org`
- **Mailing List Requests:** `mozilla-beos-request@mozilla.org`

Builds

The builds forum is for discussions on building the Mozilla source code. If you are having trouble compiling the Mozilla source, you may find help through this discussion. You can also use this forum to talk about the Mozilla build system.

- **Newsgroup:** `netscape.public.mozilla.builds`
- **Mailing List:** `mozilla-builds@mozilla.org`
- **Mailing List Requests:** `mozilla-builds-request@mozilla.org`

Calendar

The calendar forum is for discussions on the Zulu project. Zulu is an effort to create a standards-based calendar client for Mozilla.

- **Newsgroup:** `netscape.public.mozilla.calendar`
- **Mailing List:** `mozilla-calendar@mozilla.org`
- **Mailing List Requests:** `mozilla-calendar-request@mozilla.org`

Calendar Checkins

The calendar-checkins forum is for announcements of code checkins on the Zulu project. If you are working on this project and have a major checkin, you should announce it here.

- **Newsgroup:** `netscape.public.mozilla.calendar-checkins`
- **Mailing List:** `mozilla-calendar-checkins@mozilla.org`
- **Mailing List Requests:** `mozilla-calendar-checkins-request@mozilla.org`

Crash-Data

The crash-data forum is for posting summaries of reports generated by Mozilla binaries at crash-time. This is designed to help developers identify bugs in their code.

- **Newsgroup:** `netscape.public.mozilla.crash-data`
- **Mailing List:** `mozilla-crash-data@mozilla.org`
- **Mailing List Requests:** `mozilla-crash-data-request@mozilla.org`

Cryptography

The cryptography forum is for discussions about cryptography and key crypto-graphic issues pertaining to Mozilla. This is an important issue because the U.S. government restricts the distribution of cryptographic source code and as such, mozilla.org cannot distribute this code. However, other organizations are working on encryption solutions for Mozilla, and you can learn about them here.

- **Newsgroup:** `netscape.public.mozilla.crypto`
- **Mailing List:** `mozilla-crypto@mozilla.org`
- **Mailing List Requests:** `mozilla-crypto-request@mozilla.org`

Directory Services

Under the Open Source program, Netscape has published the source code for its directory services, SDK. This forum is for discussions about the directory services, SDK and the related source code.

- **Newsgroup:** `netscape.public.mozilla.directory`
- **Mailing List:** `mozilla-directory@mozilla.org`
- **Mailing List Requests:** `mozilla-directory-request@mozilla.org`

Documentation

The documentation forum is for discussions about Mozilla documentation. You'll find people talking about documenting the Mozilla source code, the hows and whys of documentation, and more.

- **Newsgroup:** `netscape.public.mozilla.documentation`
- **Mailing List:** `mozilla-documentation@mozilla.org`
- **Mailing List Requests:** `mozilla-documentation-request@mozilla.org`

Document Object Model

The W3C's Document Object Model is implemented in Mozilla's NGLayout. In this forum, you'll find people talking about the DOM and its implementation in Mozilla.

- **Newsgroup:** `netscape.public.mozilla.dom`

- **Mailing List:** `mozilla-dom@mozilla.org`

- **Mailing List Requests:** `mozilla-dom-request@mozilla.org`

Embedding

The embedding forum is for discussions about embedding Mozilla components into software applications. You'll find a separate discussion for embedding Mozilla components into handheld devices (called *Small Devices*).

- **Newsgroup:** `netscape.public.mozilla.embedding`

- **Mailing List:** `mozilla-embedding@mozilla.org`

- **Mailing List Requests:** `mozilla-embedding@mozilla.org`

General

The general forum is the catchall discussion area. The forum is for discussions about Mozilla source code and mozilla.org. If the topic or module you want to discuss doesn't have its own forum, you can discuss it here.

- **Newsgroup:** `netscape.public.mozilla.general`

- **Mailing List:** `mozilla-general@mozilla.org`

- **Mailing List Requests:** `mozilla-general-request@mozilla.org`

GTK

GTK is a Unix toolkit for creating graphical user interfaces. This forum is for discussions on implementing GTK in Mozilla and related issues.

- **Newsgroup:** `netscape.public.mozilla.gtk`

- **Mailing List:** `mozilla-gtk@mozilla.org`

- **Mailing List Requests:** `mozilla-gtk-request@mozilla.org`

HTML Editing

The HTML editing forum is for discussions about Mozillla's HTML editor, called *Composer*. Composer is a WYSIWYG HTML editor that can be embedded in HTML and XML pages.

- **Newsgroup:** `netscape.public.mozilla.editor`
- **Mailing List:** `mozilla-editor@mozilla.org`
- **Mailing List Requests:** `mozilla-editor-request@mozilla.org`

Internationalization

The internationalization forum is for discussions on internationalization and localization of the Mozilla source code. Localization is the process of adapting software to a specific language and culture. Internationalization is the writing system that enables software to be localized.

- **Newsgroup:** `netscape.public.mozilla.i18n`
- **Mailing List:** `mozilla-i18n@mozilla.org`
- **Mailing List Requests:** `mozilla-i18n-request@mozilla.org`

Java

The Java forum is for discussions about Mozilla and Java. You'll find people talking about embedding Java runtime environments in Mozilla, working with Just In Time compilers such as Electrical Fire and extending Mozilla modules using Java.

- **Newsgroup:** `netscape.public.mozilla.java`
- **Mailing List:** `mozilla-java@mozilla.org`
- **Mailing List Requests:** `mozilla-java-request@mozilla.org`

JavaScript Engine

The JavaScript Engine forum is for discussions about the Mozilla JavaScript engine and related topics. In this forum, you'll find people talking about a lot of JavaScript-related topics that all deal with implementing JavaScript-based solutions in the Mozilla source code. This means you can discuss XPConnect,

XPCOM, XPIDL, Java/JavaScript Reflection, and other key topics as they relate to the JavaScript engine.

- **Newsgroup:** `netscape.public.mozilla.jseng`
- **Mailing List:** `mozilla-jseng@mozilla.org`
- **Mailing List Requests:** `mozilla-jseng-request@mozilla.org`

NOTE
XPCOM has its own forum. It should be used to discuss cross-platform COM issues.

Layout

The layout forum is for discussions about document layout in Mozilla. You'll find people talking about the next generation layout engine and related technologies such as XML, HTML, and CSS.

- **Newsgroup:** `netscape.public.mozilla.layout`
- **Mailing List:** `mozilla-layout@mozilla.org`
- **Mailing List Requests:** `mozilla-layout-request@mozilla.org`

NOTE
Although the DOM has its own discussion forum, some limited discussions about the DOM take place in this group—especially if the discussions are directly related to document layout.

Layout Checkins

The layout checkins forum is for announcements of code checkins on the layout project. If you are working on this project and have a major checkin, you should announce it here.

- **Newsgroup:** `netscape.public.mozilla.layout.checkins`
- **Mailing List:** `mozilla-layout-checkins@mozilla.org`
- **Mailing List Requests:** `mozilla-layout-checkins-request@mozilla.org`

Licensing

The licensing forum is used to discuss licensing issues related to distributing and using the Mozilla source code. If you are interested in licensing issues or would like to discuss the Netscape Public License or the Mozilla Public License, this is the place to do it.

- **Newsgroup:** `netscape.public.mozilla.license`
- **Mailing List:** `mozilla-license@mozilla.org`
- **Mailing List Requests:** `mozilla-license-request@mozilla.org`

Macintosh

The Macintosh forum is used to discuss programming issues related to the Macintosh operating system and Mozilla. You'll find people discussing Mozilla's Mac modules and related programming issues.

- **Newsgroup:** `netscape.public.mozilla.mac`
- **Mailing List:** `mozilla-mac@mozilla.org`
- **Mailing List Requests:** `mozilla-mac-request@mozilla.org`

Mail and News Readers

The mail and news-readers forum is for discussions about the Mozilla mail and news reader and related topics. You'll find people talking about Smart Mail and thin mail clients as well as integrating Mozilla with other mail and news systems.

- **Newsgroup:** `netscape.public.mozilla.mail-news`
- **Mailing List:** `mozilla-mail-news@mozilla.org`
- **Mailing List Requests:** `mozilla-mail-news-request@mozilla.org`

Networking Libraries

The networking libraries forum is used to discuss issues related to Mozilla's netlib module. If you are interested in this topic, start following the discussion.

- **Newsgroup:** `netscape.public.mozilla.netlib`

- **Mailing List:** `mozilla-netlib@mozilla.org`

- **Mailing List Requests:** `mozilla-netlib-request@mozilla.org`

NSPR

NSPR is the portable runtime library used in Mozilla. This forum discusses NSPR and related hardware abstraction issues.

- **Newsgroup:** `netscape.public.mozilla.nspr`

- **Mailing List:** `mozilla-nspr@mozilla.org`

- **Mailing List Requests:** `mozilla-nspr-request@mozilla.org`

Open JVM Integration

Members of the Open JVM Integration (OJI) project are working to extend the plug-in architecture to enable Java virtual machines to be plugged into Mozilla. This forum discusses OJI implementations and related topics.

- **Newsgroup:** `netscape.public.mozilla.oji`

- **Mailing List:** `mozilla-oji@mozilla.org`

- **Mailing List Requests:** `mozilla-oji-request@mozilla.org`

Patches

The patches forum is for posting patches and bug fixes to the Mozilla source code. If you are posting a bug fix, be sure to enter it into Bugzilla and discuss the fixes with the module owner.

- **Newsgroup:** `netscape.public.mozilla.patches`

- **Mailing List:** `mozilla-patches@mozilla.org`

- **Mailing List Requests:** `mozilla-patches-request@mozilla.org`

Performance

Performance is a major issue in the Mozilla source code. Mozilla's performance needs to be improved in many areas, and this forum is used to discuss such issues.

- **Newsgroup:** `netscape.public.mozilla.performance`
- **Mailing List:** `mozilla-performance@mozilla.org`
- **Mailing List Requests:** `mozilla-performance-request@mozilla.org`

Quality Assurance for Browser Components

The quality assurance for browser components forum is for discussing issues related to quality assurance and testing of Mozilla's browser components. If you are interested in this effort, start following the discussion.

- **Newsgroup:** `netscape.public.mozilla.qa.browser`
- **Mailing List:** `mozilla-qa-browser@mozilla.org`
- **Mailing List Requests:** `mozilla-qa-browser-request@mozilla.org`

Quality Assurance for Editor Components

The quality assurance for editor components forum is for discussing issues related to quality assurance and testing of Mozilla's editor components. If you are interested in this effort, start following the discussion.

- **Newsgroup:** `netscape.public.mozilla.qa.editor`
- **Mailing List:** `mozilla-qa-editor@mozilla.org`
- **Mailing List Requests:** `mozilla-qa-editor-request@mozilla.org`

Quality Assurance for Mozilla

The quality assurance for Mozilla forum is for discussing issues related to general quality assurance and testing of Mozilla. If you'd like to discuss quality issues that aren't related to the browser or editor components, this is the place to do it.

- **Newsgroup:** `netscape.public.mozilla.qa.general`
- **Mailing List:** `mozilla-qa-general@mozilla.org`
- **Mailing List Requests:** `mozilla-qa-general-request@mozilla.org`

QT GUI Toolkit

QT is a toolkit for creating graphical user interfaces. This forum is for discussions on implementing QT in Mozilla and related issues.

- **Newsgroup:** `netscape.public.mozilla.qt`
- **Mailing List:** `mozilla-qt@mozilla.org`
- **Mailing List Requests:** `mozilla-qt-request@mozilla.org`

RDF

Resource Description Framework (RDF) support is built into Mozilla. It is used in many different ways and especially with the NGLayout when you want to use style elements that can be queried, modified, or superimposed from remote sources. If you are interested in RDF initiatives in the Mozilla source code, tune in to this discussion.

- **Newsgroup:** `netscape.public.mozilla.rdf`
- **Mailing List:** `mozilla-rdf@mozilla.org`
- **Mailing List Requests:** `mozilla-rdf-request@mozilla.org`

Rhapsody

The Rhapsody forum is used to help support developers who are porting Mozilla to Apple's next generation operating system, called *Rhapsody*. If you are interested in this effort, start following the discussion.

- **Newsgroup:** `netscape.public.mozilla.rhapsody`
- **Mailing List:** `mozilla-rhapsody@mozilla.org`
- **Mailing List Requests:** `mozilla-rhapsody-request@mozilla.org`

Security

The security forum is for discussions on security problems, issues, and ideas for making the code, as a whole, more secure. The discussion group is not for cryptography.

- **Newsgroup:** `netscape.public.mozilla.security`
- **Mailing List:** `mozilla-security@mozilla.org`
- **Mailing List Requests:** `mozilla-security-request@mozilla.org`

Small Devices

The small devices forum is for discussions about embedding Mozilla components into handheld devices. You'll find a separate discussion for embedding Mozilla components into software applications (called *Embedding*).

- **Newsgroup:** `netscape.public.mozilla.small-devices`
- **Mailing List:** `mozilla-small-devices@mozilla.org`
- **Mailing List Requests:** `mozilla-small-devices@mozilla.org`

User Interfaces

The user interfaces forum is for discussing issues related to Mozilla's user interfaces. You can discuss current and future user interface issues here.

- **Newsgroup:** `netscape.public.mozilla.ui`
- **Mailing List:** `mozilla-ui@mozilla.org`
- **Mailing List Requests:** `mozilla-ui-request@mozilla.org`

Unix and X11

The Unix and X11 forum is for discussions about the Unix and X11 areas of the Mozilla source code. Although you'll find a good deal of discussion about Unix and X11 issues, keep in mind that porting Mozilla to other toolkits and Unix platforms is the subject of different forums.

- **Newsgroup:** `netscape.public.mozilla.unix`

- **Mailing List:** `mozilla-unix@mozilla.org`

- **Mailing List Requests:** `mozilla-unix-request@mozilla.org`

Unix Checkins

The Unix checkins forum is for announcements of code checkins for Unix- and X11-related modules. If you are working on this project and have a major checkin, you should announce it here.

- **Newsgroup:** `netscape.public.mozilla.unix.checkins`

- **Mailing List:** `mozilla-unix-checkins@mozilla.org`

- **Mailing List Requests:** `mozilla-unix-checkins-request@mozilla.org`

Web Tools

Web-based tools used by mozilla.org include Bugzilla, Bonsai, and Tinderbox. If you are interested in developing these tools further or working with their source code, you should visit this discussion forum.

- **Newsgroup:** `netscape.public.mozilla.webtools`

- **Mailing List:** `mozilla-webtools@mozilla.org`

- **Mailing List Requests:** `mozilla-webtools@mozilla.org`

XPCOM

The XPCOM forum is for discussing issues related to XPCOM development and implementation in Mozilla. XPCOM is a cross-platform architecture that mimics COM, and it is being used to convert existing code into modules.

- **Newsgroup:** `netscape.public.mozilla.xpcom`

- **Mailing List:** `mozilla-xpcom@mozilla.org`

- **Mailing List Requests:** `mozilla-xpcom-request@mozilla.org`

XPFE

XPFE is Mozilla's cross-platform front end. This forum is for discussions about XPFE development and implementation.

- **Newsgroup:** `netscape.public.mozilla.xpfe`
- **Mailing List:** `mozilla-xpfe@mozilla.org`
- **Mailing List Requests:** `mozilla-xpfe-request@mozilla.org`

XPFE Checkins

The Cross-Platform Front-End (XPFE) checkins forum is for announcements of code checkins for XPFE-related modules. If you are working on this project and have a major checkin, you should announce it here.

- **Newsgroup:** `netscape.public.mozilla.xpfe.checkins`
- **Mailing List:** `mozilla-xpfe-checkins@mozilla.org`
- **Mailing List Requests:** `mozilla-xpfe-checkins-request@mozilla.org`

What's on the CD-ROM?

The accompanying CD-ROM contains source code for Mozilla, additional open source modules, and Mozilla developer tools. Using the source code, you can build Netscape's open-source software on Windows, Unix, Linux, and Macintosh systems.

Recommended System Requirements

The files on the CD-ROM can be accessed and used from Windows, Macintosh, Linux, and Unix environments. For Windows 95/98/NT/2000, use the Windows Explorer to access the software. For Macintosh, use the Finder to access the software. For Unix and Linux, use your favorite browser or command tool to access the software.

Before you can build Mozilla or other Open Source applications, you'll need to install the developer environment as detailed in Chapters 14–16. Source listings are designed to be used with CVS but can be viewed in any standard text editor or word processor. To copy all of the source files to your hard drive, you'll need at least 325MB of free space. If you don't plan on working on other open source applications, copy only the Mozilla source files, which require less than 95MB of free space.

The precompiled binaries can be run only on the designated Windows, Macintosh, Linux, or Unix system. The size of the precompiled binaries depends on your operating system, but you should have at least 10MB of free space for the binaries. This space is in addition to what you'll need for the source files.

Disk Contents

Source code on the CD-ROM is provided in project-specified directories. Platform-specific software is located in the appropriate directories for Windows, Macintosh, Linux, and Unix. The contents include the following items.

Source Code for Mozilla and Other Open Source Projects

On the CD-ROM, you'll find the source code for the open-source projects listed in Table D-1. Projects are listed by name, description, and CD-ROM location.

TABLE D-1: PROJECTS ON THE CD-ROM

PROJECT	DESCRIPTION	CD-ROM LOCATION
Bugzilla	Web-based bug tracking system	`Source\Bugzilla`
Calendar	Calendar client	`Source\Calendar`
Grendel	Java mail client	`Source\Grendel`
JavaScript	JavaScript Reference (JSRef) implementation	`Source\JavaScript\JSRef`
Localization	Localization Kits for Netscape Communicator	`Source\L10N`
LDAP C SDK	LDAP software development kit for C	`Source\LDAP\C`
LDAP Java SDK	LDAP software development kit for Java	`Source\LDAP\Java`
LDAP Perl SDK	LDAP software development kit for Perl	`Source\LDAP\Perl`
Messaging SDK	Netscape Messaging Access SDK	`Source\Messaging`
Mozilla	Web browser	`Source\Mozilla`
Rhino	JavaScript in Java implementation	`Source\JavaScript\Rhino`

The source code provides a starting point for coding Mozilla and other open-source applications. Use the source code in conjunction with CVS and you'll be able to update the source to the latest version quickly and easily. With CVS, only source files that have changed are downloaded. Because you already have the files on your computer, this can save many hours of downloading, especially if you want to work with multiple projects.

Precompiled Binaries for Windows, Unix, and Macintosh

The precompiled binaries enable you to run Mozilla using the binary executable. These executables are for a particular milestone in the project, such as Milestone 8. Each milestone has a particular set of features, with the latest milestone having the most recent updates. On the CD-ROM, you'll find several versions of the binaries for Windows, Macintosh, Linux, and Unix.

- Binary files for 32-bit Window systems are in `Bin\Win32`

- Archived binaries for Macintosh are in `Bin\Mac`

- Archive binaries for Linux are in `Bin\Linux`

Netscape's Windows Build Tools for Mozilla

As described in Chapter 14, Netscape provides a special set of build tools for Windows systems, which contains a modified version of GNU Make, SHMSDOS, Umake, and NSInstall. These build tools are provided on the CD-ROM in the `Bin\Win32\build` folder. Install the tools as described in Chapter 14.

CVS Clients for Unix, Windows, and Macintosh

To build Mozilla, you need a CVS client. The CVS clients provided on the CD-ROM are under the GNU open source license and are freeware.

- CVS clients for Window systems are in `CVS\Win32`

- CVS clients for Macintosh are in `CVS\Mac`

- CVS clients for Linux are in `CVS\Linux`

Install the clients on your respective system as described in Chapters 14–16.

Index

A

N

Version 2, June 1991

Preamble

The licenses for most software are designed to take away your freedom to share and change it. By contrast, the GNU General Public License is intended to guarantee your freedom to share and change free software ó to make sure the software is free for all its users. This General Public License applies to most of the Free Software Foundation's software and to any other program whose authors commit to using it. (Some other Free Software Foundation software is covered by the GNU Library General Public License instead.) You can apply it to your programs, too.

When we speak of free software, we are referring to freedom, not price. Our General Public Licenses are designed to make sure that you have the freedom to distribute copies of free software (and charge for this service if you wish), that you receive source code or can get it if you want it, that you can change the software or use pieces of it in new free programs, and that you know you can do these things.

To protect your rights, we need to make restrictions that forbid anyone to deny you these rights or to ask you to surrender the rights. These restrictions translate to certain responsibilities for you if you distribute copies of the software, or if you modify it.

For example, if you distribute copies of such a program, whether gratis or for a fee, you must give the recipients all the rights that you have. You must make sure that they, too, receive or can get the source code. And you must show them these terms so they know their rights.

We protect your rights with two steps: (1) copyright the software, and (2) offer you this license which gives you legal permission to copy, distribute and/or modify the software.

Also, for each author's protection and ours, we want to make certain that everyone understands that there is no warranty for this free software. If the software is modified by someone else and passed on, we want its recipients to know that what they have is not the original, so that any problems introduced by others will not reflect on the original authors' reputations.

Finally, any free program is threatened constantly by software patents. We wish to avoid the danger that redistributors of a free program will individually obtain patent licenses, in effect making the program proprietary. To prevent this, we have made it clear that any patent must be licensed for everyone's free use or not licensed at all.

The precise terms and conditions for copying, distribution and modification follow.

TERMS AND CONDITIONS FOR COPYING, DISTRIBUTION AND MODIFICATION

0. This License applies to any program or other work that contains a notice placed by the copyright holder saying it may be distributed under the terms of this General Public License. The "Program", below, refers to any such program or work, and a "work based on the Program" means either the Program or any derivative work under copyright law: that is to say, a work containing the Program or a portion of it, either verbatim or with modifications and/or translated into another language. (Hereinafter, translation is included without limitation in the term "modification".) Each licensee is addressed as "you".

Activities other than copying, distribution and modification are not covered by this License; they are outside its scope. The act of running the Program is not restricted, and the output from the Program is covered only if its contents constitute a work based on the Program (independent of having been made by running the Program). Whether that is true depends on what the Program does.

1. You may copy and distribute verbatim copies of the Program's source code as you receive it, in any medium, provided that you conspicuously and appropriately publish on each copy an appropriate copyright notice and disclaimer of warranty; keep intact all the notices that refer to this License and to the absence of any warranty; and give any other recipients of the Program a copy of this License along with the Program.

You may charge a fee for the physical act of transferring a copy, and you may at your option offer warranty protection in exchange for a fee.

2. You may modify your copy or copies of the Program or any portion of it, thus forming a work based on the Program, and copy and distribute such modifications or work under the terms of Section 1 above, provided that you also meet all of these conditions:

a) You must cause the modified files to carry prominent notices stating that you changed the files and the date of any change.

b) You must cause any work that you distribute or publish, that in whole or in part contains or is derived from the Program or any part thereof, to be licensed as a whole at no charge to all third parties under the terms of this License.

c) If the modified program normally reads commands interactively when run, you must cause it, when started running for such interactive use in the most ordinary way, to print or display an announcement including an appropriate copyright notice and a notice that there is no warranty (or else, saying that you provide a warranty) and that users may redistribute the program under these conditions, and telling the user how to view a copy of this License. (Exception: if the Program itself is interactive but does not normally print such an announcement, your work based on the Program is not required to print an announcement.)

These requirements apply to the modified work as a whole. If identifiable sections of that work are not derived from the Program, and can be reasonably considered independent and separate works in themselves, then this License, and its terms, do not apply to those sections when you distribute them as separate works. But when you distribute the same sections as part of a whole which is a work based on the Program, the distribution of the whole must be on the terms of this License, whose permissions for other licensees extend to the entire whole, and thus to each and every part regardless of who wrote it.

Thus, it is not the intent of this section to claim rights or contest your rights to work written entirely by you; rather, the intent is to exercise the right to control the distribution of derivative or collective works based on the Program.

In addition, mere aggregation of another work not based on the Program with the Program (or with a work based on the Program) on a volume of a storage or distribution medium does not bring the other work under the scope of this License.

3. You may copy and distribute the Program (or a work based on it, under Section 2) in object code or executable form under the terms of Sections 1 and 2 above provided that you also do one of the following:

a) Accompany it with the complete corresponding machine-readable source code, which must be distributed under the terms of Sections 1 and 2 above on a medium customarily used for software interchange; or,

b) Accompany it with a written offer, valid for at least three years, to give any third party, for a charge no more than your cost of physically performing source distribution, a complete machine-readable copy of the corresponding source code, to be distributed under the terms of Sections 1 and 2 above on a medium customarily used for software interchange; or,

c) Accompany it with the information you received as to the offer to distribute corresponding source code. (This alternative is allowed only for noncommercial distribution and only if you received the program in object code or executable form with such an offer, in accord with Subsection b above.)

The source code for a work means the preferred form of the work for making modifications to it. For an executable work, complete source code means all the source code for all modules it contains, plus any associated interface definition files, plus the scripts used to control compilation and installation of the executable. However, as a special exception, the source code distributed need not include anything that is normally distributed (in either source or binary form) with the major components (compiler, kernel, and so on) of the operating system on which the executable runs, unless that component itself accompanies the executable.

If distribution of executable or object code is made by offering access to copy from a designated place, then offering equivalent access to copy the source code from the same place counts as distribution of the source code, even though third parties are not compelled to copy the source along with the object code.

4. You may not copy, modify, sublicense, or distribute the Program except as expressly provided under this License. Any attempt otherwise to copy, modify, sublicense or distribute the Program is void, and will automatically terminate your rights under this License. However, parties who have received copies, or rights, from you under this License will not have their licenses terminated so long as such parties remain in full compliance.

5. You are not required to accept this License, since you have not signed it. However, nothing else grants you permission to modify or distribute the Program or its derivative works. These actions are prohibited by law if you do not accept this License. Therefore, by modifying or distributing the Program (or any work based on the Program), you indicate your acceptance of this License to do so, and all its terms and conditions for copying, distributing or modifying the Program or works based on it.

6. Each time you redistribute the Program (or any work based on the Program), the recipient automatically receives a license from the original licensor to copy, distribute or modify the Program subject to these terms and conditions. You may not impose any further restrictions on the recipients' exercise of the rights granted

herein. You are not responsible for enforcing compliance by third parties to this License.

7.If, as a consequence of a court judgment or allegation of patent infringement or for any other reason (not limited to patent issues), conditions are imposed on you (whether by court order, agreement or otherwise) that contradict the conditions of this License, they do not excuse you from the conditions of this License. If you cannot distribute so as to satisfy simultaneously your obligations under this License and any other pertinent obligations, then as a consequence you may not distribute the Program at all. For example, if a patent license would not permit royalty-free redistribution of the Program by all those who receive copies directly or indirectly through you, then the only way you could satisfy both it and this License would be to refrain entirely from distribution of the Program.

If any portion of this section is held invalid or unenforceable under any particular circumstance, the balance of the section is intended to apply and the section as a whole is intended to apply in other circumstances.

It is not the purpose of this section to induce you to infringe any patents or other property right claims or to contest validity of any such claims; this section has the sole purpose of protecting the integrity of the free software distribution system, which is implemented by public license practices. Many people have made generous contributions to the wide range of software distributed through that system in reliance on consistent application of that system; it is up to the author/donor to decide if he or she is willing to distribute software through any other system and a licensee cannot impose that choice.

This section is intended to make thoroughly clear what is believed to be a consequence of the rest of this License.

8. If the distribution and/or use of the Program is restricted in certain countries either by patents or by copyrighted interfaces, the original copyright holder who places the Program under this License may add an explicit geographical distribution limitation excluding those countries, so that distribution is permitted only in or among countries not thus excluded. In such case, this License incorporates the limitation as if written in the body of this License.

9.The Free Software Foundation may publish revised and/or new versions of the General Public License from time to time. Such new versions will be similar in spirit to the present version, but may differ in detail to address new problems or concerns.

Each version is given a distinguishing version number. If the Program specifies a version number of this License which applies to it and "any later version", you have the option of following the terms and conditions either of that version or of any later version published by the Free Software Foundation. If the Program does not specify a version number of this License, you may choose any version ever published by the Free Software Foundation.

10. If you wish to incorporate parts of the Program into other free programs whose distribution conditions are different, write to the author to ask for permission. For software that is copyrighted by the Free Software Foundation, write to the Free Software Foundation; we sometimes make exceptions for this. Our decision will be guided by the two goals of preserving the free status of all derivatives of our free software and of promoting the sharing and reuse of software generally.

NO WARRANTY

11. BECAUSE THE PROGRAM IS LICENSED FREE OF CHARGE, THERE IS NO WARRANTY FOR THE PROGRAM, TO THE EXTENT PERMITTED BY APPLICABLE LAW. EXCEPT WHEN OTHERWISE STATED IN WRITING THE COPYRIGHT HOLDERS AND/OR OTHER PARTIES PROVIDE THE PROGRAM "AS IS" WITHOUT WARRANTY OF ANY KIND, EITHER EXPRESSED OR IMPLIED, INCLUDING, BUT NOT LIMITED TO, THE IMPLIED WARRANTIES OF MERCHANTABILITY AND FITNESS FOR A PARTICULAR PURPOSE. THE ENTIRE RISK AS TO THE QUALITY AND PERFORMANCE OF THE PROGRAM IS WITH YOU. SHOULD THE PROGRAM PROVE DEFECTIVE, YOU ASSUME THE COST OF ALL NECESSARY SERVICING, REPAIR OR CORRECTION.

12. IN NO EVENT UNLESS REQUIRED BY APPLICABLE LAW OR AGREED TO IN WRITING WILL ANY COPYRIGHT HOLDER, OR ANY OTHER PARTY WHO MAY MODIFY AND/OR REDISTRIBUTE THE PROGRAM AS PERMITTED ABOVE, BE LIABLE TO YOU FOR DAMAGES, INCLUDING ANY GENERAL, SPECIAL, INCIDENTAL OR CONSEQUENTIAL DAMAGES ARISING OUT OF THE USE OR INABILITY TO USE THE PROGRAM (INCLUDING BUT NOT LIMITED TO LOSS OF DATA OR DATA BEING RENDERED INACCURATE OR LOSSES SUSTAINED BY YOU OR THIRD PARTIES OR A FAILURE OF THE PROGRAM TO OPERATE WITH ANY OTHER PROGRAMS), EVEN IF SUCH HOLDER OR OTHER PARTY HAS BEEN ADVISED OF THE POSSIBILITY OF SUCH DAMAGES.

*****END OF TERMS AND CONDITIONS*****

How to Apply These Terms to Your New Programs

If you develop a new program, and you want it to be of the greatest possible use to the public, the best way to achieve this is to make it free software which everyone can redistribute and change under these terms.

To do so, attach the following notices to the program. It is safest to attach them to the start of each source file to most effectively convey the exclusion of warranty; and each file should have at least the "copyright" line and a pointer to where the full notice is found.

```
one line to give the program's name and an idea of what
it does.

Copyright (C) yyyy  name of author

This program is free software; you can redistribute it
and/ormodify it under the terms of the GNU General Public
License as published by the Free Software Foundation; either
version 2 of the License, or (at your option) any later
version.

This program is distributed in the hope that it will be
useful, but WITHOUT ANY WARRANTY; without even the implied
warranty of MERCHANTABILITY or FITNESS FOR A PARTICULAR
PURPOSE.  See the GNU General Public License for more
details.

You should have received a copy of the GNU General Public
License along with this program; if not, write to the Free
Software Foundation, Inc., 59 Temple Place - Suite 330,
Boston, MA 02111-1307, USA.
```

Also add information on how to contact you by electronic and paper mail.

If the program is interactive, make it output a short notice like this when it starts in an interactive mode:

```
Gnomovision version 69, Copyright (C) yyyy name of author
Gnomovision comes with ABSOLUTELY NO WARRANTY; for details
type 'show w'.  This is free software, and you are welcome
to redistribute it under certain conditions; type 'show c'
for details.
```

The hypothetical commands 'show w' and 'show c' should show the appropriate parts of the General Public License. Of course, the commands you use may be called something other than 'show w' and 'show c'; they could even be mouse-clicks or menu items—whatever suits your program.

You should also get your employer (if you work as a programmer) or your school, if any, to sign a "copyright disclaimer" for the program, if necessary. Here is a sample; alter the names:

```
Yoyodyne, Inc., hereby disclaims all copyright
interest in the program `Gnomovision'
(which makes passes at compilers) written
by James Hacker.

signature of Ty Coon, 1 April 1989
Ty Coon, President of Vice
```

This General Public License does not permit incorporating your program into proprietary programs. If your program is a subroutine library, you may consider it more useful to permit linking proprietary applications with the library. If this is what you want to do, use the GNU Library General Public License instead of this License.

Netscape and Mozilla Public Licenses Version 1.1

With version 1.1 of the public licenses for Mozilla, Netscape add stricter wording for commercial use and distribution of the source code. You'll also find additional wording for third party claims, particularly in the areas of patents and intellectual property rights. The licenses this time around are combined into a single legal document. When you want to apply the Mozilla Public License using the version 1.1 document, you:

- Include the Mozilla Public License Version 1.1 and Exhibit A-Mozilla Public License
- Delete the Amendments and Exhibit A-Netscape Public License.

The Netscape Public License Version 1.1, on the other hand, consists of the Mozilla Public License Version 1.1 with the Amendments and Exhibit A-Netscape Public License. This means you include the entire document in the source code.

Mozilla Public License Version 1.1

1. Definitions.

1.0.1. "Commercial Use"

"Commercial Use" means distribution or otherwise making the Covered Code available to a third party.

1.1. "Contributor"

"Contributor" means each entity that creates or contributes to the creation of Modifications.

1.2. "Contributor Version"

"Contributor Version" means the combination of the Original Code, prior Modifications used by a Contributor, and the Modifications made by that particular Contributor.

1.3. "Covered Code"

"Covered Code" means the Original Code or Modifications or the combination of the Original Code and Modifications, in each case including portions thereof.

1.4. "Electronic Distribution Mechanism"

"Electronic Distribution Mechanism" means a mechanism generally accepted in the software development community for the electronic transfer of data.

1.5. "Executable"

"Executable" means Covered Code in any form other than Source Code.

1.6. "Initial Developer"

"Initial Developer" means the individual or entity identified as the Initial Developer in the Source Code notice required by Exhibit A.

1.7. "Larger Work"

"Larger Work" means a work which combines Covered Code or portions thereof with code not governed by the terms of this License.

1.8. "License"

"License" means this document.

1.8.1. "Licensable"

"Licensable" means having the right to grant, to the maximum extent possible, whether at the time of the initial grant or subsequently acquired, any and all of the rights conveyed herein.

1.9. "Modifications"

"Modifications" means any addition to or deletion from the substance or structure of either the original Code or any previous Modifications. When Covered Code is released as a series of files, a Modification is:

A. Any addition to or deletion from the contents of a file containing Original Code or previous Modifications.

B. Any new file that contains any part of the Original Code or previous Modifications.

1.10. "Original Code"

"Original Code" means Source Code of computer software code which is described in the Source Code notice required by Exhibit A as Original Code, and which, at the time of its release under this License is not already Covered Code governed by this License.

1.10.1. "Patent Claims"

"Patent Claims" means any patent claim(s), now owned or hereafter acquired, including without limitation, method, process, and apparatus claims, in any patent Licensable by grantor.

1.11. "Source Code"

"Source Code" means the preferred form of the Covered Code for making modifications to it, including all modules it contains, plus any associated interface definition files, scripts used to control compilation and installation of an Executable, or source code differential comparisons against either the Original Code or another well known, available Covered Code of the Contributor's choice. The Source Code can be in a compressed or archival form, provided the appropriate decompression or de-archiving software is widely available for no charge.

1.12. "You" (or "Your")

"You" (or "Your") means an individual or a legal entity exercising rights under, and complying with all of the terms of, this License or a future version of this License issued under Section 6.1. For legal entities, "You" includes any entity which controls, is controlled by, or is under common control with You.

For purposes of this definition, "control" means (a) the power, direct or indirect, to cause the direction or management of such entity, whether by contract or otherwise, or (b) ownership of more than fifty percent (50%) of the outstanding shares or beneficial ownership of such entity.

2. Source Code License.

2.1. The Initial Developer Grant.

The Initial Developer hereby grants You a world-wide, royalty-free, non-exclusive license, subject to third party intellectual property claims:

(a) under intellectual property rights (other than patent or trademark) Licensable by Initial Developer to use, reproduce, modify, display, perform, sublicense and distribute the Original Code (or portions thereof) with or without Modifications, and/or as part of a Larger Work; and

(b) under Patents Claims infringed by the making, using or selling of Original Code, to make, have made, use, practice, sell, and offer for sale, and/or otherwise dispose of the Original Code (or portions thereof).

(c) the licenses granted in this Section 2.1(a) and (b) are effective on the date Initial Developer first distributes Original Code under the terms of this License.

(d) Notwithstanding Section 2.1(b) above, no patent license is granted: 1) for code that You delete from the Original Code; 2) separate from the Original Code; or 3) for infringements caused by: i) the modification of the Original Code or ii) the combination of the Original Code with other software or devices.

2.2. Contributor Grant.

Subject to third party intellectual property claims, each Contributor hereby grants You a world-wide, royalty-free, non-exclusive license

(a) under intellectual property rights (other than patent or trademark) Licensable by Contributor, to use, reproduce, modify, display, perform, sublicense and distribute the Modifications created by such Contributor (or portions thereof) either on an unmodified basis, with other Modifications, as Covered Code and/or as part of a Larger Work; and

(b) under Patent Claims infringed by the making, using, or selling of Modifications made by that Contributor either alone and/or in combination with its Contributor Version (or portions of such combination), to make, use, sell, offer for sale, have made, and/or otherwise dispose of: 1) Modifications made by that Contributor (or portions thereof); and 2) the combination of Modifications made by that Contributor with its Contributor Version (or portions of such combination).

(c) the licenses granted in Sections 2.2(a) and 2.2(b) are effective on the date Contributor first makes Commercial Use of the Covered Code.

(d) Notwithstanding Section 2.2(b) above, no patent license is granted: 1) for any code that Contributor has deleted from the Contributor Version; 2) separate from the Contributor Version; 3) for infringements caused by: i) third party modifications of Contributor Version or ii) the combination of Modifications made by that Contributor with other software (except as part of the Contributor Version) or other devices; or 4) under Patent Claims infringed by Covered Code in the absence of Modifications made by that Contributor.

3. Distribution Obligations.

3.1. Application of License.

The Modifications which You create or to which You contribute are governed by the terms of this License, including without limitation Section 2.2. The Source Code version of Covered Code may be distributed only under the terms of this License or a future version of this License released under Section 6.1, and You must include a copy of this License with every copy of the Source Code You distribute. You may not offer or impose any terms on any Source Code version that alters or restricts the applicable version of this

License or the recipients' rights hereunder. However, You may include an additional document offering the additional rights described in Section 3.5.

3.2. Availability of Source Code.

Any Modification which You create or to which You contribute must be made available in Source Code form under the terms of this License either on the same media as an Executable version or via an accepted Electronic Distribution Mechanism to anyone to whom you made an Executable version available; and if made available via Electronic Distribution Mechanism, must remain available for at least twelve (12) months after the date it initially became available, or at least six (6) months after a subsequent version of that particular Modification has been made available to such recipients. You are responsible for ensuring that the Source Code version remains available even if the Electronic Distribution Mechanism is maintained by a third party.

3.3. Description of Modifications.

You must cause all Covered Code to which You contribute to contain a file documenting the changes You made to create that Covered Code and the date of any change. You must include a prominent statement that the Modification is derived, directly or indirectly, from Original Code provided by the Initial Developer and including the name of the Initial Developer in (a) the Source Code, and (b) in any notice in an Executable version or related documentation in which You describe the origin or ownership of the Covered Code.

3.4. Intellectual Property Matters

(a) Third Party Claims. If Contributor has knowledge that a license under a third party's intellectual property rights is required to exercise the rights granted by such Contributor under Sections 2.1 or 2.2, Contributor must include a text file with the Source Code distribution titled "LEGAL" which describes the claim and the party making the claim in sufficient detail that a recipient will know whom to contact. If Contributor obtains such knowledge after the Modification is made available as described in Section 3.2, Contributor shall promptly modify the LEGAL file in all copies Contributor makes available thereafter and shall take other steps (such as notifying appropriate mailing lists or newsgroups) reasonably calculated to inform those who received the Covered Code that new knowledge has been obtained.

(b) Contributor APIs. If Contributor's Modifications include an application programming interface and Contributor has knowledge of patent licenses which are reasonably necessary to implement that API, Contributor must also include this information in the LEGAL file.

(c) Representations. Contributor represents that, except as disclosed pursuant to Section 3.4(a) above, Contributor believes that Contributor's Modifications are Contributor's original creation(s) and/or Contributor has sufficient rights to grant the rights conveyed by this License.

3.5. Required Notices.

You must duplicate the notice in Exhibit A in each file of the Source Code. If it is not possible to put such notice in a particular Source Code file due to its structure, then You must include such notice in a location (such as a relevant directory) where a user would be likely to look for such a notice. If You created one or more Modification(s) You may add your name as a Contributor to the notice described in Exhibit A. You must also duplicate this License in any documentation for the Source Code where You describe recipients' rights or ownership rights relating to Covered Code. You may choose to offer, and to charge a fee for, warranty, support, indemnity or liability obligations to one or more recipients of Covered Code. However, You may do so only on Your own behalf, and not on behalf of the Initial Developer or any Contributor. You must make it absolutely clear than any such warranty, support, indemnity or liability obligation is offered by You alone, and You hereby agree to indemnify the Initial Developer and every Contributor for any liability incurred by the Initial Developer or such Contributor as a result of warranty, support, indemnity or liability terms You offer.

3.6. Distribution of Executable Versions.

You may distribute Covered Code in Executable form only if the requirements of Section 3.1-3.5 have been met for that Covered Code, and if You include a notice stating that the Source Code version of the Covered Code is available under the terms of this License, including a description of how and where You have fulfilled the obligations of Section 3.2. The notice must be conspicuously included in any notice in an Executable version, related documentation or collateral in which You describe recipients' rights relating to the Covered Code.

You may distribute the Executable version of Covered Code or ownership rights under a license of Your choice, which may contain terms different from this License, provided that You are in compliance with the terms of this License and that the license for the Executable version does not attempt to limit or alter the recipient's rights in the Source Code version from the rights set forth in this License. If You distribute the Executable version under a different license You must make it absolutely clear that any terms which differ from this License are offered by You alone, not by the Initial Developer or any Contributor. You hereby agree to indemnify the Initial Developer and every Contributor for any liability incurred by the Initial Developer or such Contributor as a result of any such terms You offer.

3.7. Larger Works.

You may create a Larger Work by combining Covered Code with other code not governed by the terms of this License and distribute the Larger Work as a single product. In such a case, You must make sure the requirements of this License are fulfilled for the Covered Code.

4. Inability to Comply Due to Statute or Regulation.

If it is impossible for You to comply with any of the terms of this License with respect to some or all of the Covered Code due to statute, judicial order, or regulation then You must: (a) comply with the terms of this License to the maximum extent possible; and (b) describe the limitations and the code they affect. Such description must be included in the LEGAL file described in Section 3.4 and must be included with all distributions of the Source Code. Except to the extent prohibited by statute or regulation, such description must be sufficiently detailed for a recipient of ordinary skill to be able to understand it.

5. Application of this License.

This License applies to code to which the Initial Developer has attached the notice in Exhibit A and to related Covered Code.

6. Versions of the License.

6.1. New Versions.

Netscape Communications Corporation (''Netscape'') may publish revised and/or new versions of the License from time to time. Each version will be given a distinguishing version number.

6.2. Effect of New Versions.

Once Covered Code has been published under a particular version of the License, You may always continue to use it under the terms of that version. You may also choose to use such Covered Code under the terms of any subsequent version of the License published by Netscape. No one other than Netscape has the right to modify the terms applicable to Covered Code created under this License.

6.3. Derivative Works.

If You create or use a modified version of this License (which you may only do in order to apply it to code which is not already Covered Code governed by this License), You must (a) rename Your license so that the phrases ''Mozilla'', ''MOZILLAPL'', ''MOZPL'', ''Netscape'', "MPL", ''NPL'' or any confusingly similar phrase do not appear in your license (except to note that your license differs from this License) and (b) otherwise make it clear that Your version of the license contains terms which differ from the Mozilla Public License and Netscape Public License. (Filling in the name of the Initial Developer, Original Code or Contributor in the notice described in Exhibit A shall not of themselves be deemed to be modifications of this License.)

7. DISCLAIMER OF WARRANTY.

COVERED CODE IS PROVIDED UNDER THIS LICENSE ON AN "AS IS" BASIS, WITHOUT WARRANTY OF ANY KIND, EITHER EXPRESSED OR IMPLIED, INCLUDING, WITHOUT LIMITATION, WARRANTIES THAT THE COVERED CODE IS FREE OF DEFECTS, MERCHANTABLE, FIT FOR A PAR-

TICULAR PURPOSE OR NON-INFRINGING. THE ENTIRE RISK AS TO THE QUALITY AND PERFORMANCE OF THE COVERED CODE IS WITH YOU. SHOULD ANY COVERED CODE PROVE DEFECTIVE IN ANY RESPECT, YOU (NOT THE INITIAL DEVELOPER OR ANY OTHER CONTRIBUTOR) ASSUME THE COST OF ANY NECESSARY SERVICING, REPAIR OR CORRECTION. THIS DISCLAIMER OF WARRANTY CONSTITUTES AN ESSENTIAL PART OF THIS LICENSE. NO USE OF ANY COVERED CODE IS AUTHORIZED HERE-UNDER EXCEPT UNDER THIS DISCLAIMER.

8. TERMINATION.

8.1.

This License and the rights granted hereunder will terminate automatically if You fail to comply with terms herein and fail to cure such breach within 30 days of becoming aware of the breach. All sublicenses to the Covered Code which are properly granted shall survive any termination of this License. Provisions which, by their nature, must remain in effect beyond the termination of this License shall survive.

8.2.

If You initiate litigation by asserting a patent infringement claim (excluding declatory judgment actions) against Initial Developer or a Contributor (the Initial Developer or Contributor against whom You file such action is referred to as "Participant") alleging that:

   (a) such Participant's Contributor Version directly or indirectly infringes any patent, then any and all rights granted by such Participant to You under Sections 2.1 and/or 2.2 of this License shall, upon 60 days notice from Participant terminate prospectively, unless if within 60 days after receipt of notice You either: (i) agree in writing to pay Participant a mutually agreeable reasonable royalty for Your past and future use of Modifications made by such Participant, or (ii) withdraw Your litigation claim with respect to the Contributor Version against such Participant. If within 60 days of notice, a reasonable royalty and payment arrangement are not mutually agreed upon in writing by the parties or the litigation claim is not withdrawn, the rights granted by Participant to You under Sections 2.1 and/or 2.2 automatically terminate at the expiration of the 60 day notice period specified above.

(b) any software, hardware, or device, other than such Participant's Contributor Version, directly or indirectly infringes any patent, then any rights granted to You by such Participant under Sections 2.1(b) and 2.2(b) are revoked effective as of the date You first made, used, sold, distributed, or had made, Modifications made by that Participant.

8.3.

If You assert a patent infringement claim against Participant alleging that such Participant's Contributor Version directly or indirectly infringes any patent where such claim is resolved (such as by license or settlement) prior to the initiation of patent infringement litigation, then the reasonable value of the licenses granted by such Participant under Sections 2.1 or 2.2 shall be taken into account in determining the amount or value of any payment or license.

8.4.

In the event of termination under Sections 8.1 or 8.2 above, all end user license agreements (excluding distributors and resellers) which have been validly granted by You or any distributor hereunder prior to termination shall survive termination.

9. LIMITATION OF LIABILITY.

UNDER NO CIRCUMSTANCES AND UNDER NO LEGAL THEORY, WHETHER TORT (INCLUDING NEGLIGENCE), CONTRACT, OR OTHERWISE, SHALL YOU, THE INITIAL DEVELOPER, ANY OTHER CONTRIBUTOR, OR ANY DISTRIBUTOR OF COVERED CODE, OR ANY SUPPLIER OF ANY OF SUCH PARTIES, BE LIABLE TO ANY PERSON FOR ANY INDIRECT, SPECIAL, INCIDENTAL, OR CONSEQUENTIAL DAMAGES OF ANY CHARACTER INCLUDING, WITHOUT LIMITATION, DAMAGES FOR LOSS OF GOODWILL, WORK STOPPAGE, COMPUTER FAILURE OR MALFUNCTION, OR ANY AND ALL OTHER COMMERCIAL DAMAGES OR LOSSES, EVEN IF SUCH PARTY SHALL HAVE BEEN INFORMED OF THE POSSIBILITY OF SUCH DAMAGES. THIS LIMITATION OF LIABILITY SHALL NOT APPLY TO LIABILITY FOR DEATH OR PERSONAL INJURY RESULTING FROM SUCH PARTY'S NEGLIGENCE TO THE EXTENT APPLICABLE LAW PROHIBITS SUCH LIMITATION. SOME JURISDICTIONS DO NOT ALLOW THE EXCLUSION OR LIMITATION OF INCIDENTAL OR CONSEQUENTIAL DAMAGES, SO THIS EXCLUSION AND LIMITATION MAY NOT APPLY TO YOU.

10. U.S. GOVERNMENT END USERS.

The Covered Code is a ''commercial item,'' as that term is defined in 48 C.F.R. 2.101 (Oct. 1995), consisting of ''commercial computer software'' and ''commercial computer software documentation,'' as such terms are used in 48 C.F.R. 12.212 (Sept. 1995). Consistent with 48 C.F.R. 12.212 and 48 C.F.R. 227.7202-1 through 227.7202-4 (June 1995), all U.S. Government End Users acquire Covered Code with only those rights set forth herein.

11. MISCELLANEOUS.

This License represents the complete agreement concerning subject matter hereof. If any provision of this License is held to be unenforceable, such provision shall be reformed only to the extent necessary to make it enforceable. This License shall be governed by California law provisions (except to the extent applicable law, if any, provides otherwise), excluding its conflict-of-law provisions. With respect to disputes in which at least one party is a citizen of, or an entity chartered or registered to do business in the United States of America, any litigation relating to this License shall be subject to the jurisdiction of the Federal Courts of the Northern District of California, with venue lying in Santa Clara County, California, with the losing party responsible for costs, including without limitation, court costs and reasonable attorneys' fees and expenses. The application of the United Nations Convention on Contracts for the International Sale of Goods is expressly excluded. Any law or regulation which provides that the language of a contract shall be construed against the drafter shall not apply to this License.

12. RESPONSIBILITY FOR CLAIMS.

As between Initial Developer and the Contributors, each party is responsible for claims and damages arising, directly or indirectly, out of its utilization of rights under this License and You agree to work with Initial Developer and Contributors to distribute such responsibility on an equitable basis. Nothing herein is intended or shall be deemed to constitute any admission of liability.

13. MULTIPLE-LICENSED CODE.

Initial Developer may designate portions of the Covered Code as ìMultiple-Licensedî. ìMultiple-Licensedî means that the Initial Developer permits you to utilize portions of the Covered Code under Your choice of the NPL or the alternative licenses, if any, specified by the Initial Developer in the file described in Exhibit A.

EXHIBIT A -Mozilla Public License.

``The contents of this file are subject to the Mozilla Public License Version 1.1 (the "License"); you may not use this file except in compliance with the License. You may obtain a copy of the License at http://www.mozilla.org/MPL/

Software distributed under the License is distributed on an "AS IS" basis, WITHOUT WARRANTY OF ANY KIND, either express or implied. See the License for the specific language governing rights and limitations under the License.

The Original Code is _____.

The Initial Developer of the Original Code is _____.

Portions created by _____ are Copyright © _____

_____. All Rights Reserved.

Contributor(s): _____.

Alternatively, the contents of this file may be used under the terms of the _____ license (the ì[___] Licenseî), in which case the provisions of [_____] License are applicable instead of those above. If you wish to allow use of your version of this file only under the terms of the [____] License and not to allow others to use your version of this file under the MPL, indicate your decision by deleting the provisions above and replace them with the notice and other provisions required by the [___] License. If you do not delete the provisions above, a recipient may use your version of this file under either the MPL or the [___] License."

[NOTE: The text of this Exhibit A may differ slightly from the text of the notices in the Source Code files of the Original Code. You should use the text of this Exhibit A rather than the text found in the Original Code Source Code for Your Modifications.]

AMENDMENTS

The Netscape Public License Version 1.1 ("NPL") consists of the Mozilla Public License Version 1.1 with the following Amendments, including Exhibit A-Netscape Public License. Files identified with "Exhibit A-Netscape Public License" are governed by the Netscape Public License Version 1.1.

Additional Terms applicable to the Netscape Public License.

I. Effect. These additional terms described in this Netscape Public License — Amendments shall apply to the Mozilla Communicator client code and to all Covered Code under this License.

II. 'Netscape's Branded Code" means Covered Code that Netscape distributes and/or permits others to distribute under one or more trademark(s) which are controlled by Netscape but which are not licensed for use under this License.

III. Netscape and logo. This License does not grant any rights to use the trademarks "Netscape", the "Netscape N and horizon" logo or the "Netscape lighthouse" logo, "Netcenter", "Gecko", "Java" or "JavaScript", "Smart Browsing" even if such marks are included in the Original Code or Modifications.

IV. Inability to Comply Due to Contractual Obligation. Prior to licensing the Original Code under this License, Netscape has licensed third party code for use in Netscape's Branded Code. To the extent that Netscape is limited contractually from making such third party code available under this License, Netscape may choose to reintegrate such code into Covered Code without being required to distribute such code in Source Code form, even if such code would otherwise be considered ''Modifications" under this License.

V. Use of Modifications and Covered Code by Initial Developer.

V.1. In General. The obligations of Section 3 apply to Netscape, except to the extent specified in this Amendment, Section V.2 and V.3.

V.2. Other Products. Netscape may include Covered Code in products other than the Netscape's Branded Code which are released by Netscape during the two (2) years following the release date of the Original Code, without such additional products becoming subject to the terms of this License, and may license such additional products on different terms from those contained in this License.

V.3. Alternative Licensing.

Netscape may license the Source Code of Netscape's Branded Code, including Modifications incorporated therein, without such Netscape Branded Code becoming subject to the terms of this License, and may license such Netscape Branded Code on different terms from those contained in this License.

VI. Litigation.

Notwithstanding the limitations of Section 11 above, the provisions regarding litigation in Section 11(a), (b) and (c) of the License shall apply to all disputes relating to this license.

EXHIBIT A-Netscape Public License.

''The contents of this file are subject to the Netscape Public License Version 1.1 (the "License"); you may not use this file except in compliance with the License. You may obtain a copy of the License at http://www.mozilla.org/NPL/

Software distributed under the License is distributed on an "AS IS" basis, WITH-OUT WARRANTY OF ANY KIND, either express or implied. See the License for the specific language governing rights and limitations under the License.

The Original Code is Mozilla Communicator client code, released March 31, 1998.

The Initial Developer of the Original Code is Netscape Communications Corporation. Portions created by Netscape are Copyright © 1998-1999 Netscape Communications Corporation. All Rights Reserved.

Contributor(s): _____.

Alternatively, the contents of this file may be used under the terms of the _____ license (the ì[___] Licenseî), in which case the provisions of [_____] License are applicable instead of those above. If you wish to allow use of your version of this file only under the terms of the [____] License and not to allow others to use your version of this file under the NPL, indicate your decision by deleting the provisions above and replace them with the notice and other provisions required by the [___] License. If you do not delete the provisions above, a recipient may use your version of this file under either the NPL or the [___] License.''

NETSCAPE PUBLIC LICENSE Version 1.0

1. Definitions.

1.1. "Contributor"

"Contributor" means each entity that creates or contributes to the creation of Modifications.

1.2. "Contributor Version"

"Contributor Version" means the combination of the Original Code, prior Modifications used by a Contributor, and the Modifications made by that particular Contributor.

1.3. "Covered Code"

"Covered Code" means the Original Code or Modifications or the combination of the Original Code and Modifications, in each case including portions thereof.

1.4. "Electronic Distribution Mechanism"

"Electronic Distribution Mechanism" means a mechanism generally accepted in the software development community for the electronic transfer of data.

1.5. "Executable"

"Executable" means Covered Code in any form other than Source Code.

1.6. "Initial Developer"

"Initial Developer" means the individual or entity identified as the Initial Developer in the Source Code notice required by Exhibit A.

1.7. "Larger Work"

"Larger Work" means a work which combines Covered Code or portions thereof with code not governed by the terms of this License.

1.8. "License"

"License" means this document.

1.9. "Modifications"

"Modifications" means any addition to or deletion from the substance or structure of either the Original Code or any previous Modifications. When Covered Code is released as a series of files, a Modification is:

   A. Any addition to or deletion from the contents of a file containing Original Code or previous Modifications.

   B. Any new file that contains any part of the Original Code or previous Modifications.

1.10. "Original Code"

"Original Code" means Source Code of computer software code which is described in the Source Code notice required by Exhibit A as Original Code, and which, at the time of its release under this License is not already Covered Code governed by this License.

1.11. "Source Code"

"Source Code" means the preferred form of the Covered Code for making modifications to it, including all modules it contains, plus any associated interface definition files, scripts used to control compilation and installation of an Executable, or a list of source code differential comparisons against either the Original Code or another well known, available Covered Code of the Contributor's choice. The Source Code can be in a compressed or archival form, provided the appropriate decompression or de-archiving software is widely available for no charge.

1.12. "You"

"You" means an individual or a legal entity exercising rights under, and complying with all of the terms of, this License or a future version of this License issued under Section 6.1. For legal entities, ``You" includes any entity which controls, is controlled by, or is under common control with You. For purposes of this definition, ``control" means

   (a) the power, direct or indirect, to cause the direction or management of such entity, whether by contract or otherwise, or

   (b) ownership of fifty percent (50%) or more of the outstanding shares or beneficial ownership of such entity.

2. Source Code License.

2.1. The Initial Developer Grant.

The Initial Developer hereby grants You a world-wide, royalty-free, non-exclusive license, subject to third party intellectual property claims:

(a) to use, reproduce, modify, display, perform, sublicense and distribute the Original Code (or portions thereof) with or without Modifications, or as part of a Larger Work; and

(b) under patents now or hereafter owned or controlled by Initial Developer, to make, have made, use and sell (``Utilize'') the Original Code (or portions thereof), but solely to the extent that any such patent is reasonably necessary to enable You to Utilize the Original Code (or portions thereof) and not to any greater extent that may be necessary to Utilize further Modifications or combinations.

2.2. Contributor Grant.

Each Contributor hereby grants You a world-wide, royalty-free, non-exclusive license, subject to third party intellectual property claims:

(a) to use, reproduce, modify, display, perform, sublicense and distribute the Modifications created by such Contributor (or portions thereof) either on an unmodified basis, with other Modifications, as Covered Code or as part of a Larger Work; and

(b) under patents now or hereafter owned or controlled by Contributor, to Utilize the Contributor Version (or portions thereof), but solely to the extent that any such patent is reasonably necessary to enable You to Utilize the Contributor Version (or portions thereof), and not to any greater extent that may be necessary to Utilize further Modifications or combinations.

3. Distribution Obligations.

3.1. Application of License.

The Modifications which You create or to which You contribute are governed by the terms of this License, including without limitation Section 2.2. The Source Code version of Covered Code may be distributed only under the terms of this License or a future version of this License released under Section 6.1, and You must include a copy of this License with every copy of the Source Code You distribute.

You may not offer or impose any terms on any Source Code version that alters or restricts the applicable version of this License or the recipients' rights hereunder. However, You may include an additional document offering the additional rights described in Section 3.5.

3.2. Availability of Source Code.

Any Modification which You create or to which You contribute must be made available in Source Code form under the terms of this License either on the same media as an Executable version or via an accepted Electronic Distribution Mechanism to anyone to whom you made an Executable version available; and if made available via Electronic Distribution Mechanism, must remain available for at least twelve (12) months after the date it initially became available, or at least six (6) months after a subsequent version of that particular Modification has been made available to such recipients. You are responsible for ensuring that the Source Code version remains available even if the Electronic Distribution Mechanism is maintained by a third party.

3.3. Description of Modifications.

You must cause all Covered Code to which you contribute to contain a file documenting the changes You made to create that Covered Code and the date of any change. You must include a prominent statement that the Modification is derived, directly or indirectly, from Original Code provided by the Initial Developer and including the name of the Initial Developer in (a) the Source Code, and (b) in any notice in an Executable version or related documentation in which You describe the origin or ownership of the Covered Code.

3.4. Intellectual Property Matters

(a) Third Party Claims. If You have knowledge that a party claims an intellectual property right in particular functionality or code (or its utilization under this License), you must include a text file with the source code distribution titled ``LEGAL'' which describes the claim and the party making the claim in sufficient detail that a recipient will know whom to contact. If you obtain such knowledge after You make Your Modification available as described in Section 3.2, You shall promptly modify the LEGAL file in all copies You make available thereafter and shall take other steps (such as notifying appropriate mailing lists or newsgroups) reasonably calculated to inform those who received the Covered Code that new knowledge has been obtained.

(b) Contributor APIs. If Your Modification is an application programming interface and You own or control patents which are reasonably necessary to implement that API, you must also include this information in the LEGAL file.

3.5. Required Notices.

You must duplicate the notice in Exhibit A in each file of the Source Code, and this License in any documentation for the Source Code, where You describe recipients' rights relating to Covered Code. If You created one or more Modification(s), You may add your name as a Contributor to the notice described in Exhibit A. If it is not possible to put such notice in a particular Source Code file due to its structure, then you must include such notice in a location (such as a relevant directory file) where a user would be likely to look for such a notice.

You may choose to offer, and to charge a fee for, warranty, support, indemnity or liability obligations to one or more recipients of Covered Code. However, You may do so only on Your own behalf, and not on behalf of the Initial Developer or any Contributor. You must make it absolutely clear than any such warranty, support, indemnity or liability obligation is offered by You alone, and You hereby agree to indemnify the Initial Developer and every Contributor for any liability incurred by the Initial Developer or such Contributor as a result of warranty, support, indemnity or liability terms You offer.

3.6. Distribution of Executable Versions.

You may distribute Covered Code in Executable form only if the requirements of Section 3.1-3.5 have been met for that Covered Code, and if You include a notice stating that the Source Code version of the Covered Code is available under the terms of this License, including a description of how and where You have fulfilled the obligations of Section 3.2. The notice must be conspicuously included in any notice in an Executable version, related documentation or collateral in which You describe recipients' rights relating to the Covered Code.

You may distribute the Executable version of Covered Code under a license of Your choice, which may contain terms different from this License, provided that You are in compliance with the terms of this License and that the license for the Executable version does not attempt to limit or alter the recipient's rights in the Source Code version from the rights set forth in this License. If You distribute the Executable version under a different license You must make it absolutely clear that any terms which differ from this License are offered by You alone, not by the Initial Developer or any Contributor.

You hereby agree to indemnify the Initial Developer and every Contributor for any liability incurred by the Initial Developer or such Contributor as a result of any such terms You offer.

3.7. Larger Works.

You may create a Larger Work by combining Covered Code with other code not governed by the terms of this License and distribute the Larger Work as a single product. In such a case, You must make sure the requirements of this License are fulfilled for the Covered Code.

4. Inability to Comply Due to Statute or Regulation.

If it is impossible for You to comply with any of the terms of this License with respect to some or all of the Covered Code due to statute or regulation then You must: (a) comply with the terms of this License to the maximum extent possible; and (b) describe the limitations and the code they affect. Such description must be included in the LEGAL file described in Section 3.4 and must be included with all distributions of the Source Code. Except to the extent prohibited by statute or regulation, such description must be sufficiently detailed for a recipient of ordinary skill to be able to understand it.

5. Application of this License.

This License applies to code to which the Initial Developer has attached the notice in Exhibit A, and to related Covered Code.

6. Versions of the License.

6.1. New Versions.

Netscape Communications Corporation (``Netscape") may publish revised and/or new versions of the License from time to time. Each version will be given a distinguishing version number.

6.2. Effect of New Versions.

Once Covered Code has been published under a particular version of the License, You may always continue to use it under the terms of that version. You may also choose to use such Covered Code under the terms of any subsequent version of the License published by Netscape. No one other than Netscape has the right to modify the terms applicable to Covered Code created under this License.

6.3. Derivative Works.

If you create or use a modified version of this License (which you may only do in order to apply it to code which is not already Covered Code governed by this License), you must (a) rename Your license so that the phrases ``Mozilla'', ``MOZILLAPL'', ``MOZPL'', ``Netscape'', ``NPL'' or any confusingly similar phrase do not appear anywhere in your license and (b) otherwise make it clear that your version of the license contains terms which differ from the Mozilla Public License and Netscape Public License. (Filling in the name of the Initial Developer, Original Code or Contributor in the notice described in Exhibit A shall not of themselves be deemed to be modifications of this License.)

7. DISCLAIMER OF WARRANTY.

COVERED CODE IS PROVIDED UNDER THIS LICENSE ON AN ``AS IS'' BASIS, WITHOUT WARRANTY OF ANY KIND, EITHER EXPRESSED OR IMPLIED, INCLUDING, WITHOUT LIMITATION, WARRANTIES THAT THE COVERED CODE IS FREE OF DEFECTS, MERCHANTABLE, FIT FOR A PARTICULAR PURPOSE OR NON-INFRINGING. THE ENTIRE RISK AS TO THE QUALITY AND PERFORMANCE OF THE COVERED CODE IS WITH YOU. SHOULD ANY COVERED CODE PROVE DEFECTIVE IN ANY RESPECT, YOU (NOT THE INITIAL DEVELOPER OR ANY OTHER CONTRIBUTOR) ASSUME THE COST OF ANY NECESSARY SERVICING, REPAIR OR CORRECTION. THIS DISCLAIMER OF WARRANTY CONSTITUTES AN ESSENTIAL PART OF THIS LICENSE. NO USE OF ANY COVERED CODE IS AUTHORIZED HEREUNDER EXCEPT UNDER THIS DISCLAIMER.

8. TERMINATION.

This License and the rights granted hereunder will terminate automatically if You fail to comply with terms herein and fail to cure such breach within 30 days of becoming aware of the breach. All sublicenses to the Covered Code which are properly granted shall survive any termination of this License. Provisions which, by their nature, must remain in effect beyond the termination of this License shall survive.

9. LIMITATION OF LIABILITY.

UNDER NO CIRCUMSTANCES AND UNDER NO LEGAL THEORY, WHETHER TORT (INCLUDING NEGLIGENCE), CONTRACT, OR OTHERWISE, SHALL THE INITIAL DEVELOPER, ANY OTHER CONTRIBUTOR, OR ANY DISTRIBUTOR OF COVERED CODE, OR ANY SUPPLIER OF ANY OF SUCH PARTIES, BE LIABLE TO YOU OR ANY OTHER PERSON FOR ANY INDIRECT, SPECIAL, INCIDENTAL, OR CONSEQUENTIAL DAMAGES OF ANY CHARACTER INCLUDING, WITHOUT LIMITATION, DAMAGES FOR LOSS OF GOODWILL, WORK STOPPAGE, COMPUTER FAILURE OR MALFUNCTION, OR ANY AND ALL OTHER COMMERCIAL DAMAGES OR LOSSES, EVEN IF SUCH PARTY SHALL HAVE BEEN INFORMED OF THE POSSIBILITY OF SUCH DAMAGES. THIS LIMITATION OF LIABILITY SHALL NOT APPLY TO LIABILITY FOR DEATH OR PERSONAL INJURY RESULTING FROM SUCH PARTY'S NEGLIGENCE TO THE EXTENT APPLICABLE LAW PROHIBITS SUCH LIMITATION. SOME JURISDICTIONS DO NOT ALLOW THE EXCLUSION OR LIMITATION OF INCIDENTAL OR CONSEQUENTIAL DAMAGES, SO THAT EXCLUSION AND LIMITATION MAY NOT APPLY TO YOU.

10. U.S. GOVERNMENT END USERS.

The Covered Code is a ``commercial item,'' as that term is defined in 48 C.F.R. 2.101 (Oct. 1995), consisting of ``commercial computer software'' and ``commercial computer software documentation,'' as such terms are used in 48 C.F.R. 12.212 (Sept. 1995). Consistent with 48 C.F.R. 12.212 and 48 C.F.R. 227.7202-1 through 227.7202-4 (June 1995), all U.S. Government End Users acquire Covered Code with only those rights set forth herein.

11. MISCELLANEOUS.

This License represents the complete agreement concerning subject matter hereof. If any provision of this License is held to be unenforceable, such provision shall be reformed only to the extent necessary to make it enforceable. This License shall be governed by California law provisions (except to the extent applicable law, if any, provides otherwise), excluding its conflict-of-law provisions. With respect to disputes in which at least one party is a citizen of, or an entity chartered or registered to do business in, the United States of America:

(a) unless otherwise agreed in writing, all disputes relating to this License (excepting any dispute relating to intellectual property rights) shall be subject to final and binding arbitration, with the losing party paying all costs of arbitration;

(b) any arbitration relating to this Agreement shall be held in Santa Clara County, California, under the auspices of JAMS/EndDispute; and

(c) any litigation relating to this Agreement shall be subject to the jurisdiction of the Federal Courts of the Northern District of California, with venue lying in Santa Clara County, California, with the losing party responsible for costs, including without limitation, court costs and reasonable attorneys fees and expenses.

The application of the United Nations Convention on Contracts for the International Sale of Goods is expressly excluded. Any law or regulation which provides that the language of a contract shall be construed against the drafter shall not apply to this License.

12. RESPONSIBILITY FOR CLAIMS.

Except in cases where another Contributor has failed to comply with Section 3.4, You are responsible for damages arising, directly or indirectly, out of Your utilization of rights under this License, based on the number of copies of Covered Code you made available, the revenues you received from utilizing such rights, and other relevant factors. You agree to work with affected parties to distribute responsibility on an equitable basis.

AMENDMENTS

Additional Terms applicable to the Netscape Public License.

I. Effect. These additional terms described in this Netscape Public License -- Amendments shall apply to the Mozilla Communicator client code and to all Covered Code under this License.

II. ``Netscape's Branded Code" means Covered Code that Netscape distributes and/or permits others to distribute under one or more trademark(s) which are controlled by Netscape but which are not licensed for use under this License.

III. Netscape and logo. This License does not grant any rights to use the trademark ``Netscape", the ``Netscape N and horizon" logo or the Netscape lighthouse logo, even if such marks are included in the Original Code.

IV. Inability to Comply Due to Contractual Obligation. Prior to licensing the Original Code under this License, Netscape has licensed third party code for use in Netscape's Branded Code. To the extent that Netscape is limited contractually from making such third party code available under this License, Netscape may choose to reintegrate such code into Covered Code without being required to distribute such code in Source Code form, even if such code would otherwise be considered ``Modifications" under this License.

V. Use of Modifications and Covered Code by Initial Developer.

V.1. In General. The obligations of Section 3 apply to Netscape, except to the extent specified in this Amendment, Section V.2 and V.3.

V.2. Other Products. Netscape may include Covered Code in products other than the Netscape's Branded Code which are released by Netscape during the two (2) years following the release date of the Original Code, without such additional products becoming subject to the terms of this License, and may license such additional products on different terms from those contained in this License.

V.3. Alternative Licensing. Netscape may license the Source Code of Netscape's Branded Code, including Modifications incorporated therein, without such additional products becoming subject to the terms of this License, and may license such additional products on different terms from those contained in this License.

VI. Arbitration and Litigation. Notwithstanding the limitations of Section 11 above, the provisions regarding arbitration and litigation in Section 11(a), (b) and (c) of the License shall apply to all disputes relating to this License.

EXHIBIT A.

``The contents of this file are subject to the Netscape Public License Version 1.0 (the "License"); you may not use this file except in compliance with the License. You may obtain a copy of the License at http://www.mozilla.org/NPL/

Software distributed under the License is distributed on an "AS IS" basis, WITHOUT WARRANTY OF ANY KIND, either express or implied. See the License for the specific language governing rights and limitations under the License.

The Original Code is Mozilla Communicator client code, released March 31, 1998.

The Initial Developer of the Original Code is Netscape Communications Corporation. Portions created by Netscape are Copyright © 1998 Netscape Communications Corporation. All Rights Reserved.

Contributor(s): _____."

[NOTE: The text of this Exhibit A may differ slightly from the text of the notices in the Source Code files of the Original Code. This is due to time constraints encountered in simultaneously finalizing the License and in preparing the Original Code for release. You should use the text of this Exhibit A rather than the text found in the Original Code Source Code for Your Modifications.]

MOZILLA PUBLIC LICENSE Version 1.0

1. Definitions.

1.1. "Contributor"

"Contributor" means each entity that creates or contributes to the creation of Modifications.

1.2. "Contributor Version"

"Contributor Version" means the combination of the Original Code, prior Modifications used by a Contributor, and the Modifications made by that particular Contributor.

1.3. "Covered Code"

"Covered Code" means the Original Code or Modifications or the combination of the Original Code and Modifications, in each case including portions thereof.

1.4. "Electronic Distribution Mechanism"

"Electronic Distribution Mechanism" means a mechanism generally accepted in the software development community for the electronic transfer of data.

1.5. "Executable"

"Executable" means Covered Code in any form other than Source Code.

1.6. "Initial Developer"

"Initial Developer" means the individual or entity identified as the Initial Developer in the Source Code notice required by Exhibit A.

1.7. "Larger Work"

"Larger Work" means a work which combines Covered Code or portions thereof with code not governed by the terms of this License.

1.8. "License"

"License" means this document.

1.9. "Modifications"

"Modifications" means any addition to or deletion from the substance or structure of either the Original Code or any previous Modifications. When Covered Code is released as a series of files, a Modification is:

    A. Any addition to or deletion from the contents of a file containing Original Code or previous Modifications.

    B. Any new file that contains any part of the Original Code or previous Modifications.

1.10. "Original Code"

"Original Code" means Source Code of computer software code which is described in the Source Code notice required by Exhibit A as Original Code, and which, at the time of its release under this License is not already Covered Code governed by this License.

1.11. "Source Code"

"Source Code" means the preferred form of the Covered Code for making modifications to it, including all modules it contains, plus any associated interface definition files, scripts used to control compilation and installation of an Executable, or a list of source code differential comparisons against either the Original Code or another well known, available Covered Code of the Contributor's choice. The Source Code can be in a compressed or archival form, provided the appropriate decompression or de-archiving software is widely available for no charge.

1.12. "You"

"You" means an individual or a legal entity exercising rights under, and complying with all of the terms of, this License or a future version of this License issued under Section 6.1. For legal entities, ``You'' includes any entity which controls, is controlled by, or is under common control with You. For purposes of this definition, ``control'' means

(a) the power, direct or indirect, to cause the direction or management of such entity, whether by contract or otherwise, or

(b) ownership of fifty percent (50%) or more of the outstanding shares or beneficial ownership of such entity.

2. Source Code License.

2.1. The Initial Developer Grant.

The Initial Developer hereby grants You a world-wide, royalty-free, non-exclusive license, subject to third party intellectual property claims:

(a) to use, reproduce, modify, display, perform, sublicense and distribute the Original Code (or portions thereof) with or without Modifications, or as part of a Larger Work; and

(b) under patents now or hereafter owned or controlled by Initial Developer, to make, have made, use and sell (``Utilize'') the Original Code (or portions thereof), but solely to the extent that any such patent is reasonably necessary to enable You to Utilize the Original Code (or portions thereof) and not to any greater extent that may be necessary to Utilize further Modifications or combinations.

2.2. Contributor Grant.

Each Contributor hereby grants You a world-wide, royalty-free, non-exclusive license, subject to third party intellectual property claims:

(a) to use, reproduce, modify, display, perform, sublicense and distribute the Modifications created by such Contributor (or portions thereof) either on an unmodified basis, with other Modifications, as Covered Code or as part of a Larger Work; and

(b) under patents now or hereafter owned or controlled by Contributor, to Utilize the Contributor Version (or portions thereof), but solely to the extent that any such patent is reasonably necessary to enable You to Utilize the Contributor Version (or portions thereof), and not to any greater extent that may be necessary to Utilize further Modifications or combinations.

3. Distribution Obligations.

3.1. Application of License.

The Modifications which You create or to which You contribute are governed by the terms of this License, including without limitation Section 2.2. The Source Code version of Covered Code may be distributed only under the terms of this License or a future version of this License released under Section 6.1, and You must include a copy of this License with every copy of the Source Code You distribute. You may not offer or impose any terms on any Source Code version that alters or restricts the applicable version of this License or the recipients' rights hereunder. However, You may include an additional document offering the additional rights described in Section 3.5.

3.2. Availability of Source Code.

Any Modification which You create or to which You contribute must be made available in Source Code form under the terms of this License either on the same media as an Executable version or via an accepted Electronic Distribution Mechanism to anyone to whom you made an Executable version available; and if made available via Electronic Distribution Mechanism, must remain available for at least twelve (12) months after the date it initially became available, or at least six (6) months after a subsequent version of that particular Modification has been made available to such recipients. You are responsible for ensuring that the Source

Code version remains available even if the Electronic Distribution Mechanism is maintained by a third party.

3.3. Description of Modifications.

You must cause all Covered Code to which you contribute to contain a file documenting the changes You made to create that Covered Code and the date of any change. You must include a prominent statement that the Modification is derived, directly or indirectly, from Original Code provided by the Initial Developer and including the name of the Initial Developer in

(a) the Source Code, and

(b) in any notice in an Executable version or related documentation in which You describe the origin or ownership of the Covered Code.

3.4. Intellectual Property Matters

(a) Third Party Claims. If You have knowledge that a party claims an intellectual property right in particular functionality or code (or its utilization under this License), you must include a text file with the source code distribution titled ``LEGAL'' which describes the claim and the party making the claim in sufficient detail that a recipient will know whom to contact. If you obtain such knowledge after You make Your Modification available as described in Section 3.2, You shall promptly modify the LEGAL file in all copies You make available thereafter and shall take other steps (such as notifying appropriate mailing lists or newsgroups) reasonably calculated to inform those who received the Covered Code that new knowledge has been obtained.

(b) Contributor APIs. If Your Modification is an application programming interface and You own or control patents which are reasonably necessary to implement that API, you must also include this information in the LEGAL file.

3.5. Required Notices.

You must duplicate the notice in Exhibit A in each file of the Source Code, and this License in any documentation for the Source Code, where You describe recipients' rights relating to Covered Code. If You created one or more Modification(s), You may add your name as a Contributor to the notice described in Exhibit A. If it is not possible to put such notice in a particular Source Code file due to its structure, then you must include such notice in a location (such as a relevant directory file) where a user would be likely to look for such a notice.

You may choose to offer, and to charge a fee for, warranty, support, indemnity or liability obligations to one or more recipients of Covered Code. However, You may do so only on Your own behalf, and not on behalf of the Initial Developer or any Contributor. You must make it absolutely clear than any such warranty, support, indemnity or liability obligation is offered by You alone, and You hereby agree to indemnify the Initial Developer and every Contributor for any liability incurred by the Initial Developer or such Contributor as a result of warranty, support, indemnity or liability terms You offer.

3.6. Distribution of Executable Versions.

You may distribute Covered Code in Executable form only if the requirements of Section 3.1-3.5 have been met for that Covered Code, and if You include a notice stating that the Source Code version of the Covered Code is available under the terms of this License, including a description of how and where You have fulfilled the obligations of Section 3.2. The notice must be conspicuously included in any notice in an Executable version, related documentation or collateral in which You describe recipients' rights relating to the Covered Code.

You may distribute the Executable version of Covered Code under a license of Your choice, which may contain terms different from this License, provided that You are in compliance with the terms of this License and that the license for the Executable version does not attempt to limit or alter the recipient's rights in the Source Code version from the rights set forth in this License. If You distribute the Executable version under a different license You must make it absolutely clear that any terms which differ from this License are offered by You alone, not by the Initial Developer or any Contributor. You hereby agree to indemnify the Initial Developer and every Contributor for any liability incurred by the Initial Developer or such Contributor as a result of any such terms You offer.

3.7. Larger Works.

You may create a Larger Work by combining Covered Code with other code not governed by the terms of this License and distribute the Larger Work as a single product. In such a case, You must make sure the requirements of this License are fulfilled for the Covered Code.

4. Inability to Comply Due to Statute or Regulation.

If it is impossible for You to comply with any of the terms of this License with respect to some or all of the Covered Code due to statute or regulation then You must:

(a) comply with the terms of this License to the maximum extent possible; and

(b) describe the limitations and the code they affect.

Such description must be included in the LEGAL file described in Section 3.4 and must be included with all distributions of the Source Code. Except to the extent prohibited by statute or regulation, such description must be sufficiently detailed for a recipient of ordinary skill to be able to understand it.

5. Application of this License.

This License applies to code to which the Initial Developer has attached the notice in Exhibit A, and to related Covered Code.

6. Versions of the License.

6.1. New Versions.

Netscape Communications Corporation (``Netscape'') may publish revised and/or new versions of the License from time to time. Each version will be given a distinguishing version number.

6.2. Effect of New Versions.

Once Covered Code has been published under a particular version of the License, You may always continue to use it under the terms of that version. You may also choose to use such Covered Code under the terms of any subsequent version of the License published by Netscape. No one other than Netscape has the right to modify the terms applicable to Covered Code created under this License.

6.3. Derivative Works.

If you create or use a modified version of this License (which you may only do in order to apply it to code which is not already Covered Code governed by this License), you must

(a) rename Your license so that the phrases ``Mozilla'', ``MOZILLAPL'', ``MOZPL'', ``Netscape'', ``NPL'' or any confusingly similar phrase do not appear anywhere in your license and

(b) otherwise make it clear that your version of the license contains terms which differ from the Mozilla Public License and Netscape Public License.

(Filling in the name of the Initial Developer, Original Code or Contributor in the notice described in Exhibit A shall not of themselves be deemed to be modifications of this License.)

7. DISCLAIMER OF WARRANTY.

COVERED CODE IS PROVIDED UNDER THIS LICENSE ON AN ``AS IS'' BASIS, WITHOUT WARRANTY OF ANY KIND, EITHER EXPRESSED OR IMPLIED, INCLUDING, WITHOUT LIMITATION, WARRANTIES THAT THE COVERED CODE IS FREE OF DEFECTS, MERCHANTABLE, FIT FOR A PARTICULAR PURPOSE OR NON-INFRINGING. THE ENTIRE RISK AS TO THE QUALITY AND PERFORMANCE OF THE COVERED CODE IS WITH YOU. SHOULD ANY COVERED CODE PROVE DEFECTIVE IN ANY RESPECT, YOU (NOT THE INITIAL DEVELOPER OR ANY OTHER CONTRIBUTOR) ASSUME THE COST OF ANY NECESSARY SERVICING, REPAIR OR CORRECTION. THIS DISCLAIMER OF WARRANTY CONSTITUTES AN ESSENTIAL PART OF THIS LICENSE. NO USE OF ANY COVERED CODE IS AUTHORIZED HEREUNDER EXCEPT UNDER THIS DISCLAIMER.

8. TERMINATION.

This License and the rights granted hereunder will terminate automatically if You fail to comply with terms herein and fail to cure such breach within 30 days of becoming aware of the breach. All sublicenses to the Covered Code which are properly granted shall survive any termination of this License. Provisions which, by their nature, must remain in effect beyond the termination of this License shall survive.

9. LIMITATION OF LIABILITY.

UNDER NO CIRCUMSTANCES AND UNDER NO LEGAL THEORY, WHETHER TORT (INCLUDING NEGLIGENCE), CONTRACT, OR OTHERWISE, SHALL THE INITIAL DEVELOPER, ANY OTHER CONTRIBUTOR, OR

ANY DISTRIBUTOR OF COVERED CODE, OR ANY SUPPLIER OF ANY OF SUCH PARTIES, BE LIABLE TO YOU OR ANY OTHER PERSON FOR ANY INDIRECT, SPECIAL, INCIDENTAL, OR CONSEQUENTIAL DAMAGES OF ANY CHARACTER INCLUDING, WITHOUT LIMITATION, DAMAGES FOR LOSS OF GOODWILL, WORK STOPPAGE, COMPUTER FAILURE OR MALFUNCTION, OR ANY AND ALL OTHER COMMERCIAL DAMAGES OR LOSSES, EVEN IF SUCH PARTY SHALL HAVE BEEN INFORMED OF THE POSSIBILITY OF SUCH DAMAGES. THIS LIMITATION OF LIABILITY SHALL NOT APPLY TO LIABILITY FOR DEATH OR PERSONAL INJURY RESULTING FROM SUCH PARTY'S NEGLIGENCE TO THE EXTENT APPLICABLE LAW PROHIBITS SUCH LIMITATION. SOME JURISDICTIONS DO NOT ALLOW THE EXCLUSION OR LIMITATION OF INCIDENTAL OR CONSEQUENTIAL DAMAGES, SO THAT EXCLUSION AND LIMITATION MAY NOT APPLY TO YOU.

10. U.S. GOVERNMENT END USERS.

The Covered Code is a ``commercial item," as that term is defined in 48 C.F.R. 2.101 (Oct. 1995), consisting of ``commercial computer software" and ``commercial computer software documentation," as such terms are used in 48 C.F.R. 12.212 (Sept. 1995). Consistent with 48 C.F.R. 12.212 and 48 C.F.R. 227.7202-1 through 227.7202-4 (June 1995), all U.S. Government End Users acquire Covered Code with only those rights set forth herein.

11. MISCELLANEOUS.

This License represents the complete agreement concerning subject matter hereof. If any provision of this License is held to be unenforceable, such provision shall be reformed only to the extent necessary to make it enforceable. This License shall be governed by California law provisions (except to the extent applicable law, if any, provides otherwise), excluding its conflict-of-law provisions. With respect to disputes in which at least one party is a citizen of, or an entity chartered or registered to do business in, the United States of America:

(a) unless otherwise agreed in writing, all disputes relating to this License (excepting any dispute relating to intellectual property rights) shall be subject to final and binding arbitration, with the losing party paying all costs of arbitration;

(b) any arbitration relating to this Agreement shall be held in Santa Clara County, California, under the auspices of JAMS/EndDispute; and

(c) any litigation relating to this Agreement shall be subject to the jurisdiction of the Federal Courts of the Northern District of California, with venue lying in Santa Clara County, California, with the losing party responsible for costs, including without limitation, court costs and reasonable attorneys fees and expenses.

The application of the United Nations Convention on Contracts for the International Sale of Goods is expressly excluded. Any law or regulation which provides that the language of a contract shall be construed against the drafter shall not apply to this License.

12. RESPONSIBILITY FOR CLAIMS.

Except in cases where another Contributor has failed to comply with Section 3.4, You are responsible for damages arising, directly or indirectly, out of Your utilization of rights under this License, based on the number of copies of Covered Code you made available, the revenues you received from utilizing such rights, and other relevant factors. You agree to work with affected parties to distribute responsibility on an equitable basis.

EXHIBIT A.

``The contents of this file are subject to the Mozilla Public License Version 1.0 (the "License"); you may not use this file except in compliance with the License. You may obtain a copy of the License at http://www.mozilla.org/MPL/

Software distributed under the License is distributed on an "AS IS" basis, WITHOUT WARRANTY OF ANY KIND, either express or implied. See the License for the specific language governing rights and limitations under the License.

The Original Code is _____.
The Initial Developer of the Original Code is _____.
Portions created by _____ are Copyright © _____
_____. All Rights Reserved.
Contributor(s): _____."

my2cents.idgbooks.com

CD-ROM Installation Instructions

See Appendix D, "What's on the CD-ROM?" for detailed instructions.

Note that all CD-ROM files are read-only. When you copy a file from the CD-ROM to your hard drive, it retains its read-only attribute. To change this attribute after copying a file, right-click the filename or icon and select Properties from the shortcut menu. In the Properties dialog box, click the General tab and remove the checkmark from the Read-only check box.

Limited Warranty

IDG Books Worldwide, Inc. ("IDGB") warrants that the Software and Software Media are free from defects in materials and workmanship under normal use for a period of sixty (60) days from the date of purchase of this Book. If IDGB receives notification within the warranty period of defects in materials or workmanship, IDGB will replace the defective Software Media.

IDGB AND THE AUTHOR OF THE BOOK DISCLAIM ALL OTHER WARRANTIES, EXPRESS OR IMPLIED, INCLUDING WITHOUT LIMITATION IMPLIED WARRANTIES OF MERCHANTABILITY AND FITNESS FOR A PARTICULAR PURPOSE, WITH RESPECT TO THE SOFTWARE, THE PROGRAMS, THE SOURCE CODE CONTAINED THEREIN, AND/OR THE TECHNIQUES DESCRIBED IN THIS BOOK. IDGB DOES NOT WARRANT THAT THE FUNCTIONS CONTAINED IN THE SOFTWARE WILL MEET YOUR REQUIREMENTS OR THAT THE OPERATION OF THE SOFTWARE WILL BE ERROR FREE.

This limited warranty gives you specific legal rights, and you may have other rights that vary from jurisdiction to jurisdiction.